The Politics of International Telecommunications Regulation

James G. Savage

Westview Press
BOULDER, SAN FRANCISCO, & LONDON

The opinions expressed in this book are those of the author and do not necessarily reflect the official position of the Department of Communications, Canada.

This Westview softcover edition is printed on acid-free paper and bound in softcovers that carry the highest rating of the National Association of State Textbook Administrators, in consultation with the Association of American Publishers and the Book Manufacturers' Institute.

Published in 1989 in the United States of America by Westview Press, Inc., 5500 Central Avenue, Boulder, Colorado 80301, and in the United Kingdom by Westview Press, Inc., 13 Brunswick Centre, London WC1N 1AF, England

Library of Congress Cataloging-in-Publication Data
Savage, James G., 1963–
   The politics of international telecommunications regulation / by
James G. Savage.
      p.   cm.
   Includes index.
   ISBN 0-8133-7682-3
   1. International Telecommunication Union.   2. Telecommunication—
International cooperation—Political aspects.   I. Title.
HE7700.S28   1989
384′.041—dc19   88-20564
                                                                                    CIP

Printed and bound in the United States of America

The paper used in this publication meets the requirements of the American National Standard for Permanence of Paper for Printed Library Materials Z39.48-1984.

10   9   8   7   6   5   4   3   2   1

Contents

Acknowledgments

Many individuals and organizations have provided invaluable assistance to me in the research and writing of this book. To my mentor, adviser, editor, and friend, Professor Mark W. Zacher, Director, Institute of International Relations, University of British Columbia, I offer my deepest and most sincere thanks. Without Mark's generous support and confidence, this project would never have become a reality.

Several individuals were especially helpful to me in providing insights, opportunities, and comments. I would particularly like to thank Ed DuCharme of the Department of Communications, Canada; Gary Brooks, International Frequency Registration Board (IFRB), Geneva; and Arnold Matthey, formerly of the IFRB and a veteran of the International Telecommunication Union (ITU). I have also benefited from the information and insights obtained from the following people: in Ottawa—Gaby Warren, Don Fraser, John Gilbert, Keith Hoffmann, Robert Jones, Jeffrey Crelinsten, and Vernon MacDonald; in Montreal—Paul Morneault, Andre Vermette, Ian MacFarland, and Ram Jakhu; and in Washington, D.C.— Don Abelson, Doug Davis, Michael Gardner, Domenick Iacovo, Harold Kimball, Lawrence Palmer, Anthony Rutkowski, and Kalmann Schaefer. Much assistance was also received from many people at the ITU in Geneva and from several organizations here in London.

For their generous financial assistance, I am deeply indebted to the Institute of International Relations, University of British Columbia; the Donner Canadian Foundation; and the Department of Communications, Canada. I would also like to thank Gaby Warren at the Department of Communications for permitting me the unique opportunity of attending, within the Canadian delegation, the 1987 ITU World Administrative Radio Conference for the Planning of the High Frequency Bands Allocated to the Broadcasting Service. Here in London, my employer, the International Institute of Communications, has shown unusual understanding in granting me time and the use of facilities in completing this work.

I am indebted to my friends in Vancouver and London for many happy times associated with the period spent on this project. Finally, I reserve special thanks for my parents, whose encouragement, faith, and support could not have been greater.

James G. Savage
London

Introduction

If trade is the life blood of an economy, then telecommunications can truly be regarded as the nervous system of both the economy and society.
—C.R. Dickerson

What is telecommunications? This word, used by all of us in everyday speech, in fact lacks any clear meaning. The International Telecommunication Union (ITU), the UN specialized agency empowered to oversee telecommunications regulation, has struggled through the 1970s and 1980s attempting to forge an acceptable definition.

Telecommunications comprises all aspects of voice and data transmission by radio, television, wire, microwave, and satellite. To people in the industry there is a sharp distinction between "telecommunications" (referring to all two-way services such as telephony, data traffic, etc.) and "broadcast communications" (such as radio and television). At both the national and international level, "telecoms" and broadcasting are subject to the same regulatory frameworks. But any umbrella definition of telecommunications must consider that "there are no two things in the universe that are more different to each other in their pure states than broadcasting and telecommunications. One of them is all content with a minimum degree of carriage, the other is all carriage with no content. . . . We are under an overriding disability when we come to talk about both broadcasting and telecommunications . . . in that the arguments, issues and concerns that apply to the one will almost never apply to the other."[1]

Having said that, the 1980s have also seen the emergence of what has come to be termed the "convergence" of the new technologies of telecommunications and broadcasting. This trend started with cable television and has evolved into broadband systems, fiber optics, satellite delivery means, and so forth. The boundary lines demarcating "telecom" services, broadcast services, and, indeed, certain computer technologies are no longer that distinct. Broadcasters will be able to provide data services and telephone carriers will be able to provide radio and television services. To an extent, this is already happening.

1

While this convergence is still largely inchoate, the *status quo* of telecommunications remains that of a perpetual state of change, in both technology and in the regulatory and political environment.[2] The pace of change and the boundaries of change are now unprecedented. Regulatory structures must encompass—albeit flexibly—these high velocity changes to telecoms and broadcasting.

For the purposes of this volume, telecommunications will comprise both "telecoms" and broadcasting. In other words, telecommunications is everything within the purview of the International Telecommunication Union.

This book seeks to explain the ITU and its central role in the politics of international telecommunications. It focuses on the key areas of frequency spectrum allocation, the avoidance of deliberate interference, and the setting of international telecommunications standards. These areas are all vital to the operation of the international economy. The ability of the ITU to facilitate international communications has a direct and immediate impact on every aspect of political economy. The ITU oversees international telecommunications which, however one defines it, is at the heart of all aspects of the modern economy and polity. Nothing is more central to the economic and political infrastructures of daily life.

The origins of international telecommunications, and the speed with which these technologies became central to our lives, must be noted in any attempt to understand how telecommunications are governed today. Telegraphy originated with the experiments of Morse and Wheatstone in the 1830s. Within twenty years telegraphy had grown rapidly and pervasively across Europe and North America. International telegraphy became possible on both continents (though not between them) by 1850.

Telephony originated with the experiments of Alexander Graham Bell in 1876. This technology took a while longer to become accepted as a serious means of communication. For years it was seen as a fad or what today would be called an "executive toy." Nevertheless, telephone networks steadily grew and the technology proved its legitimacy and value during World War I.

As Chapter 1 describes, the evolution of an international telephone network was a difficult and frustrating process. Virtually every country had a uniquely different telephone system and possessed an equipment manufacturing industry to go with it. As a consequence of their economic and political value, these differences between countries were cherished by national administrations, making the ITU's efforts at international standardization and coordination remarkably difficult. It was not until the completion of the first transatlantic telephone cables in the 1950s that serious attempts at standardization began.

International radio communications began with the efforts of several scientists, the most famous of whom was Marconi. In its early years radio existed as radiotelegraphy, largely employed for maritime use. Regular broadcasting did not begin until the establishment of commercial operations in Britain, Canada, and the United States in 1919–20. Unlike telephony, this new communications medium, which could bring instant and free news and entertainment to every home, was immediately accepted as a central feature of mass culture.

The most prominent developments since World War II have been the emergence and pervasive growth of television and the globalization of international telephony and data communications. This latter development has been a major catalyst for postwar economic growth, creating over $250 billion in annual revenues and stimulating over $100 billion in annual investment. Moreover, the world market for telecommunications services continues to grow at an astounding 12 percent a year. This figure shoots up to 20 percent for certain specialized new services.[3]

This "world" market remains, however, a First World market. There is a marked and growing disparity in the level of telecommunications service between the developed and developing worlds. Various figures are put forward to illustrate this gap. For instance, countries comprising 10 percent of the world's population control 90 percent of the available frequency spectrum. It would require an investment of at least $12 billion annually for fifteen years to extend basic telephone service to the bulk of the world's population. While various proposals, technology-disseminating organizations, cooperative programs, and so forth have been put forward and/or implemented, the North-South technology gap shows no signs of shrinking.

Indeed, as Chapter 1 explains, quite the opposite is occurring in the last two decades of the twentieth century. The unprecedented velocity of technological progress guarantees the permanence and growth of this disparity. Without basic telecommunications, no other aspect of infrastructural development—roads, agriculture, schools—can take hold. But many developing countries are only slowly recognizing just how crucial telecommunications are for development. A well-educated West African information technology student told me that it would be wrong for his small country to divert its scarce resources into telecommunications "as we already have a good postal system."

The great danger here rests in the possibility that the Third World will virtually drop out of the ever-advancing telecommunications environment. As Larry Martinez pointed out in discussing communications satellites, telecom systems work synergistically with military forces, multinational corporations, global financial networks, and other information technologies as "projectors of power." The asymmetrical distribution of these systems results in the widening of the economic, social, cultural, and strategic power gaps between North and South. "While developed country telecommunications planners worry about meeting demand with high capacity fiber optic networks, their Lesser-Developed Country (LDC) counterparts are concerned with how to get one telephone into a remote village."[4]

Chapter 1 puts today's problems in a historical perspective by describing the enormous difficulties encountered in establishing interconnection between Europe and North America. The acceptance of telephony as a viable, efficient means of international communications did not take hold until well after World War II. Herculean efforts were required to achieve harmonization just within Western Europe, much less between continents. Transoceanic telephone traffic did not become practical until the late 1950s. Since that time, the velocity and magnitude of advancement in telecommunications technology has easily outstripped any international efforts to regulate or even supervise these changes. It would sometimes seem that if there actually is some sort of "order" or "regime" that may be applied to international telecommunications, it is chiefly the result of the momentum of change. In other words, the pace of advancement does not even permit chaos to become entrenched.

To this day, the role of telecommunications, here applied in its narrow sense of telephony, telex, facsimile, data traffic, etc., remains either underestimated or taken for granted, even by those most reliant on it. Likewise, the complexity and fragility of the international arrangements that make international communications possible are not fully appreciated, nor is the significance of these new telecommunications technologies. The structure of the ITU, still reflective of yesterday's technology, has nevertheless made recent efforts to directly address the technological and political concerns of developing countries. As Chapter 1 explains, this has sometimes occurred at the expense of good relations with certain advanced states and has led to accusations of the ITU betraying its own apolitical, technological heritage. The survey of the ITU's history in Chapter 1 clearly shows these latter accusations to be nonsense. As will be repeated throughout the book, the ITU is at heart a political organization. It does not operate in a political vacuum. Chapter 1 introduces the issues, their historical background and political salience.

Chapter 2 demonstrates this truism by analyzing the ITU's work in managing the radio frequency spectrum. Radio began with the pioneering efforts of Marconi at the turn of the twentieth century. Until the 1920s radio meant radiotelegraphy, and despite the obvious complementarity with the International *Telegraphy* Union, radio was not a part of the ITU for the first three decades of its development. This can only be attributed to radio's commercial origins, as opposed to the ITU's intergovernmental heritage. The ITU did not become the International *Telecommunication Union*—today's ITU—until it merged with the heretofore semi-autonomous International Radio Conferences in 1932. This merger would have itself been unthinkable had Europe's governments not by that point taken firm control over their domestic radio bands, making the medium acceptable to the Eurocentric Union.

While the 1932 merger was not that dramatic, it was indicative of several developments. Radio had come of age and the technical work of the ITU's consultative committees, along with the prestige of the ITU, could greatly assist in the establishment of orderly arrangements for the medium. That such steps were necessary was beyond doubt. Even by the early 1930s, the radio broadcasting bands were becoming crowded and difficult to regulate, particularly within Europe.

Following a brief historical overview, Chapter 2 moves, literally, up the radio frequency spectrum in surveying the postwar political challenges confronting management of the spectrum. These were the formative years for the ITU's current "doctrine" of frequency registration and planning. This doctrine is analyzed through its evolution, from the Cold War–ridden world of postwar international high frequency (shortwave) broadcasting to the challenges of the 1990s as international direct broadcasting by satellite (DBS) and competitive international telecommunications carriers come into play.

Chapter 3 expands upon the seemingly minor point of deliberate interference to international broadcasting. In its traditional guise, deliberate interference is most often associated with the "jamming" of international radio stations such as the Voice of America or Radio Free Europe. While this is serious enough, the issue in fact involves the power of the state to regulate international satellite television broadcasting and the contradictions between the ITU's commitment to the free flow of communications and its equal commitment to the supremacy of the sovereign rights of states.

In essence, Chapter 3 is a journey into the murky world of the role of specialized international organizations vis-à-vis the accepted limits of state sovereignty. The developing countries, who have provided a catalyst and impetus to the "new" ITU of the 1980s and 1990s, have also reaffirmed their overwhelming faith in the concept of sovereignty and the rights of states over the dissemination of information. This faith is manifested through the New World Information and Communications Order (NWICO), which has gone through many guises since its inception in the mid-1970s but remains dogma for most developing states. The ITU continues to have problems reconciling its own commitment to NWICO, which seeks a "controlled, balanced" flow of information, with Article 4 of the ITU International Telecommunication Convention, which states unequivocally the ITU's central function in facilitating unrestricted international communications.

In the past three decades the ITU has played a pivotal, if low-key, role in facilitating the advancement and development of international telecommunications. In doing so, it has become one of the most important of the UN specialized agencies. Yet, unlike the GATT, ICAO, or UNCLOS, the machinations and politics of the Union are not the stuff of newspaper headlines or analysis. This is not a result of any lack of drama in the subject matter. It is more the consequence of fear; journalists and social scientists often approach technological matters with trepidation, just as engineers and technical experts find the discovery of "politics" in their work to be distasteful and corrupting.

Nowhere is this more evident than in the thorny field of telecommunication standard-setting. Standards are at the basis of all international communications. They are the most difficult, yet, in many ways, the most successful area of ITU endeavor. Chapter 4 focuses on the ITU's two consultative committees (known by their French acronyms CCIR and CCITT). These committees provide the rules of the road for the world's telecommunications highways.

The deliberations of the consultative committees are deceptively low-keyed. The stakes, in fact, may often involve the future of national telecommunications industries, entire fields of research and development, thousands of jobs, and billions of dollars. A favorable CCI decision can be itself a commercial seal of approval guaranteeing the international success of a technology and great political prestige. These implications are rarely discussed by those involved in the technological standard-setting process and rarely appreciated by those who are not.

                                        *   *   *

The objective of this study is to address several key questions regarding the politics of international telecommunications regulation; questions that have not been adequately analyzed in the past.

The first question looks at the ties between the ITU and the member states of which it consists: how strong have the regulatory arrangements been with respect to spectrum and orbital management, the right of control over international telecommunications, and operational and technical standards? If these arrangements *have* been effective, why?

A second question looks at the doctrine behind the regulations: what jurisdictional principles have tended to be embodied in the regulation and why? Finally, which states (or groups of states) have had the greatest influence in shaping the regulatory arrangements, and on what resources is such influence based? The focus of the study is not so much on the

ITU as an organization—although organizational structure and function are covered—but on regulatory and regime politics within the ITU.

These questions are addressed through the analyses of three major issues: radio frequency spectrum management, the free flow of international communications versus the principle of prior consent, and the establishment of technical and operational standards. Prior to these analyses there is a chapter introducing the structure, history, and decision-making processes of the ITU. This first chapter also looks at other major issues and influences that are shaping the ITU as it enters the twenty-first century. Finally, the conclusion identifies those factors common to the issue areas, surveys why and where the ITU is successful, and how a handful of key principles allow the ITU to achieve international accord.

Notes

1. Gordon Haase, in T. McPhail and S. Hamilton, *Communication in the Eighties: Major Issues* (Calgary: University of Calgary Press, 1984).

2. Denis Gilhooly, "Telecom 87—At the Crossroads of Change," *Telecommunications*, International Edition, 21:10 (October 1987), p. 9.

3. Gilhooly, loc. cit.

4. Larry Martinez, *Communications Satellites: Power Politics in Space* (Dedham, MA: Artech House Inc., 1985), p. 42.

1

The International
Telecommunication Union

Over twenty years ago, Karl Deutsch proposed that the new centers of political power were to be found among those who controlled the dissemination of information and the means of communication. Deutsch argued that communications infrastructure constitutes the nervous system of modern society, and that the groups that gain control over this nervous system will come to control society.[1] Two decades later the importance of communication, particularly by electronic means, has grown significantly in both scope and complexity. This growth has led many observers to posit that we are entering—or have entered—a post-industrial, post-modern information age. While an entire academic industry has arisen to chart and interpret the effects that the "information age" will have upon humankind, one common element can be identified from the many discordant theorists: electronic communications, particularly telecommunications, harbors the greatest potential of all communications media and will have a dramatic and increasing impact upon the world's population. The nature of this impact differs from country to country— many countries are only now, in the 1980s, discovering the overwhelming difference basic telephone service can make to the quality of life—but progress in telecommunications technology has an influence on every country and every individual.

From the earliest developments in international telecommunications there has existed a need to coordinate development, communicate policy, and exchange information in the field. As early as the 1840s, an international regulatory order was envisaged for international telegraphy. Even at that early date one could see the necessity for technical standardization, for active efforts to avoid the disruption of telegraph lines, and for the creation of cooperative agreements between states. As a result, there first emerged the International Telegraph Union, then the International Radio Conferences, and ultimately the International Telecommunication Union—today's ITU. Specialized uses of technologies begot International Consultative Committees within the ITU to study and issue recommendations on technical aspects of radio, telephone, and telegraph use. Outside the ITU, broadcasters formed their own regional cooperative bodies, and commercial satellite users created their own uniquely structured global organizations.

Today a plethora of institutions, organizations, and groupings exist to manage international telecommunications. Paramount among them is the ITU, since 1947 a United Nations specialized agency. The ITU, which dates back to 1865, is the sole global body empowered to supervise and manage the international telecommunications order. Its purposes are: "(1) to maintain and extend international cooperation for the improvement and rational use of telecommunications of all kinds as well as to promote and offer technical assistance; (2) to promote the use of technical facilities and their most efficient operations . . . improving their efficiency . . . increasing their usefulness . . . and making them, so far as possible, generally available to the public; (3) to harmonize the actions of nations in the attainment of these common ends."[2]

These appear to be upstanding, dispassionate, politically neutral objectives. The ITU, while increasingly cognizant of its greater social responsibilities, has traditionally viewed itself as a technical body operating in an atmosphere of engineering professionalism and scientific objectivity. More often than not ITU personnel decry the existence of "politics" in the organization as an unnecessary hindrance to their work. Others deny the political salience of the international telecommunications organizations, arguing that the ITU and the other organizations merely wish to promote technical progress and must not be tainted by the "politicization" manifest in UNESCO or the United Nations General Assembly. Such arguments are motivated by a sincere desire to maintain the effectiveness of the ITU against political threats, but illustrate a failure on the part of both observers and participants within the international telecommunications regime to appreciate the political saliency *inherent* in the dissemination of communication and information technologies. Twenty-five years ago, French sociologist Jacques Ellul catalogued a few of the greater implications of the spread of technology:

> All technical progress exacts a price: that is, while it adds something on the one hand, it subtracts something on the other. All technical progress raises more problems than it solves, tempts us to see the consequent problems as technical in nature, and prods us to seek technical solutions to them.
>
> The negative effects of technological innovation are inseparable from the positive. It is naive to say that technology is neutral, that it may be

used for good or bad ends: the good and bad effects are, in fact, simultaneous and inseparable.

All technological innovations have unforeseeable effects.[3]

As the velocity of change in telecommunications technology increases, so too does the political significance of international telecommunication regulation. At both the national and international level, the evolution of telecommunications technology has been and continues to be one of the paramount developments of the twentieth century. The significance of telecommunications for virtually every aspect of modern life is now usually taken for granted and yet still cannot be overestimated.

At the heart of international telecommunications rests the ITU, which sets the "rules of the road," the code of behavior, and the specific technical criteria that enable international telecommunications to take place. The ITU regulates or supervises three main spheres of telecommunications activity: (1) the coordination and allocation of radio services and assignments, as well as the apportionment of the geostationary orbit for communication satellite services; (2) the recommendation of international technical standards enabling or frustrating international telecommunications; and (3) the defining and regulation of international telephony, telegraphy, and new "telecommunications services" such as computer data exchanges. The ITU is also increasingly active in promoting and conducting telecommunications development and assistance to developing countries. It is, in essence, the sum of its member countries, and so is as subject to coalition-forming, reciprocity, personality conflicts, interdepartmental rivalry, and prejudicial behavior as any body comprised of mere mortals. It is *not* "above politics" simply by nature of its technical basis.

The ITU has been described in print before. Several excellent reference works have been written over the years which are familiar to those active in the international telecommunications order.[4] There is a tendency, however, to consider the ITU in a vacuum, and to disregard the issues within international telecommunications in favor of describing the regulatory regime. This can contribute to an impression that the order determines the issue, and not vice versa. In addition, it deprecates the political significance of ITU activity. There is a politics of international telecommunications that exists independently of any "politicization"— the label given to any non-telecommunications issues introduced into the ITU.

But the "politics of international telecommunications" obviously involves far more than those issues key to the ITU. Within the amorphous, indistinct definition of the word "telecommunications" there are issues of sovereignty over transborder data flows, the legal and moral implications of international program exchanges, copyright and royalty disputes over audio and video piracy, and, of course, 160 different domestic telecommunications administrations with particular objectives and methods. To deal comprehensively with both the specific politics of the ITU and the political implications of all other salient aspects of the information age is beyond the scope of this and perhaps any other single book.

The primary objective of this book is to identify the political saliency of the ITU and those issues which dominate its activity: the management of the radio frequency spectrum and the geostationary orbit, the control of harmful interference and protection of the so-called "right to communicate," and the establishment of international technical standards which enable international telecommunications to take place at all and permit new technologies to be brought into the field. In looking at the specific issues I trace the technical and political developments that have led to demands for international regulation. The ITU has traditionally been viewed as an organization reactive to technical progress and the technical needs of its members. In fact, political influences promote change in the ITU at least as frequently as do technical changes. In surveying the issues I hope to explain the policies that certain major ITU actors—key states and coalitions of states—have promoted. There have always been alignments of states within the Union. These alignments reflect both greater political groupings as well as commonalities of technical interests.

This latter point is of particular note as the ITU, to a far greater extent than other specialized agencies, has often made a point of following the rule of consensus in decision-making.[5] Collective action through the ITU increases the individual state's economic self-interest as, to a large extent, a tacit unanimity rule exists in all voting fora of the ITU. The unanimity rule, seen by Buchanan and Tullock as comparatively rare in international behavior, is in fact a norm within the ITU, particularly in frequency spectrum management and the establishment of technical standards. Using Buchanan and Tullock's analysis, a state's membership in the ITU involves two types of costs. The cost of participation and decision-making depends on the individual state's power and influence—determined in the ITU by technical leadership and capability—as well as the size of the membership. As the ITU has grown collective decision-making has become, at the very least, a more cumbersome process. The ITU has certainly lost all but the vestiges of the "clubby" Eurocentrism that characterized the prewar Union. The second type of cost, external cost, involves the costs a state will incur through decisions taken by other members or through votes in which it found itself in minority opposition. The unanimity rule minimizes the degree of external cost involved in ITU membership. This is not to say external costs do not exist. As the ITU, like most international organizations, features a majority of Third World members, those states that will find an opposing or dissenting minority view in their interest are those states best able to shoulder the supplementary external costs, i.e., the developed countries.[6]

The "technical" positions of major states and groupings also involve, to a surprising extent, the economic influence of major private telecommunications enterprises. The resultant alignments can thus vary from issue to issue. Similarly, the centers of power and influence vary with—and within—issue areas. Over time, the sources of bargaining leverage within the ITU have varied as well. The type and definition of this leverage varies within the issue areas. What constitutes power in achieving technical standards may be irrelevant in dealing with deliberate interference to international broadcasting. The decision-making process of the ITU and its agencies, along with the prevailing rules set by the ITU International Telecommunication Convention and the ITU Regulations for radio and wired telecommunication, has been largely shaped by the interests and efforts of key states and key groupings during certain time periods. Once set, however, these rules have in turn greatly determined the functions and powers of the ITU, as well as the sort of leverage a state or a group of states will have in attempting to effect change.

The ITU is an old, highly structured organization attempting to regulate a new, dynamic, rapidly expanding technology at the global level. But the ITU has not been static. It is an international organization unique in many ways, including in its flexibility and reactiveness to changing demands. In the 1980s, however, signs of strain emerged between the greatly disparate telecommunication needs of North and South and the ability of the ITU to reconcile them in order to form global telecommunications policy. The areas of conflict within the branches and agencies of the ITU have, as will be illustrated, shifted markedly over the years.

The limits of the ITU's jurisdiction thus limit the scope of this book. This chapter focuses on introducing the ITU, the three major political issues that dominate international telecommunications regulation, and tracing the development of the international regulatory regime that has emerged over the past century to control and coordinate international telecommunications. In order to gauge how the function and power of the ITU has changed since 1945, the chapter concludes with an overview of the six dominant areas of change—and hence contention—within ITU activity. These are: (1) the authority of ITU organization regarding management of the radio frequency spectrum; (2) the influence of the regulatory regime on deliberate interference and controls on the free flow of information; (3) changes in the ITU's technical standard-setting function; (4) changes in the structure and legal status of the ITU itself;

(5) the emergence of technical assistance to developing countries as a central ITU function; and (6) actions taken within the ITU concerning non-telecommunications issues such as South African apartheid or the status of Israel. Some of these issues are dealt with specifically in later chapters and are mentioned here in order to introduce the reader to the general political saliency of the topic and how the particular issue fits into the wider context of ITU activity. Our goal is *not* to emphasize problems within the ITU or show the Union as an organization in peril. The ITU is confronting issues of unprecedented complexity, but it would be melodramatic to suggest that this is threatening the Union's survival or even the core of its effectiveness. Our approach seeks to discuss and analyze problems and crises within the text as a means of achieving a better understanding of the status quo.

The ITU

The International Telecommunication Union is the international organization entrusted with the harmonizing and coordinating of world telecommunications. It is the only organization so mandated, and all other international telecommunication bodies are complementary to it. If there can be said to be a "control center" for the provision, maintenance, operation, and coordination of international telecommunications, the ITU is it. Given the importance of what the ITU does, it is both surprising and revealing how little is commonly known or understood about the Union. Paradoxically, this lack of visibility and the ITU's low profile are often cited as the chief reasons for the success of ITU work.[7] ITU delegates and personnel often believe it is in the interests of both facilitated international telecommunication and the survival of the Union to minimize visible conflict, to emphasize compromise, to obviate stormy issues, and avoid clear-cut polarization over issues. When this becomes inevitable the ITU is thrust into a role of arbiter with which it is not comfortable, even though it has sometimes been quite successful in this role.[8] The conscious efforts to minimize conflict help explain *why* the ITU achieves many of its objectives successfully, but does not explain *how* the ITU fulfills its mandate. This process takes place through the complicated but effective current structure of the ITU. As will be seen, this structure has evolved over the history of the Union, and the ITU has been physically remolded over the years to accommodate the changing needs and desires of ITU members.

ITU Structure

The ITU stands out within the UN system. ITU structure is generally described as "federal" in that it possesses semi-autonomous consultative committees and a frequency registration board. Unlike most UN specialized agencies, where an elected Secretary General appoints his directorate, in the ITU there are nine elected officials. The complexity of ITU structure often frightens off many would-be observers. For those courageous or tenacious enough to closely study ITU structure, the challenge of explaining the Union without over-simplifying or inundating the reader with detail may appear insurmountable.

But a basic understanding of how the ITU works is indispensable if one is to appreciate the political saliency of the international telecommunications order. Perhaps the best method of describing the Union is through an admittedly imperfect analogy, that of a private corporation.[9] The 160 member countries may be viewed as shareholders. The "General Meeting" of the ITU is the *Plenipotentiary Conference*, held every few years. The chief objective of the Plenipotentiary Conference is the review and, if necessary, revision of the International Telecommunication Convention, the governing document of the Union. The Plenipotentiary also establishes general policies and priorities concerning the ITU, and, as of the 1989 Plenipotentiary, elects the nine electable officials (the Secretary-General, the Deputy Secretary-General, the five IFRB members, and the two CCI Directors). This closely resembles a corporate Annual General Meeting, and can be equally contentious. As Plenipotentiary resolutions and proposals are firmly rooted to the one-country one-vote principle, the building of winning coalitions and voting blocs may comprise a good deal of the behind-the-scenes activity at a Plenipotentiary. As with a corporate meeting, an ability to engage in "horse-trading" is often necessary to achieve, for example, a resolution establishing a technical training program or a resolution criticizing a recalcitrant member. The vociferous exchanges that take place at a Plenipotentiary are about as stormy as the ITU ever gets. Dissent and debate usually lead to a post-Plenipotentiary period of introspection and questioning of the basic premises and validity of the Union. This, like the machinations of a group of unhappy shareholders, may create a basis for change within the Union, but it does not normally threaten the survival of the Union.

The "Board of Directors" of the ITU is made up of the 41 members of the *Administrative Council*. The 41 are elected by the membership at the Plenipotentiary. The Administrative Council is the supreme body of the organization in the periods between Plenipotentiary Conferences. The Council is responsible for implementing decisions of the Plenipotentiary Conference and other conferences, as well as deciding on the agenda of these conferences. It determines the ITU's position on matters of technical assistance, budgeting, relations with the United Nations, and many other concerns. The Administrative Council may decide upon a myriad of issues which are unrelated except for their connection to the maintenance of international telecommunications.

The Administrative Council directs all matters stemming from the decisions of the Plenipotentiary Conferences and the resolutions of the International Telecommunication Convention. The ITU is, however, also responsible for the International Radio Regulations and the International Telephone and Telegraph Regulations. The Radio Regulations comprise two sizeable volumes containing quite specific provisions. The Telephone and Telegraph regulations set global technical principles governing the use of wired telecommunications and provide a regulatory framework for international telephone and telegraph routing, performance, and even rate-setting requirements. To an increasing extent, these regulations are encompassing new computer data flow regulations as well, for much data flow activity takes place over telephone lines. The establishment, review, and revision of the regulations takes place at the *administrative conferences*, which are divided into radio spectrum (WARCs and, at the regional level, RARCs) and telecommunications branches (WATTCs). World administrative radio conferences (WARCs) and RARCs deal with all aspects of radio communication. For example, the two-session WARC covering the allotment of the geostationary orbit and services using it (GSO-WARC), which met in 1985 and 1988, assigned specific services, including broadcasting, aviation, and radiotelex, to segments of the radio frequency spectrum used by satellites, as well as determining an allotment plan for the allocation of satellites to spaces in the geostationary orbit. Clearly, this is highly technical work, and delegates to WARCs and RARCs tend to be skilled technicians who are averse to talking about issues of equitability in telecommunication use or greater non-technical principles of "justice" or "democratization." These greater concerns are important, however, particularly to the Third World. They have, consequently, come to dominate the discussions of recent WARCs and, to a lesser extent, RARCs, and thus lead to accusations from some Western developed countries that the ITU is becoming "politicized." Developing countries insist, however, that this is a process of "democratization."

The World Administrative Telephone-Telegraph Conference, or WATTC, is somewhat unrelated to the concerns of the WARCs or RARCs. The Telephone-Telegraph Regulations now comprise only a brief volume of general principles. The conferences are infrequent: the last was held in 1973, the next is to be held in 1988. In 1973 many of the duties of the Telephone-Telegraph Regulations were transferred to the relevant ITU Consultative Committee, the CCITT. The role and mandate of the WATTC is somewhat unclear as the 1980s progress. One outcome of the 1988 WATTC was the drafting of a volume of international telecommunications regulations, which encompass all aspects of wired (i.e., non-radio) telecommunication technology—such as computer data flows—instead of remaining limited to telephones and telegraphs.

The Radio Regulations resulting from the WARCs and RARCs, along with the less sizeable Telephone and Telegraph regulations, are adhered to by all ITU members. Likewise, all ITU members must adhere to the Convention as it is decided upon by the Plenipotentiary. A safety valve exists, however, to prevent members from seceding from the Union when matters do not go their way. Members have the ability to place a "reservation" within the Convention or Regulation Final Protocols. A country may therefore sign the Final Acts of a WARC or the Convention at a Plenipotentiary yet reserve the right to "take any necessary steps" to ensure domestic telecommunication or disagree with specific resolutions, or merely to criticize the actions of a fellow ITU member.

The Administrative Conferences do not fit satisfactorily in our analogy of the private corporation, as they perform a specific technical task. In the case of WARCs and RARCs, they must oversee the distribution of two limited common resources: the radio frequency spectrum and the geostationary orbit. The closest parallel might be that of a company's product planning division, in that such a division must gauge future needs and attempt to shape the company's production accordingly.

The "Chief Executive Officer" overseeing the entire operation of the Union is the ITU's *Secretary-General*. His department, the *General Secretariat*, performs all of the tasks of a secretariat, such as organizing conferences, publications, and documentation. The Secretary-General and his deputy have a role much like that of the Secretary-General of the United Nations. The power of the ITU Secretary-General's office has been enhanced markedly over the past decade, chiefly as a result of conscious efforts on the part of the last two Secretaries-General to placate LDC concerns. The Secretary-General's office is responsible for technical cooperation and training programs as well as the external relations of the Union. Some observers have suggested that recent Secretaries-General have actively sought to increase their personal power and their profile in the Union.[10] The decision of the 1982 Plenipotentiary to elect CCI directors at Plenipotentiary Conferences instead of at CCI Assemblies or WARCs has been a prominent example of power being centralized in the Plenipotentiary and hence within the greater bailiwick of the Secretary-General. Likewise, it was feared that the establishment of new development bodies such as the Center for Telecommunications Development (see below), set up under the aegis of the ITU, may not evolve in as desirably an autonomous pattern as their proponents had originally intended.

The "subsidiaries" of the ITU corporate body are the semi-autonomous or "federal" *International Frequency Registration Board (IFRB)* and the

International Consultative Committees (CCIs). The IFRB is a five-member board entrusted with the considerable task of recording, registering, publishing, and assessing the legality of every radio frequency used in the spectrum. In recent years the IFRB has also been mandated to conduct orbital allotment planning exercises for the geostationary orbit. The IFRB is largely responsible for the work between sessions of the two-session WARCs and, not surprisingly, is responsible for much of the preparation in advance of WARCs. The IFRB also advises members on frequency assignment issues and other technical matters, and has served as an arbiter in coordinating bilateral and multilateral frequency plans among countries that would not otherwise cooperate with one another (e.g., Israel and its neighbors, South Africa and the "Frontline" states).

There are two consultative committees (CCIs), each of which is quite unique. The basic distinction between the two is that the CCIR studies issues relating to all aspects of radio communication, while the CCITT studies all aspects of wired telecommunication. The result of all this study, in the CCIR case, is a compendium of Study Groups and Interim Working Parties issuing recommended global standards and codes of conduct on every radio communications topic from basic point-to-point radio service to highly advanced high-definition television systems. In addition, CCIR Conference Preparatory Meetings (CPMs) precede every WARC and provide conferences with necessary technical information. The CCIR views its role as more than just standardization of radio systems or methods. In its Conference preparatory faculty, it prefers to see itself as an active participant in ITU technical policy formation. The CCITT is the committee more purely concerned with "standardization" of technical systems. Dealing with wired communications, the CCITT Study Groups research technologies which are at the cutting edge of telecommunications advancement, such as computer data transmissions or fiber optics.

The recommendations of the CCIs do not carry the force of law. They are *recommended* worldwide standards, however, and most countries adhere to these recommendations. Every few years, the CCIs publish the sum total of all recommendations in a series of volumes known by the color of their binding, e.g., CCITT Yellow Books. Many countries, as a matter of course, incorporate the recommendations into national legislation. Others, however, cannot even afford the price of the books and have not the technical personnel to interpret the recommendations. The CCITT has also formed a Conference Preparatory Meeting for the 1988 WATTC (see Chapter 4) but this preparatory role is not as significant to the CCITT as it is to its radio communications counterpart.

ITU structure, despite its apparent complexity, follows a logical and, among UN specialized agencies, familiar pattern. To summarize, the Plenipotentiary Conference is the supreme organ which reviews and revises the Convention and hence determines the scope and direction of ITU activity. The Administrative Council completes the tasks directed to it by the Plenipotentiary, sets the agenda for the Conferences, and directs the Union between Plenipotentiaries. The actual regulatory work concerning telecommunications takes place through periodic administrative conferences at the world and regional level. There are three semi-autonomous bodies that exist to facilitate the tasks set by conferences. The IFRB registers all employed radio frequencies on its master list and assesses the legal right of an ITU member to use a given frequency. The Board also provides indispensable work in developing frequency plans and, in recent years, plans for geostationary orbit use. The CCIR also conducts technical preparatory work for WARCs, but its chief objective remains standardization of worldwide radio communication systems. The CCITT's work is even more specifically technical, often relating to nascent technologies involving data flow issues. At the center of ITU infrastructure is the General Secretariat, which does everything from ensuring the supply of paper clips at conferences to determining the size of draft budgets to be submitted to the Administrative Council.

ITU Issues

The subsequent three chapters focus on the paramount issues confronting the ITU during the last two decades of this century. Each chapter centers on one of the central functions and objectives of the Union—the management of the spectrum and geostationary orbit, the avoidance of interference and promotion of equitability, and the global standardization of telecommunications technology—and the political issues that are inherent in these roles as well as political challenges that accompany changes in these roles.

Management of the Radio Frequency Spectrum and the Geostationary Orbit

At the heart of the spectrum management issue described in Chapter 2 is control of a common but limited resource. Unlike other common heritage resources, however, the radio frequency spectrum possesses an enviable degree of flexibility. Technological advancement enables the spectrum—itself an intangible entity determined by the emission of radio waves—to be enlarged, permitting far more efficient use of existing radio frequencies. Even so, the ITU finds the job of allocating segments of the spectrum to certain services, e.g., broadcasting radionavigation, to be a strong challenge, particularly given the increased demands of the developing countries. International regulation emerged in this area at the turn of the twentieth century as a natural consequence of a growing need for basic rules of the road governing international radio use. In the early years of radio communications there were few conflicts directly related to the technology save the overcrowding of certain portions of the radio spectrum and the perceived inability of the pre–World War II ITU spectrum management system to cope with these changes.

Since the war, one central point of division has emerged: whether or not the ITU should actively *plan*—that is, allocate—each frequency on a given band within the spectrum for specific member countries. This method, known as *a priori* planning, has been employed by the ITU before and is now advocated by the majority of LDCs, who believe it is a vital part of guaranteeing their access to the radio frequency spectrum. The status quo of the ITU for most bands is found in a system developed by the IFRB in 1959 known as *a posteriori* or *first-come, first-served* frequency registration. Under this system a user commences operation on a frequency, notifies the IFRB, and if no interference takes place within a two-month period, the frequency is automatically approved and entered into the master frequency list with full legal rights.

But what are the "legal rights" of a frequency? They are *not* ownership or property rights. The ITU is unambiguous in regarding the spectrum as a common heritage resource. Nevertheless, a *de facto* priority right does exist. The longer a country has occupied a given radio frequency or orbital allotment, the less likely it is that a newcomer will win any dispute over that frequency in the IFRB. This does not imply actual state acquisition or sovereignty over a frequency. But *a priori* and *a posteriori* schemes, in their purest forms, are both flawed in that they suggest property-like claims to frequencies or allotments. There is considerable evidence to suggest that from the earliest attempts to manage the spectrum many—if not most—countries have regarded control of the radio frequency spectrum to be an integral part of sovereign control over domestic communications, and have been willing to only yield a portion of their authority to the supranational ITU.

Yet state sovereignty is based on territorial jurisdictions. The radio frequency spectrum is non-territorial in nature and cannot fall within complete sovereign authority. States still may have difficulty coming to terms with it, but the radio frequency spectrum is a global common heritage resource encompassing the four aspects described twenty years ago by Ambassador Pardo of Malta in describing the sea bed and oceans floor:

1. Such areas are not subject to appropriation by states;
2. All states must share in the management of them;
3. There must be an active sharing of the benefits reaped from the exploitation of their resources; and
4. The areas must be dedicated exclusively to peaceful purposes.[11]

The ITU and its components delegated to manage the radio frequency spectrum, WARCs, the IFRB, and the CCIR, remain firmly committed to these precepts. Even Pardo's last point concerning "peaceful use," perhaps a questionable point given extensive military use of the spectrum, is nevertheless valid as far as the jurisdiction of the ITU is concerned. Military communications are not addressed by the ITU and are labelled "government services" at ITU frequency management conferences.

The ITU has provided an indispensable role in managing the limited common resource that is the spectrum. It has done so despite the ownership-like implications of *a priori* planning and the perception of priority rights conferred through *a posteriori* methods. Claims of direct sovereign control have not completely disappeared, as certain equatorial countries continue to claim sovereignty over portions of the geostationary orbit, a radio frequency spectrum issue by reason of its connection with the ITU spectrum management regime. With this apparently high degree of confusion over the nature of spectrum management and given the turbulent "trial and error" evolution of the current order (see Chapter 2) it seems remarkable that the ITU could have achieved any substantial success in keeping spectrum use from descending into chaos. The ITU, through the complex network of conferences, radio regulations, and semi-autonomous organs evolved over twelve years of activity, has been able to secure at least a minimal measure of compliance and order from the world's radio frequency spectrum users. Even the most recalcitrant members notify the IFRB of their frequency-use plans.

Yet, as will be shown, certain portions of the spectrum are more amenable to compromise and international regulation than others. Certain aviation and maritime bands are assigned and registered without a hint of dissent or contention. In such cases all countries realize the danger and futility of disagreement. On less vital bands, however, or bands more international in nature—like the international high frequency (HF) broadcast band or direct broadcast by satellite bands—countries are more likely to be willing to risk subordination of the technical order to political principles. Where countries believe international cooperation will hinder their access to certain portions of the spectrum or will require a costly subordination of authority to the ITU, such cooperation is not likely to take place unless the technical order of the band in question is seriously threatened.

The threat of chaos on the airwaves provides a strong incentive to permit international regulation of the resource. The fact that regulatory cooperation is not always forthcoming illustrates that this threat is in itself not sufficient to preclude more particular, less technical concerns. The ability of the ITU, whether at a WARC or within the IFRB, to forge successful outcomes in spectrum management is dependent upon two central factors (mentioned here but described in Chapter 2):

1. *The nature of the band or portion of the spectrum being assigned.* The more international the band, the more contentious the conference assigning it. These more contentious bands are nevertheless usually those that require the strongest ITU voice and are in greatest need of international coordination.
2. *Development in technology that may assuage global spectrum demands and hence facilitate the management role of the ITU.* Successful planning of the bands for direct broadcast satellites was largely possible because the technology was as yet not widely employed and the bulk of relevant spectrum space was unused. Such was also the case in the proposed allotment plan developed in the mid-1980s for the GSO and frequencies using it. This "success," however, also invites the question of the need for planning bands for technologies not advanced enough to be widely employed.

This question is of particular interest to countries located at the wrong end of the technology gap, whose ability to employ assignments granted may not be realized for several decades after the planning of the band. But waiting for the telecommunications technology to develop before attempting to plan it is no answer either. This occurred in the case of international high frequency (HF) broadcasting. Once a band is in widespread use, however inefficiently, attempts to develop a frequency plan are largely doomed. In the case of HF broadcasting, technical innovations that would enable far more efficient use of the spectrum[12] cannot be established as the current technology is intractably entrenched.

Spectrum management issues have historically taken on an East-West or North-South dimension, with each side accusing the other of inordinately benefiting from ITU decisions, manipulating WARCs, or dominating the discussion within CCIRs or IFRB. The accusations stem from misconceptions concerning what constitutes bargaining leverage and power within the spectrum management process. Three elements contribute to the real sources of this leverage: technical ability to use the spectrum and demands for spectrum space; the power of sovereignty; and the power of Third World voting bloc unity. The first element is without doubt the chief determinant of how much spectrum space a country will employ. The telecommunication requirements of the United States or Soviet Union are far higher than those of India or China, irrespective of population and potential future demands. The United States largely shaped the direction of the ITU in the immediate postwar era because it had by far the greatest spectrum demands and the greatest ability to use the spectrum. As other countries have enhanced their own technical prowess, they have played a significantly greater role within the ITU and have, to a large degree, successfully achieved their objectives at ITU conferences. Noteworthy in this respect are recent technical powers such as Japan, Canada, Australia, as well as newly industrializing countries such as India, Brazil, Indonesia, and China.

The power of sovereignty has grown within the radio frequency spectrum issue as the number of sovereign states has grown. The position of the ITU concerning "sovereignty" over frequencies is discussed above. Countries have a right of access to the spectrum, but no ownership rights. Unfortunately, both the *a priori* and *a posteriori* systems imply ownership of frequencies, leading to confusion. In addition, the tenets of the New World Information Order (NWIO) along with the intergovernmental one-country, one-vote structure of the ITU lead to a considerable importance being given to the position of sovereign states. The smaller developing countries have formed a strong coalition within the ITU and have successfully pressed for increases in the scope and degree of spectrum planning in order to ensure their right of access to the spectrum. This third element, the unity of the Third World voting bloc within the ITU, has become stronger in the late 1980s than it was at the height of NWIO rhetoric at the end of the 1970s. Countries as divergent as Costa Rica, Algeria, and Malaysia have sought to affirm *a priori* planning in the name of equitability and justice. Certain developing country spokesmen have come to be among the leading personalities of recent WARCs and others have been chosen for secondment into the ITU General Secretariat, leading to greater developing country representation.

Deliberate Interference and Control over Information Flows

This issue warrants discussion as it illustrates the relationship of the international telecommunications regulatory regime vis-à-vis the legitimacy of state control over domestic and international information flows. Unlike the other telecommunications issues discussed in this book, this issue has not been strongly influenced by ITU activity. Many other international organizations, as Chapter 3 explains, consider the realm of international information flows. Where telecommunications are involved the issue enters ITU jurisdiction. It will be seen that the ITU has nonetheless been loath to actively involve itself in the resolution of the jamming of broadcasts, the specter of deliberate interference against satellite television, or restrictions against the free flow of news and information. The issue is seen as purely political and thus beyond ITU competence. Yet deliberate interference to broadcasts constitutes a technical process which contravenes specific articles of the ITU Convention and Radio Regulations. Controls on information flows are completely at odds with the purpose of the ITU.

There are, in fact, two elements within this issue. The first, of an East-West dimension, is the jamming of international radio and satellite broadcasts and efforts within the ITU and other organizations to control jamming. Regulation in this area has been motivated by the frustrating cost and inefficiency suffered by administrations targeted by jammers, the damage done to entire broadcasting bands, and the realization that any control—even mild censure—can only have an impact if it takes place through an international forum respected by even the most recalcitrant of jammers.

The second element of the issue is more recent and less specific: it involves the tenets of the New World Information Order (NWIO) which propose rigorous controls on international information flows in order to redress the heavy imbalance in telecommunications flows. The Northern industrialized countries dominate world production of information and communications. The South is fairly united in believing that the "free flow" norm perpetuates this imbalance, and that "balanced flow" and "free flow" are incompatible. Consequently, developing countries have sought to use fora such as the UN General Assembly, UNESCO, and the ITU to legitimize controls and restrictions on the flow of information. This is a form of deliberate interference stemming from different motives than those of the jammers—although even some LDCs will perceive the danger of free flow to rest in its political threat, not in its threat to indigenous socio-cultural development. Regulation of this aspect of deliberate interference has largely *affirmed* the position of those who wish to restrict information flows, namely the developing countries, with voting assistance from the Eastern bloc. While Eastern bloc motives differ from those of the South, many LDCs—including many non-Marxist states—are attracted to the Soviet view of government and people as a single entity.[13]

To the extent that the ITU has been able to achieve successful outcomes in the area of jamming, that success has been largely attributable not to the force of international regulation or censure, but to the sheer cost and inconvenience of jamming. Restricting the flow of information is not an easy process, as Chapter 3 explains. International regulations outside of the ITU which sanction the blockage of incoming information flows make the ITU's role more difficult, particularly if these new restrictions emanate from within the UN system, as several have. The fortunate fact that jamming and other restrictions are not more prevalent is in fact not indicative of a desire on the part of the majority to open up the borders, but instead the grudging realization that controls demand a higher cost than the yielded "benefits" justify.

The states with political leverage in this issue area are thus those states which can afford to jam or otherwise control information flows. This, as far as jamming of international broadcasting goes, has permitted the Soviets to defeat or deflect any concerted international attempt to get the ITU to explicitly censure jamming. Smaller states can gain leverage through collaboration. The power of the NWIO is in the resolutely *collective* position it promotes. The collective hostility of the South toward Northern dominance of international information flows has been keenly reflected in the one-nation, one-vote fora of the UN and its agencies. This is less evident in the ITU than in UNESCO or General Assembly resolutions. Developing country leverage is thus not based upon any technical ability to jam but upon a consensual distrust of the free flow of information principle and the collective ability to act upon that distrust.

Technical Standard-Setting

The role of the ITU consultative committees (CCIR and CCITT) in establishing recommendations for telecommunication technical standards is, along with spectrum management, one of the twin pillars of ITU activity. Standardization is an obvious prerequisite to international telecommunications. This is especially true in radio communications, where the global codes of conduct and technical criteria set by the CCIR are vital to international communications. The CCITT, likewise, has enabled worldwide telephone linkage to occur through sometimes quite specific recommendations. The basis for the bulk of CCI Recommendations and the reason why these recommendations—which do not carry the force of law—are adhered to may be found in a universal recognition of the desirability of standardized telecommunications systems. A related factor is the strong imperative for technical homogeneity, as technical incompatibilities are disquieting to the experts who comprise CCI delegations and personnel.

The need for technical compatibility is the obvious reason for CCI success and, indeed, the explicit rationale behind its recommendations. A less evident but equally important motive behind CCI technical regulation is the ability for countries to obtain access to export markets. A CCI Recommendation confers worldwide approval upon a technology and, if the technology is competing against non-standard rivals, will confer an export advantage. If the technology is developed by a single large firm, particularly a multinational corporation, this too facilitates standardization and CCI approval, as such standards are often developed from their inception with global use in mind.

The CCI norm, as may be apparent by this point, is to set standards in largely a reactive manner. A technology is developed in a specific country or by a certain firm. When worldwide approval of the new technology is sought, it is presented to the CCI which will in turn allocate it to one of its Study Groups or, if the issue is important enough, the CCI will create a new Study Group for it. The result of this research is the unanimous proposal of a "Recommendation" at the CCI Plenary Assemblies, held every four years. Recommendations are not binding, but they must have the consensual approval of members at the Plenary Assembly.

This process, while not flawless, is generally successful (as is described in Chapter 4). The above factors predicate that success. But instances occur that serve to discourage standardization. When heavy investments in incompatible technologies are made and when telecommunications manufacturing industries are threatened by foreign competition, the maintenance of incompatibility may be seen as both desirable and vital as a means of economic protectionism. In effect, differing standards can constitute non-tariff barriers to trade. Only advanced technological powers will possess the leverage necessary to maintain this sort of situation. Likewise, a large firm with a sizeable share of the global market will be able to sway standardization in its favor, irrespective of the technical merits or demerits of its technology.

Developing countries are keenly aware of the leverage of the technological powers within the CCI standardization process. The resultant distrust and hostility on the part of Third World countries toward the CCIs leads to an entrenched belief that LDC interests and needs are not adequately addressed within the Northern "club" atmosphere of the CCIs. As a consequence, the high quality CCIR technical preparatory work for WARCs may be neglected at conferences by developing countries who could greatly benefit from it. Likewise, the 1984 Maitland Commission on Telecommunications Development, which focused chiefly on the development of telephone in the Third World, did not once mention a role for the CCITT in this development. Unlike the situation in spectrum management or information flows, developing countries have not amassed leverage in the ITU standard-setting bodies. At the heart of their inability to do so is the technical nature of the CCIs. Delegations must, by and large, possess considerable technical acumen and be able to contribute to the Study Groups and working parties. Moves to increase developing country involvement through reducing the price of CCI publications or subsidizing the travel costs of Third World delegations have come from the Administrative Council. This "reform from above"[14] is not indicative of a Third World impetus to become involved in the CCIs as much as it is reflective of an ITU fear that without such LDC involvement the CCIs might face a precarious future. The problem of reconciling Third World aspirations to the reality of CCI standardization is discussed in Chapter 4, as are forthcoming changes in CCI structure and function which may dramatically alter the political position of the developing countries within the ITU technical standard-setting regime.

*　　*　　*

The above brief overview covers the three central issue areas which are explained in the subsequent three chapters. Each chapter attempts to illustrate the political salience of the issue area as a consequence of the evolution of groupings and alignments of forces within the issue, why regulations have emerged, and why they have or have not been successful. The ITU is not solely a technical body. There is a politics of international telecommunications that is quite unrelated to what has been termed "politicization" of the international telecommunications regime. By identifying this "politics," explaining why it must exist, and why certain countries or groups of countries have at different times and on different issues dominated it, I hope to dispel the fallacious notion that the ITU is in decline or under threat of abduction by one state or group of states. At the same time, the self-congratulatory "professionalism" with which many of those active in the international telecommunications regime attempt to approach the ITU may be equally misguided. It is popular to look at the ITU as a purely technical, dispassionate forum in which technical professionals base decisions upon engineering principles and hence serve the greater good. There is much to be said of this view, but the "professionalism" of the ITU does not go far in explaining many of the actions of the Union or its members when discussing the three issue areas. By removing the blinkers of "dispassionate professionalism," New World Information Order ideology, or Western fears of "politicization," it is hoped that we might gain a better understanding of the ITU, *why* it does what it does, and why the political nature of the Union need not be ignored, denigrated, or feared.

Politics are not new to international telecommunications issues. The remainder of this chapter will briefly describe the central issues, conflicts, and alignments that have dominated the 150 year history of the technology. We will conclude by surveying the changes within ITU power and function since the momentous ITU conferences of 1947, and how the output and scope of ITU activity have changed, by looking at seven areas of change within the international telecommunications order. Before launching into the issue areas it is important to have a sense of the dynamism of telecommunications and how the ITU of the 1980s is dramatically unlike the ITU of 1906, or 1956.

The ITU: Evolution of
an International Organization

Electric telegraphy, the fruition of the efforts of Morse, Wheatstone, and Cooke, commenced regular operations in England in 1837 and in the United States in 1844.[15] Most European countries established domestic telegraphy networks by the early 1850s, usually under the auspices of the national post office. When, in the earliest days of European telegraphy, messages for neighboring countries were sent, they were duly telegraphed to the border, transcribed, literally handed across the border, then recoded and sent on to their destination. Clearly this was a slow, costly, and inefficient method which demanded international cooperation to rectify.

The first such effort to link the telegraph systems of neighboring states occurred in October 1849 between Prussia and Austria. These two countries went on one year later to reach multilateral agreements with Bavaria and Saxony to create the Austro-German Telegraph Union. While this was formally an international agreement, it was seen at the time as a complementary part of the economic and political integration of the German *Zollverein*. The organization promoted the interconnection of national telegraphy systems, standardized coding and tariff agreements, and guaranteed the autonomy of member states to reach telegraphy agreements with "foreign" powers.[16]

France soon consolidated the non-Germanic European states into a similar union.[17] From the beginning there was a close correspondence between the Western and Central European unions. The Convention of the West European Telegraph Union, as this French-led organization was called, was to serve as the model for the first ITU Convention.

It is of interest to note that Britain was purposely excluded from both continental unions as its telegraphs were privately owned. The French administration in particular, and most European administrations in general, found the idea of privately owned telegraphs abhorrent and antithetical to administrative logic and international cooperation. This disapproval was manifested in 1858 by the exclusion of English as an official language for international telegrams—only French or German would be acceptable.[18]

By the mid-1860s the level of telegraph traffic and the inefficiency inherent in having two separate European telegraph unions made governments receptive to the idea of a single centralized union. It is perhaps not surprising, given France's leadership role in the "Concert of Europe" and its proclivities toward the centralizing of power in domestic matters, that it was the French Imperial government that first promoted the idea of the ITU. Keith Clark, writing in the early 1930s, somewhat bombastically ascribed the following motives to France's call for one Union: "The Emperor Napoleon III, at the height of his imperial glory, and neglecting no means which would centralize the world in France, moved then to secure a European entente by the scarcely visible wires of telegraphic solidarity."[19]

The French government convened an International Telegraph Conference in Paris in May 1865 to draft a convention for a new Union. Twenty European states attended.[20] Great Britain remained excluded. France put forth a complete draft Convention, largely based on the West European Telegraph Union Convention of 1858. The central achievements of the founding conference of the ITU were the establishment of a European telegraphy network through the standardization of Morse code, the setting of an acceptable rate structure, and the decision to hold periodic meetings of the European telegraphy administrations. In addition, other countries could join the Convention through notifying the French government of their implementation of the Convention and Regulations.[21]

The ITU at first did not possess a permanent secretariat. However, the Vienna Telegraph Conference of 1868 decided to accept a Swiss proposal to establish an "International Bureau of Telegraph Administrations." This new permanent bureau was entrusted solely with administrative duties: gathering technical information, publishing rate tables, statistics, and a journal on telegraphy matters (the *Journal Telegraphique*).[22] There appeared to be little controversy involved in the decision to allow neutral Switzerland to be the permanent home of what came to be known as the Bern Bureau, nor in the decision to let the Swiss government run the Bureau. The Vienna Conference also extended the authority of the telegraph convention to private telegraph agencies in member states. One consequence of the recognition of private operators was the accession by Great Britain to the Convention.[23] This change of heart appeared motivated by the need to "internationalize" the Union.[24] Moving the headquarters of the Union to Switzerland had been a first step in this regard.

The issue of deliberate interference—in this case the physical destruction of telegraph lines during the Franco-Prussian War of 1870—was first raised by the ITU at the 1871 Rome Telegraph Conference, with telegraph pioneer Samuel Morse expressing the hope "that the conference will not adjourn without adopting a resolution asking the universal protection of all nations for this powerful agent of civilization."[25] Such a resolution was considered outside the jurisdiction of the ITU Plenary Assembly.

Four years later a growing ITU, boasting 24 member countries and 16 recognized private companies, held a major telegraphy conference at St. Petersburg. The conference drafted a new, simplified convention that was to remain in force for 60 years. This draft, compiled by the Bern Bureau, introduced Administrative Conferences to periodically revise the telegraph regulations and permitted members to "reserve" the right to abrogate portions of the Convention in order to ensure domestic tele-communications objectives. This power was opposed by the Italian delegate who argued that such an option, if exercised by one or more members, could render the entire Convention useless.[26] While it may be true that this reservation power creates enforcement problems for the ITU, it is difficult to determine how the ITU could have survived, particularly in the more politically turbulent twentieth century, without the flexibility such an option offers to dissenting members.

The longevity of the St. Petersburg Convention is attributable to several unique factors. The world system of states was then fairly Eurocentric, and European practices were largely accepted by others. However, the ITU did grow from 24 countries at St. Petersburg to 48 members by 1914.[27] But growing telecommunications users such as the United States and China remained out of the Union during this time. In the American case the highly domestic nature of its telecommunications traffic made accession to the Eurocentric Union a fairly unimportant objective to US communications policy.[28] Nevertheless, the United States sent observers to each of the six ITU conferences held between 1875 and 1914.[29]

Another factor promoting stability was the nature of development in telecommunications technology. Unlike recent decades, in which technical progress has become a constant process featuring an incessant flow of developments in a myriad of areas, technical progress in the early years of telecommunications tended to consist of infrequent but momentous discoveries and inventions. This compelled the regulatory order to retain at least a modicum of flexibility in order to accommodate such change. One such technological breakthrough was the implementation of tele-phony, which was recognized by the ITU at the 1903 London Telegraphy Conference as falling under ITU jurisdiction.[30] At London fifteen articles dealing with telephone services were added to the regulations. The important development of radio communications was, however, not considered by the ITU but by autonomous radio conferences (see below). This is particularly curious as any sort of regular sound broadcasting was still years in the future. Early radio traffic consisted of wireless telegraphy, and there seemed to exist an obvious role for the ITU. This point was expressed by the British delegate to the 1908 Lisbon Telegraph Conference,[31] but was not fully addressed by the ITU until 1932.

The ITU saw the first challenge to its authority during World War I. The war resulted in the complete breakdown of the telecommunications order in Europe. Many international telegraphy services were suspended. The increased use of radio by the combatting forces served as a harbinger of radio's growing power, and of the need of any post–World War I regime to address the international control of this technology.

Telecommunication "Recovery Conferences" were held in 1920 and 1921, but the most significant ITU Conference convened in this period was the Paris Telegraph Conference of 1925. At this conference the ITU added two new bodies to its existing structure: the International Consultative Committee on Long-distance Telephones (CCIF—its French acronym), which had been founded independently by a group of European telephone administrations one year earlier, and the International Consultative Committee on Telegraphs (CCIT). The history and political salience of the CCIs are detailed in Chapter 4. The role of the CCIs was to issue recommendations regarding the standardization of telephone and telegraph equipment, systems, and circuits between countries. The impetus behind the creation of the CCIs was the strong desire, particularly on the part of France, to establish a single European telephone network. While this may have been motivated by a French desire to guarantee its supremacy in European technological development, most of the delegates to the new committees merely believed that the technology had evolved to a point where an international network was feasible and desirable, and that these cooperative committees were a natural and ideal way of facilitating the realization of this goal.

The 1925 Paris Conference also considered two other major issues: revision of the St. Petersburg Convention and merger with the International Radio Conferences. The two issues were quite related. The British delegate suggested that any revision to the Convention should include the incorporation of the Radio Conferences into the ITU.[32] This sentiment was reiterated at the 1928 Brussels Telegraph Conference, where the ITU accepted Spain's invitation to hold the next conference five years hence in Madrid concurrently with the next International Radio Conference. This was a deliberate final step taken to establish a merger between the ITU and the Radio Conferences.

These Radio Conferences had existed autonomously for 29 years. Yet the complementarity of radio to telegraphy was obvious from the first experimental wireless transmissions of Marconi in 1896. The international potential of the medium was first demonstrated by Marconi one year later with the transmission of a wireless telegraphy signal from England to Newfoundland. Why was this new technology, so relevant to future international telecommunications, not immediately incorporated into the ITU? Unlike the telephone, early radio was in fact merely "wireless telegraphy"—sound broadcasting was still far off in the future. As a type of telegraphy, radio was subject to many of the same principles of coding, transmission, and standardization as "wired" telegraphy. Yet the ITU embraced telephony but rejected radio communications for nearly three decades—or until it became overwhelmingly evident that radio was becoming a rival to wired telegraphy as the dominant means of international telecommunications.

Reluctance to embrace radio within the ITU was in part a consequence of the technology's historical development. The most obvious consumer for this new technology was transoceanic shipping, where the ability to communicate with other vessels and with shore-based stations could provide immeasurable improvements in maritime safety and efficiency. But the development of maritime radio did not occur through government administrations as had European telegraphy or telephony. It was instead the Anglo-Italian Marconi Wireless Company which quickly established a virtual global monopoly on maritime radio communications. Within six years of his first demonstration of international wireless telegraphy, Marconi possessed 45 coast stations, three high-powered land stations in England, Canada, and the United States, as well as innumerable stations on military and commercial vessels traversing the North Atlantic.

National telecommunications administrations had little to say about these developments in the early years of radio technology. The first competition to Marconi came not from governments but from two private competitors.[33] It was soon obvious that radio communications were developing along commercial lines quite unlike their telephone and telegraph predecessors. Yet the dominance of Marconi seemed to obviate the need for an international organization or affiliation with the ITU. By 1903 Marconi controlled international and maritime communications in Great Britain, France, Italy, Canada, Newfoundland, and the United States.[34]

Marconi was, by the early 1900s, actively attempting to establish a global monopoly over maritime radio. Part of this endeavor involved requiring that ships with Marconi equipment ban all communications with any radio station employing non-Marconi equipment.[35] After the occurrence of several incidents which jeopardized the general safety of the Atlantic shipping routes, the German government, never having been pleased with the Marconi monopoly from either an economic or nationalistic standpoint, took the initiative and called for the convening of a conference to study the international regulation of radio. The fact that the administrations of France, Austria, Britain, Hungary, Italy, Imperial Russia, Spain and the United States all responded positively to the invitation demonstrates that Germany was not the only country worried about the growth of "Marconi-ism."[36]

When the Preliminary Radio Conference of 1903 met in Berlin, however, it soon became apparent that Britain and Italy were attending the conference in order to defend Marconi against the "prejudicial" German and central European administrations. Both employed the argument that the Marconi system was the most efficient and should, therefore, be universally adopted and standardized. The French delegate questioned the wisdom of implementing any regulations given the infant state of the technology. Nevertheless a final protocol was laboriously drafted, with the most important resolution calling for "Coast stations (to be) bound to receive and transmit telegrams for ships at sea . . . without distinction as to the system of radio used by the latter."[37] This was a non-binding protocol, however, and Britain and Italy may have anticipated being able to sway an actual Convention in their favor.

The German government wished to quickly follow up this international protocol with the establishment of a Convention and Radio Regulations while an anti-Marconi majority could be sustained. The Conference was nevertheless postponed until 1906 by the Russo-Japanese War. In that year, 29 nations met in Berlin to draft a Convention and Radio Regulations. The third article of the 1906 Convention reiterated the obligation of radio operators to disregard the type of system employed when exchanging radiograms.[38] Nine of the countries present, including Britain and Italy, reserved the right to exempt themselves from this Article.

The structure of the international radio order was a contentious issue at the 1906 conference. The German government proposed the establishment of a permanent International Radio Union on the lines of the ITU administrative Bern Bureau. The majority of other delegates, recognizing the complementarity of the two organizations, preferred to entrust the administration of radio conferences to the ITU Bern Bureau and the Swiss government, which directed the Bureau.

The central achievement of the 1906 radio conference was the first assignment of parts of the existing radio frequency spectrum for specific radio services.[39] This function—the assignment of "Bands"—quickly evolved into a central function of the radio conferences. So too did the implementation of basic radio use standards, as became apparent at the next Radio Conference in London in 1912. In view of the then recent Titanic disaster, in which a ship less than 20 miles from the scene could not be summoned as her radio operator had gone to bed,[40] the 1912 London Conference was preoccupied with the promotion of safety standards and codes of conduct for maritime radio communications.

While telegraphy was thrown into disorder and decline with the advent of World War I, radio flourished during the Great War. Radio was found indispensible for military use, including communication with aircraft. Radio technology rapidly developed during the war years as governments increasingly appreciated the medium's value for military communications.

The value of amalgamating radio and telegraph unions was not lost on the victorious powers. The optimism created by perceptions of a new postwar social and economic order and the spirit of cooperation exemplified by the new League of Nations prompted the allied victors to envisage something greater and more ambitious than a mere incorporation of the radio conferences into the ITU. In November 1920, the Allied and Associated Powers (Britain, France, Japan, Italy, and the United States) met in Washington, D.C., at the invitation of the United States government to establish a "Universal Electric-Communications Union" which would have jurisdiction over all aspects of telecommunications.[41] Over twelve days the conference rapidly drew up a Draft Convention and formulated specific telephone-telegraph, cable, and radio regulations. In addition, an International Technical Committee on Radiocommunications was established to "study and advise on all problems pertaining to radio."[42]

But the proposal for the "Universal Electric-Communications Union" was never ratified, and the Union never came to be. It was in fact the panoramic scope of its proposed jurisdiction which doomed it. While the United States had been the key promoter of the union, the American delegates soon realized that accession to the proposed global telegraph-telephone, cable, and radio regulations would require consultation and approval from each and every private telecommunications operator in the United States.[43] Neither the United States nor Canada would accept the rate tables negotiated by the conference as telegraph rates were set by private companies in North America and only supervised within non-specific guidelines by governments. Yet the Washington Preliminary Conference of 1920 remained a significant step in the development of an international regulatory regime for, despite its failure, many of the proposals made by participants were later adopted by the ITU. The 1920 Washington Conference may be credited with envisaging a single telecommunications union with a centralized authority, an interim governing council, consultative committees, the need to allocate radio frequency bands, the adoption of schemes to avoid harmful interference, and the need to somehow recognize major private telecommunications operators[44]

The failure of the Washington conference of 1920 affected attitudes toward future conferences. There seemed no urgency to convene an international radio conference to address the growth of sound broadcasting. Yet, by the mid-1920s virtually every European country had a national radio broadcasting service, and North America was becoming rapidly inundated by a large number of private broadcasters. Since the Radio Conferences remained blinkered to all but point-to-point radio communications, national and regional solutions had to be found to rectify a situation in which radio broadcast frequency and power allocations were occurring in a haphazard, uncoordinated manner, with a consequent high degree of harmful interference burdening the European and North American broadcast bands.

In 1925 British broadcasters invited their major European counterparts to gather in London to form the Union Internationale de Radiodiffusion (UIR) and bring about a voluntary redistribution of broadcast frequencies. It was a remarkably successful endeavor. Likewise, in the United States the level of interference on the broadcast band prompted the 1924 remark of Secretary of Commerce Herbert Hoover that "broadcasting is probably the only industry of the US that is unanimously in favour of having itself regulated."[45] The US Federal Radio Commission was founded in 1927 to undertake the difficult task of "cleaning up" the broadcast band.[46] Two years later a multilateral agreement regarding service allocations on the broadcast band was reached with Canada and Mexico: the North American Regional Broadcast Agreement (NARBA) of 1929, which survived intact for 52 years.

The "last hurrah" of the non-ITU radio conferences was the Washington Radio conference of 1927, the first major IRU conference since 1912. Delegates from over 80 countries convened to draft a new Convention and Radio Regulations. For the first time the entire known radio spectrum was allocated to various radio services, thus establishing what was to become the central function of ITU Administrative Conferences. The 1927 Radio Conference brought forward some of the basic philosophical differences between the European administrations, which dominated the conference, and the Americans, who were hosting the conference. Neither the United States nor Canada were members of the ITU due to the dominance of private companies in their telegraph and telephone communications. They were, however, signatory to radio conferences, and were therefore opposed to being obligated to any sections of the Washington Convention that concerned radiotelegraph tariff and rate structures or the routing of radiograms.[47] The United States proposed a means by which the North American countries could adhere to the Convention and remain consistent to American principles of free enterprise. This was done by placing all contentious provisions into a separate set of "Supplemental Regulations" while leaving general articles adhered to by all members in the Convention per se.[48]

For perhaps the first time, overtly political influences unassociated with the use of telecommunications were present at the Washington Conference. The United States government, as host of the conference, refused to allow the government of the USSR to attend. Predictably, the Soviets submitted a formal protest, claiming that as full members of the IRU and signatories to the 1912 Convention they could not be excluded from the Conference.[49] Despite its exclusion, the Soviets were allowed to submit proposals to the conference. Much to the chagrin of the United States, later expulsions and exclusions of American allies such as Israel, Spain, and Portugal by LDC majorities were given legitimacy by this 1927 American precedent.

The brief and unhappy life of the 1920 International Technical Committtee on Radiocommunications did not prevent the proposal at the 1927 Conference of a Radio Conference-affiliated Radio Consultative Committee (CCIR), although a great deal of controversy surrounded the proposal. In place of the enthusiasm delegations had shown in 1920 for such a committee, the major powers now actively opposed such a body. The motives behind this opposition are described in Chapter 4. In the end, with some compromise and the active support of Italy and Germany, the CCIR was established by a close vote.[50] The 1927 Washington Conference concluded as had the 1929 Paris ITU Conference, with the passage of a resolution calling for an examination of the possibility of a merger of the International Radio Conferences with the ITU.[51] Both orders recognized that the growing degree of duplication and the complementarity of objectives indicated the extent to which the maintenance of this separation was proving to be both unnecessary and costly.

The merger of the ITU and Radio Conferences into the International Telecommunication Union occurred at the 1932 Madrid Telegraph and Radiotelegraph Conferences. Not the least of the difficulties in drafting a new Convention was the accommodation of American and Canadian interests to ensure they would join the Union. The Convention was modified to incorporate only general principles and its telephone and telegraph section was pared down and generalized to satisfy the North American administrations.[52] Yet the concessions made for the United States and Canada required, if only for the sake of political equitability, that similar concessions be allowed for others. Therefore the Conference, at the suggestion of France, placated others by providing for the power of reservation—countries could reserve the right to modify or abrogate parts of the agreement.[53] Not all were satisfied with this compromise, and Canada, the United States, the Netherlands, and Nicaragua voted against what became, by a fifty-to-four vote, the first Convention of the ITU.

Modification to the radio regulations merely reiterated principles and methods employed at the 1927 Radio Conference. Yet broadcasting remained on the margins of ITU activity through the 1930s. A European Broadcasting Conference of the UIR was held in Brussels in 1933 to create a full *a priori* broadcast plan for Europe. A similar and equally successful conference was held for the Americas in 1938—the "First

Inter-American Radio Conference"—to allocate frequencies on the lines of the 1929 North American Radio Broadcasters Agreement (NARBA). The remainder of the 1930s witnessed several evolutionary changes to the ITU. Not until the end of the decade, however, did the Union address the increasingly contentious issue of broadcasting frequency assignments and the avoidance of harmful interference on the broadcast bands. It had been hoped that regional cooperative agreements would resolve disputes between broadcasters. The inability of European broadcasting organizations to reach an agreement similar to the 1938 Havana Regional Agreement for the Americas led the 1938 Cairo ITU Administrative Radio and Telephone and Telegraph Conferences to schedule the first European Regional Administrative Radio Conference for the spring and summer of 1939. As is illustrated in the following chapter, the Cairo conference was perhaps best known for the frequency management issues that dominated it.

Five months before the outbreak of World War II the ITU finally turned its attention to radio broadcasting, holding a conference at Montreux to revise the 1933 and 1925 broadcasters' voluntary plans for Europe. The European Broadcasting Union (UIR) remained the resident technical expert and broadcaster's voice at the Conference. A full *a priori* allocation plan, replacing the 1933 plan, was achieved with surprisingly little difficulty. The plan was scheduled to take effect on the somewhat unfortunate date of September 1, 1939, at one minute after midnight.[54] For obvious reasons the plan never came into effect.

World War II brought about the unprecedented disruption of all telecommunications systems. Telecommunications networks throughout much of Europe and Asia were destroyed. Existing services adopted cavalier survivalist tactics concerning frequency allocation and deliberate interference. Despite the destruction, radio proved itself as the paramount communications medium of the era. From propaganda broadcasting to maritime radar, radio technology became central to the war efforts of both sides. It was at this time that maritime and aviation radio, high frequency (shortwave) broadcasting, and most other radio technologies experienced dramatic technical advancement. In addition, new radio technologies such as teleprinters and radar were introduced through military use.

The regulatory order, however, came out of the war in a devastated state. The Bern Bureau, in neutral Switzerland, had kept the ITU alive—if only as a letterhead—during the war. A short-lived 1942 Axis "European Postal and Telecommunications Union," sponsored by the German administration, was made subordinate to the ITU at the insistence of Italy. As early as 1943 the United States had commenced studying possible priorities and organization for a postwar ITU. By the Third Inter-American

Radio Conference in the autumn of 1945, the Americans had ready an explicit plan for the re-establishment of the ITU. It was at this conference that the United States proposed the establishment of an International Frequency Registration Board (IFRB).[55] (See Chapter 2) At a meeting of the Great Powers at Moscow in 1946 the USSR supported the idea of an IFRB whereas Britain and France, fearing loss of European control over the Union, were lukewarm in their support.

The optimism surrounding the new United Nations organization prompted the Moscow conference to promote ITU affiliation with the UN. It was hoped that the ITU could give the new UN the credibility of an established organization while the UN could give the ITU a modern, internationalist atmosphere. The Soviet Union was the chief promoter of strong ITU-UN links and automatic membership in the ITU of UN members. But the United States was the only country among the five to suggest a meeting place for the planned 1947 Conferences, namely Atlantic City.

The final step in the evolution of the modern ITU occurred at the Atlantic City Conferences of 1947. Atlantic City was a watershed in the history of the ITU, changing the nature, structure, and—to an extent—the function of the ITU. Three conferences were held to reconstruct the moribund Union: a Plenipotentiary Conference to revise the 1932 Madrid Convention, an Administrative Radio Conference to revise the 1938 Cairo Radio Regulations, and an Administrative High Frequency (HF, or shortwave) Radio Conference. The magnitude and scope of the meeting was of unparalleled proportions.[56]

The extent to which the old ITU had been devastated by the war and the amount of rebuilding required to restore the Union promoted serious discussion within the United States concerning the feasibility of scrapping the ITU and starting anew. Admittedly, the norms and principles which governed the prewar Union seemed, in light of the new postwar political and economic order, to be hopelessly Eurocentric and archaic. A precedent for establishing a new body had been set when the prewar international civil aviation body CINA (Comite Internationale de Navigation Aerienne) was scrapped and a new organization introduced with a larger, more international scope and UN affiliation (ICAO—the International Civil Aviation Organization).[57] However, it was decided that the Atlantic City Conferences would not have to be quite so revolutionary. The objectives of the Union did not require major alterations as much as a "fresh impulse".[58] The Plenipotentiary held in 1947 was perhaps the most significant such conference ever held by the Union. Members had already agreed to affiliate the ITU to the UN as a UN specialized agency and to modify ITU structure along UN lines. However, when the USSR proposed a UN-style two-thirds majority voting procedure several countries objected. In the end, the two-thirds formula was accepted.

In general, the ITU and the International Telecommunications Convention were reorganized along UN lines. An Administrative Council of 18 members was established to act on behalf of the Plenipotentiary Conference in the intervals between Plenipotentiaries (Article 5). A General Secretariat responsible to the Administrative Council superceded the Bern Bureau. No longer would the administration of the ITU be the sole responsibility of the Swiss government and hence dominated by Swiss nationals: "Due regard must be paid to the importance of recruiting staff on as wide a geographical basis as possible."[59]

What has been termed "the most important development of the 1947 Atlantic City Convention"[60] occurred with the creation of the International Frequency Registration Board (IFRB), envisaged by its American proponents as an "international FCC (US Federal Communications Commission) with power to police the air."[61] The 1947 Convention mandates the independent body to "effect an orderly recording of frequency assignments made by the different countries . . . and to furnish advice to members and associate members" regarding allocation issues.[62] Members of the Board do not sit on behalf of their countries but as independent members. The goal of the IFRB was to be the creation of a Master Frequency List of a planned, *a priori* spectrum. This was clearly a far more active role than the old Bern Bureau's recording of frequencies in use. The evolution of the IFRB and the frequency management order is detailed in Chapter 2.

The ITU Consultative Committees (CCIs) were merely recognized by the 1947 Convention and their arrangements were left to the Regulations.[63] The structures of the CCIT and CCIR (the telephone and radio committees) were slightly modified to more closely resemble that of the CCIF (long-distance telephone) which, as the Swiss delegate pointed out, was noteworthy for its past success.[64] The CCIF was then itself brought closer to the ITU. A proposal by Norway to merge the CCIF and CCIT was opposed, but an Italian proposal to study the feasibility of such a move was adopted.[65] This merger was finally achieved nine years later.

At the Atlantic City Conferences, the ITU became a UN specialized agency. Some concern was expressed over ITU linkage with the essentially political UN—best illustrated by the remarks of the Belgian delegate:

Our Union is an essentially technical and administrative body and that, as a result, international politics must continue to be excluded from its discussions. Belgium is favorable to our Union being connected with the UN, but under the formal stipulation that the complete independence of the ITU shall be maintained.[66]

Under Article 26 and Annex 5 of the 1947 Convention, the ITU is guaranteed full autonomy subject to general coordination and correspondence with the UN. The UN may propose items for discussion at ITU Plenipotentiary and Administrative Council Conferences.[67] This article by itself may have introduced a new political element to the ITU. As a UN specialized agency the ITU is under some obligation to consider its relationship with countries condemned by the UN and to discuss certain issues considered by the UN General Assembly to be of high priority. Such issues have over the years included condemnation of colonial powers and of countries employing discriminatory or racist policies (e.g., South Africa and Israel). The discussion of these nontechnical issues at Plenipotentiary Conferences has, particularly in recent years, led to accusations that the ITU is becoming unduly "politicized" and is straying from its chief purpose.

Changes in the ITU Since 1947

The changes that took place at the 1947 Atlantic Conferences were revolutionary. No less important, however, have been the evolutionary changes that have occurred in the four decades since Atlantic City. New issues, unforeseen in 1947, have emerged to compete with the traditional roles of spectrum management, avoidance of interference, and standardization. These traditional issues have themselves changed in scope and nature, and have in turn acted to change the ITU itself. As subsequent chapters focus on the effects of the regime on selected issue areas, a few words are needed regarding the influence of changes in both the traditional and more recent issue areas on the regulatory regime.

The Authority of Organization in Spectrum Management

The order emergent from the 1947 Conferences established a tripartite frequency management regime. WARCs and RARCs would periodically revise the Radio Regulations as they pertained to specific bands and services within the spectrum. The CCIR would provide technical preparation for these conferences, and the IFRB would register and monitor frequency use. An ill-fated fourth component, the Provisional Frequency Board (PFB), was a product of postwar optimism that sought to assign in advance (i.e., a priori planning) every frequency in use on every part of the spectrum. The technical impossibility of this task was quickly realized, and any minimal success the Provisional Frequency Board might have accomplished was largely precluded by Soviet bloc accusations of, among other things, American domination of the Board, unfair distribution of frequencies, and refusal to acknowledge the Soviet claims on the

1939 Bern Bureau List (these claims were regarded by all but the USSR as excessive). The Soviets withdrew from the Board late in 1949, hastening the Board's death.

Until the mid-1960s, the chief area of contention within spectrum management was conflict between East and West. Ironically, this may have served as a catalyst for the emergence of a workable frequency registration system, which was established at the 1959 General WARC and has been in force since that time. While this is described in Chapter 2, it will suffice here to say that the postwar spirit that led otherwise reasonable technicians and engineers to believe that they would allocate and assign every frequency was terminated not by a recognition of the immense technical difficulty of the endeavor but by the general state of Soviet-American relations in the early 1950s. The hostility of the USSR toward the Union was based on a belief that the ITU was, like the UN General Assembly at that time, dominated by a US-Western allied voting bloc. In addition, the Soviets had recorded frequency assignments on virtually every usable frequency on the old 1939 Bern List. They realized that any comprehensive review of this list would threaten these registrations. This East-West stand-off dominated frequency management concerns throughout the 1950s, and is held culpable for the demise of the Provisional Frequency Board—even though that may have been inevitable for technical reasons as well—and for the poorly defined mandate of the IFRB up to 1959. After the PFB was officially wound up in 1951, there was a half-hearted transfer of its mandate to the IFRB, so at least in a nominal sense the IFRB was committed to *a priori* allocation of the entire spectrum until 1959. In that year a General WARC was held and a new frequency registration system hammered out. The machinations resulting in this system are described in Chapter 2.

As the 1960s progressed the role of developing countries in the ITU increased dramatically. The emergence of direct broadcast satellite (DBS) technology and the need to allocate new portions of the spectrum led to a resumption of calls for *a priori* planning in these new bands. Unlike past efforts, which had been based upon motives of technical efficiency, these new calls were motivated by a collective Third World belief in *a priori* versus *a posteriori* (the first-come, first-served status quo) planning. This debate has led the ITU to consider and implement *a priori* plans on some bands and for some services, while not substantially altering the status quo. WARCs were becoming tangibly more concerned with the needs and aspirations of developing countries. Equitability came to match efficiency in ITU spectrum management criteria.

After 1959 the IFRB quickly established itself as the arm of the ITU most responsive to developing country concerns. This was in part due to its role as advisor on spectrum matters to countries not possessing the domestic resources for independent spectrum management. Third World countries came to rely on the IFRB. But instead of resenting such dependence, developing countries viewed the Board as their permanent ally within the ITU spectrum management system. Not all countries shared this laudatory view of the IFRB, however. Some observers, not realizing how the IFRB was changing, viewed the Board as merely an embarrassing holdover from the days of 1950s attempts to plan the entire spectrum. Others criticized the Board as being bloated, inefficient, and unable to "carry its weight" within the ITU. Still others feared Third World domination of the Board as a future possibility. Even within the ITU itself not everyone was pleased with the autonomy of the Board, and periodically the Secretary-General's office would propose bringing the Board under the Secretary-General's authority. This would enhance the power and prestige of the Secretary-General while not actually affecting the Board's ability to do its job, at least from a technical standpoint. Nevertheless, little support could be found for this idea outside of the Secretary-General's office.

The IFRB remained the most contentious element within the ITU well into the 1960s. At the 1965 Montreux Plenipotentiary Conference the United States along with several other countries proposed abolishing the IFRB and replacing it with a "frequency registration department" within the General Secretariat to be headed by a single director elected at a WARC.[68] The arguments for the abolition were not based on the failure of the PFB or the lack of a planned spectrum. It was argued that the IFRB had successfully achieved the goals of establishing a master register and norms for frequency use and that, as the German delegate stated, "11 highly paid experts were no longer necessary to manage the IFRB."[69] But it was not obvious that the IFRB had completed its task. LDCs increasingly viewed the IFRB as their voice within the ITU due to the Board's broad geographic base and its perceived independence and impartiality. The IFRB was considered by LDCs as an essential tool for the development of efficient telecommunications since the Board's staff offered them technical advice. The 1965 Plenipotentiary was thus pervaded with grandiloquent speeches from LDC members lauding the IFRB.

A compromise was finally reached paring the IFRB from 11 to five members. This occurred after the LDCs had "saved" the Board by voting for its retention by a vote of 64 to 39.[70] It was recognized by all members, however, that a certain degree of inefficiency had crept into the Board and that, as the Mexican delegate bluntly put it, "the most notable shortcoming . . . was that the workload of the Board had been distributed over only half its members."[71]

Since 1965 the IFRB has become universally recognized as a vital, indispensable component of ITU spectrum management activity. As the LDCs have become a greater force within the Union, the trend has been to transfer greater responsibility to the IFRB. This has been especially pronounced in the 1980s due to the implementation of two-session WARCs in which the lion's share of the intersessional work becomes the IFRB's responsibility. The IFRB, as a consequence, now takes a more active and involved role in WARCs and the ITU than has ever been the case in the past.

While the reputation of the IFRB might appear in the late 1980s to be at a zenith, certain resource limitations and time constraints, discussed in Chapter 2, have taxed the Board's ability to act effectively. Moreover, it must be recalled that the radio frequency spectrum is not a static resource, but can be periodically expanded—as technology warrants—to encompass new bands. This means the IFRB's bailiwick is constantly growing, although its monetary resources and size are fixed. By the mid-1980s the IFRB was entrusted with a new and considerable task: developing an allotment plan for satellite positions in the geostationary orbit in time for the Second Session of the GSO-WARC. While the IFRB has come to increasingly rely on computer technology for much of its technical work, it is the five members of the Board who must make the essentially juridical decisions regarding assignments. The velocity of technical change, and concerns about the Board's ability to keep pace with it, led in 1982 to Resolution 68 of that year's Plenipotentiary, which promises "A Review in the Light of Changing Circumstances of the Long-Term Future of the IFRB."[72]

Change to the ITU spectrum management order has been the result of two dramatic developments. First, the scope of the IFRB and the activity of WARCs and RARCs has been enlarged by rapid technological progress, particularly in the emergence of new satellite bands, new segments of the spectrum, and the need to allot the GSO. Secondly, the growth in ITU membership since 1947—almost exclusively from the emergent developing countries—has created a metamorphosis in the voting patterns and tone of ITU conferences. The ITU is now compelled to consider in frequency management the needs and concerns of those countries which are at the "wrong end" of the technology gap and who must rely on the ITU to maintain their unhindered access to the spectrum, if necessary by reserving frequencies–or orbit allotments–to specific developing countries. Such reservations, in other words *a priori* planning, have been given a new impetus in the latter part of the century by both the developing country belief in *a priori* planning as a means of achieving a just redistribution of a common resource and by the technical feasibility of developing *a priori* plans for new, and as yet unexploited bands. This latter factor motivated Western Europe into favoring *a priori* assignment of the DBS television bands. Equitability of access, fairness in distribution, and then efficiency of operation are the goals of the WARCs, the IFRB, and that element of the CCIR involved in this area.

Organizational Effects of Deliberate Interference and "New World Information Order" Tenets on the ITU

This issue is the focus of Chapter 3. Prior to the emergence of the LDCs, the ITU position on deliberate controls on the free flow of information was as unambiguous as it was remonstrative. Deliberate "controls" consisted chiefly of the jamming of radio signals directed from abroad. This jamming violated several specific ITU radio regulations as well as contravening the spirit of the International Telecommunication Convention. As far as jamming of radio signals is concerned, this situation is largely still the case, as Chapter 3 describes. The extent of jamming and actual deliberate interference is determined above all by the state of East-West relations.

Since the late 1950s, however, a new element has given the issue of control over information flows a new political salience and an increased relevance for the ITU. In the late 1960s and early 1970s the ascendency of the Third World in many international organizations, particularly the UN General Assembly and UNESCO, was accompanied by a concern on the part of these countries that the coming telecommunications "global village" was in fact threatening the development of their indigenous cultures. The New World Information Order (NWIO) emerged in the mid-1970s as an organized manifestation of these concerns. The NWIO is a part of the New International Economic Order, which seeks to redress the imbalance of economic progress and wealth. The NWIO has had a myriad of implications for the ITU, some of which are discussed below. Where information flows are concerned, the NWIO reaffirms the sovereign rights of states to control the dissemination of information to its citizenry. This is a natural progression of the dominant belief within the Third World that the Northern media have not well served the "South" and must be supplanted by domestic or regional media to as great an extent as possible. Regulatory constraints, including those at the international level, are the favored means of achieving this end.

The ITU has thus departed from its strict "free flow" commitment to one tempered by allowances for a respect for sovereignty and the resolutions of UNESCO concerning a balanced information flow. Restrictions to information flows, however well motivated, can only be accommodated by the ITU to a limited extent, as the premise of NWIO borders on violating the basic purpose of the ITU: to *facilitate* telecommunications media. The ITU thus has traditionally considered the means and media of telecommunications, not the actual message being transmitted or sent over a given medium. Unfortunately, attempts by the ITU to encompass tenets of the NWIO have jeopardized the Union's ability to control the fifty-year-old East-West problem of deliberate interference with international radio signals. While the LDCs recognize that their motives for attempting to control incoming information flows are different from Soviet bloc motives, the Third World has generally been supportive of Soviet efforts to legitimize the restricting of the free flow of information and vice versa.

Chapter 3 traces attempts to reconcile these positions with the free flow principle and the functions of the ITU. In effect, the ITU's ability to deal with deliberate interference has not greatly changed over the past four decades. A two-session High Frequency Broadcasting WARC held in 1984 and 1987 has attempted to identify and censure sources of deliberate interference, but a controversial computer program that would have stripped jammers of any facade of legitimacy by transferring a stronger frequency assignment role to the IFRB, while agreed to in principle at the 1987 conference, is not expected to have an impact upon the management of deliberate interference until the mid-1990s at the earliest. This series of events surrounding the HFBC WARC is reminiscent of a similar High Frequency WARC at Florence in 1950 which attempted many of the same objectives. The Florence Conference was less successful in addressing the jamming issue in its study groups and meetings, but the final result—or lack of results—resembled the 1984/87 Conference. These past failures have left the ITU wary of addressing the jamming issue. Moreover, any real efforts on the ITU's part would inevitably antagonize the jamming countries and create an atmosphere of hostility within the ITU.

Despite being a strong technical hindrance to facilitated communications, both traditional radio jamming and the potential "protective" deliberate interference with satellite television systems are potential minefields for the ITU regulatory order. This, as Chapter 3 explains, is why the ITU has not altered its regulatory system appreciably in order to accommodate either increases in jamming or the interference-legitimizing resolutions of other international organizations.

Organizational Changes in
the ITU Standard-Setting Regime

The growth in international trade since 1947 has made the need for international standardization more significant than at any time in the past. It might be said that the CCIR and CCITT, the ITU standard-setting consultative committees, were not genuinely global components of the ITU until 1956. In that year the first transatlantic telephone cable became operational, linking the European and North American telephone systems. Significantly, this was also the year the old separate telephone and telegraph committees (CCIF and CCIT) merged into the CCITT.

The nature of the functions and output of the CCIs have not changed significantly since that time. What has changed has been the importance of telecommunications to society and the demand for international telecommunications. Therefore, the *importance* of the CCIs has been considerably enhanced over the past three decades as a consequence of the unprecedented growth in telecommunications technology. Despite criticism of CCI structure as remaining somewhat stagnant, the CCIs are considered to be adequately reactive to the emergence of new technologies through their ability to create new study groups and working parties (see Chapter 4). This system guarantees that the CCIs will be able to encompass developments in new telecommunications technologies.

While CCI structure has not changed markedly over the years, the pressures for change have increased considerably. In both committees it is now considered imperative to find means for enhancing Third World involvement. Subsidies for publication costs and travel grants for developing country delegations are among ideas that have been implemented. But Third World involvement in the CCIs remains at a considerably lower level than in any other component of the ITU. This is due to factors discussed above and in Chapter 4. Recent changes that have come about as a consequence of the North-South conflict within the standard-setting regime possess implications for the CCIs which will not become apparent until well into the 1990s. Several of these changes were made at the 1982 ITU Plenipotentiary Conferences, and consist of transferring the election of CCI Directors from the periodic CCI Plenary Assembly to the Plenipotentiary Conference itself. This gives many more countries a say in electing the Directors and makes it more likely that Directors will come from the Third World.

Changes in the Juridical Status of the ITU

In a speech to a private conference held late in 1985 to analyze and review the decisions of that year's GSO-WARC First Session, Ambassador Diana Lady Dougan of the US State Department spoke on the need to pursue means by which the ITU might improve its ability to work within "our increasingly political world." [73] One of her recommendations was the establishment of an ITU *charter* similar in kind to the Universal Postal Union "General Congress" system, which meets every five years to revise, review, and draft resolutions, but does not encompass a core set of inviolable articles. This was the first time in several years that anyone had proposed a permanent constitution for the ITU. It is not a new idea, and has been suggested periodically since the founding of the Union.

Advocates of an ITU "constitution" argue that the current system is inadequate. Currently, the entirety of the International Telecommunication Convention, the governing document of the ITU, is reviewed and revised every few years at the Plenipotentiary Conference. The inadequacy of this system stems from its potential instability, in that voting blocs of countries may dominate the Plenipotentiary and revise the Union's central articles in such a way as to entirely alter the Union and damage its effectiveness and credibility. Usually cited as an example in this regard are "maneuverings" of the Third World at the 1982 Plenipotentiary which resulted in a change to Article Four—*the* core article of the Convention delineating the basic purposes of the ITU. This change made the promotion and offering of technical assistance to developing countries in the field of telecommunications one of the central purposes of the ITU. This amendment was accomplished only over the vociferous opposition of the United States and several other Western countries. Ambassador Douglas and others may believe that a permanent constitution or charter that could not be revised periodically in this way could create a stronger legal basis for ITU decision-making as well as creating as a greater sense of stability and permanence in the Union.

The advantage of the status quo, however, is that it guarantees at least the potential for flexibility and adaptability within the Convention. The majority of ITU members believed technical assistance, for example, should be made one of the central purposes of the Union, so Article Four was altered to reflect this belief. The danger of this admirably democratic structure being harnessed to a voting bloc to irrevocably alter the Union in an adverse manner led the 1965 Montreux Plenipotentiary Conference to establish a study group to investigate how to better prepare a basic instrument governing the Union. The recommendation of that group led the 1973 Plenipotentiary to establish, in Resolution 41 of the Convention, a division of the International Telecommunication Convention into "basic provisions"—texts of a permanent character such as those explaining the purposes of the Union and the functions of ITU components—and "General Regulations" more likely to encounter revision. These General Regulations specify how organs of the ITU function—provisions for conferences, duties of plenaries, etc.[74]

This Resolution eliminated much of the rationale behind advocacy of a constitution. By 1973 even proponents of an ITU constitution, such as the authors of a report on the subject issued that year by the American

Society of International Law Panel on International Telecommunication Policy, advised that a permanent constitution would only be beneficial if other structural changes accompanied its introduction. Neither these changes nor a constitution have come about as most ITU members are satisfied with the status of the Convention—which carries the weight of an international treaty and is considered as such by most countries— and have long since reconciled themselves to the Resolution 41 compromise.

This nevertheless leaves the question of the legal status and weight of ITU decisions. ITU regulations have tended to follow general patterns in international law and, like most international regulations, rely heavily upon the goodwill and cooperation of signatory countries. If a country violates the Radio Regulations or the Convention, or fails to adopt a CCI recommendation, the ITU may censure the violating party but can do little beyond that. Fortunately, most countries believe it is in their interest to comply and cooperate with ITU regulations. In turn, the Regulations are largely successful because they reflect the needs and interests of the majority.

The Role and Function of Technical Assistance in the ITU

As has been mentioned, the 1982 Plenipotentiary altered the first paragraph of Article Four of the International Telecommunication Convention to include the promotion and offering of technical assistance to developing countries in the field of telecommunications as one of the central purposes of the ITU. This development was the culmination of a long, often contentious gestation period which has seen the evolution of a direct developmental role for the ITU.

Dr. Brian Segal has identified four major considerations in this area which are addressed by ITU activity: (1) increasing the self-reliance of developing countries through the strengthening of technical and administrative infrastructures and facilitating the transfer of technology; (2) increasing developing country access to international development finance; (3) increasing the Third World role in the ITU decision-making process; and (4) decentralizing decision-making to the regional level where possible in order to improve ITU reactiveness to Third World concerns.[75] On this last point much discussion has taken place at ITU Plenipotentiaries and within the Administrative Council but little substantive action has been realized. Decentralizing would require either an increase in the ITU budget—unacceptable to some members—or an unacceptable relinquishing of administrative control on the part of the General Secretariat. The other points serve as an effective framework for discussing specific changes effected both by and to the ITU in the technical assistance field.

Increasing the self-reliance of developing countries through development, strengthening of technical and administrative infrastructures, and facilitating the transfer of technology. At the 1982 Nairobi Plenipotentiary, the ITU established an Independent Commission for World Wide Telecommunications Development, known as the Maitland Commission after its chairman, Sir Donald Maitland. The Maitland Commission report, issued at the end of 1984, made several strongly worded recommendations which it declared as vital to reaching the commission's objective of bringing the whole of humankind within easy reach of a telephone.[76] One of the main goals of the commission was to force both developing and developed countries to recognize that any sort of national advancement—whether in agriculture, industry, or society—cannot occur without a telecommunications infrastructure. To increase the technical abilities of the Third World would decrease the sense of North-South conflict within the ITU by lessening the division between the haves and have-nots of telecommunications technology.

Developing countries recognize this fact and have taken steps to ensure the ITU works to not only provide them with advice "from above" but also to act as a catalyst for domestic development within. The IFRB has come to be regarded highly by LDCs because of its work in designing frequency management systems for the Third World. The potential role for the CCIs in facilitating the development of LDC telephone and radio communication systems has not been fully exploited, however, and Third World participation in and regard of the CCIs remains a problem. Curiously, the Maitland Commission report could have proposed such a role for the CCIs but chose not to, perhaps to illustrate the "independent" commission's autonomy from the ITU. The Commission was organized such that its mandate will be one of the central themes of the 1989 Plenipotentiary.[77] Therefore, while the ITU can clearly do more to facilitate telecommunications development within the Third World, the Union is at least aware of the problem and is actively seeking to improve developing country self-reliance through programs such as the Center for Telecommunications Development (CTD). At the end of the 1980s, however, the number of countries contributing to these programs remains too small, and efforts by the ITU to mobilize resources for development have been difficult.

Increasing developing country access to international development finance. Financing of international telecommunications development projects administered by the ITU has traditionally taken place through the UNDP (United Nations Development Program). Several Western countries, particularly the United States, have been wary of the ITU assuming a greater or more direct role in the financing of specific telecommunications development projects. It is felt that other organizations such as UNDP, UNESCO's International Program for the Development of Communications (IPDC), and the International Bank for Reconstruction and Development (IBRD—The World Bank) International Development Association are the proper sources for such funding and that any ITU venture must not be funded directly from the ITU budget. Given the importance of telecommunications development, however, reliance on UNDP funding for such development is seen by most countries as inadequate. In 1983, only 3.9% of total UNDP expenditures went to ITU projects. Moreover, UNDP funding often does not even cover the costs of the ITU activities it is supposed to fund, in part due to fluctuations between UNDP commitments in US dollars and ITU commitments in Swiss francs.[78]

Finding a solution to providing adequate funding for telecommunications development has not been an easy quest. The Americans, along with several other ITU members, believe that direct ITU funding of projects is beyond ITU competence, would endanger the ITU zero-growth budget policy established in 1982, and would threaten the credibility of the ITU in the way that allegedly "politicized" funding authority has threatened the credibility of UNESCO.[79] Western observers and ITU personnel do not want to have to combat accusations of "Third World pork barrelling."[80]

A proposal to establish a voluntary ITU fund to supplement UNDP monies was accepted at the 1973 ITU Plenipotentiary as Resolution 21.[81] This fund still exists, and is modelled on a similar and highly successful Universal Postal Union program which funds development through a pool of voluntary contributions. The ITU "Special Fund for Technical Cooperation" has not been a success, however, due to the entrenched belief of many that the ITU should not directly fund development projects, as well as the inability of those who were committed to the fund— namely the developing countries—to make contributions to it. These problems were compounded by the period of recession following the 1973 oil embargo which made countries even less likely to voluntarily contribute.

Two potential solutions are now seen as the most viable alternatives to the politically unacceptable direct ITU funding of telecommunications development. One is a product of the Maitland Commission known as the Center for Telecommunications Development (CTD). The CTD, while established under the aegis of the ITU, is not a part of the ITU and will not impinge upon the ITU budget. It will nevertheless work in close coordination with the Technical Cooperation Department of the ITU. Proponents of the CTD hope it will rationalize the currently variegated and somewhat unsatisfactory array of telecommunications development bodies. TV Srirangan, a Senior Counsellor at the ITU and for many years a leading spokesman for Third World concerns within the Union, has defined the CTD as "a means for strengthening and expanding such multilateral advisory activities of the Union through a novel mechanism which permits the induction of resources, both financial and technical, principally from sources other than those hitherto drawn upon by the Union."[82] Other observers, however, believe the CTD can only work if it maintains a distant autonomy from the ITU General Secretariat. The success of the CTD will be highly dependent upon its as yet unpromising budgetary performance, and several meetings both inside and outside the ITU are taking place in the years up to the 1989 Plenipotentiary Conference in an effort to shape a cogent and feasible program for development that will incorporate some of the tenets and recommendations of the Maitland Commission.

The second "solution" proposed concerning financing international telecommunications development and strengthening Third World self-reliance in telecommunications is through independent, voluntary, private programs, such as the United States Telecommunication Training Institute (USTTI), a small but growing joint venture between private American firms and the United States government. Established in 1982, the USTTI is not formally affiliated with the ITU and, despite its success, is not popular with some ITU personnel.[83] The ITU would rather see all telecommunications development aid channeled through the new CTD, while directors of the USTTI believe that the "hands-on" approach of the USTTI allows sizeable numbers of students from the Third World to be trained at minimal cost to governments. Other developed countries are looking at the success of the USTTI as a model for new telecommunications development assistance programs outside of ITU structures. Even strong supporters of the ITU may be wary of the prospects of the CTD if it becomes too reliant on the ITU General Secretariat, as that would then limit the Center in both its budgetary effectiveness and could expose it to potential political "capture" by the more militant developing countries that have similarly endangered UNESCO's relations with certain developed countries.

Increasing the role of developing countries in the decision-making process in order to facilitate technical assistance. The one-nation, one-vote electoral structure of the Plenipotentiary has been the pivotal factor in the achievement of numerous resolutions at the 1965, 1973, and 1982 Plenipotentiary Conferences which have secured a technical assistance role for the ITU. Certain Third World spokesmen, such as Algeria's Mr. Bouharied and India's Mr. Srirangan, became quite well known in the 1970s as the "Group of 77" opinion leaders within the ITU decision-making process. The voice of the Third World has steadily strengthened within the Administrative Council as it has grown from 18 members in 1947 to 41 members by the late 1980s. Likewise, ITU representation in the General Secretariat has grown in a parallel fashion to the growth of the LDC presence within the UN system and the international community. In fact, in most respects Third World involvement in the ITU decision-making process has been exemplary, particularly given the fact that the ITU regulates an essentially technical field.

The one exception to the high degree of developing country involvement is in the CCIs, where a "club" of the twenty or so advanced telecommunications powers dominate the proceedings. Given the structure and functions of the CCIs, discussed above, it is difficult to estimate how meaningful Third World involvement might be enhanced without damaging the effectiveness or credibility of the CCIs. Some decisions that have been made and some proposals that have been forwarded in this area are discussed in Chapter 4.

ITU Actions on Non-telecommunication Issues

Just as the 1927 Washington Radio Conference was hindered by the American refusal to allow Soviet participation, hostility and prejudices based upon non-technical, non-telecommunications grounds have continued and increased over the decades. As part of its duties as a UN specialized agency, the ITU, through the Administrative Council and the Plenipotentiary, must routinely address certain UN General Assembly resolutions and must work within the basic political norms of the UN system. The results are often difficult to justify within the ITU's technical context. From 1950 until 1971, parallelling UN directives, the People's Republic of China was not an ITU member nor allowed to participate in the Union in any way. While China was unhappy about this, this exclusion did allow them to conduct a sort of telecommunications anarchy in the Southeast Asian region without fear of censure. Taiwan had the unenviable task of gauging and submitting frequency requirements and usage plans for all of China. From 1965 to 1975, Portugal was excluded from all ITU conferences due to its "colonial racialist policy" in its African territories. Rhodesia was kept out as a consequence of its discriminatory policies until Zimbabwean independence in 1980. Today, only the Republic of South Africa remains excluded from ITU conferences and meetings. South Africa has been *persona non grata* in the Union since 1965 due to ITU recognition of UN General Assembly resolutions condemning the white minority regime, the apartheid policies of the government, and aggressive actions against its neighbors. South Africa is nevertheless Africa's largest telecommunications user—by a wide margin—and, as Chapter 2 describes, the Republic must go to great lengths to discreetly secure ITU recognition of its technical telecommunications requirements while remaining "invisible" in Geneva.

The 1973 and 1982 Plenipotentiary Conferences were largely dominated by discussions of topics of a non-technical nature. This consumes sizeable amounts of time and money, but also serves as an important safety valve for countries that might otherwise air their complaints at the more technical WARCs or RARCs. In other words, the real work of the ITU is not necessarily threatened by the rhetoric of the Plenipotentiary Conferences. This fact is often not appreciated at the time of the Plenipotentiary.

At the 1982 Nairobi Plenipotentiary, two issues dominated the Conference. First was selection of the Secretary-General and the Deputy Secretary-General, the members of the Administrative Council, and the five members of the IFRB. While this was a more lengthy and contentious process than had been the case in past Conferences, a successful and equitable solution was eventually found. Of greater controversy was an Algerian proposal to expel Israel due to its military invasion of Lebanon. The LDCs were "unusually united in Nairobi in support of this proposal."[84] Discussion of this proposal was both heated and lengthy. Eventually the US delegate declared that if Israel were expelled, the United States would immediately withdraw from the Union. Despite the potential implication of what an American withdrawal would do to the credibility of the ITU, the proposal was only defeated by four votes in the final ballot.[85]

The actions taken at the Nairobi Conference were in fact quite similar to events at the Malaga or Montreux conferences, and "the nature of the ITU Plenipotentiary has not changed much over the years."[86] Notwithstanding the maintenance of the Plenipotentiary's "nature," voting patterns within the Plenipotentiary are now such that the development assistance resolutions mentioned above were all swept into the Convention in a manner that would have been impossible at Montreux and difficult at Malaga. Several countries expressed fears that a leap in ITU expenditures might result from these resolutions, particularly those independent of UNDP assistance. Consequently Canada, Britain, the USSR, and the United States, along with several other countries, issued reservations with respect to the acceptance of financial obligations.[87]

The US reservation was by far the most strongly worded. Shock over the near adoption of the proposal to expel Israel combined with American antipathy toward the perceived anti-US LDC voting bloc[88] led to this statement:

The United States of America, deeply troubled by developments at the 1982 ITU Plenipotentiary Conference, reserves the right to make appropriate specific reservations and statements prior to ratification of the ITU Convention. The general concern of the US is based on the Union's regrettable and pervasive lack of realistic fiscal planning, the politicization of the Union, and a requirement that the Union provide technical cooperation and assistance which should be appropriately provided through the UNDP and the private sector. This reservation is necessarily general in nature due to the Conference's inability to complete its substantive work by the time required for submission of reservation. By this reservation the United States serves notice of its right to modify to any degree its future participation in the ITU.[89]

Within a year after the 1982 Plenipotentiary several developments had taken place. Consistent with growing resentment by the American Administration toward "politicization" within UN agencies and the UN General Assembly,[90] the United States announced its decision to withdraw from UNESCO. In 1983 a lengthy report was published by the US National Telecommunications and Information Administration (NTIA) which viewed continued US involvement in the ITU as contingent upon the achievement of two long-range goals: "First, by 1990 the politicization trend must be reversed and the US and other like-minded major donors must re-establish influence over the direction of the ITU as an international organization that serves the needs of its members. . . . Second, as a parallel effort in the event unacceptable politicization continues, the US must have available a fully developed and workable alternative to the ITU."[91]

The obvious disenchantment with which some official circles in the United States viewed the ITU in the years after the 1982 Plenipotentiary became a strong cause for concern within the Union. The NTIA Report in particular "is said to have had considerable impact in Geneva."[92] Nevertheless, the consensus of American opinion, as abroad, maintains "US withdrawal from the ITU would be a disaster for the long-term development of national and international communications."[93] Most ITU member states were greatly worried at the prospect of a US withdrawal. Some observers believed, however, that Amercian calls for withdrawal from the ITU were never completely serious and were intended more as a method of augmenting State Department and NTIA bargaining leverage in negotiations with the US Congress. Using this logic, it can be seen that a "controversial" ITU requires a larger commitment of strategic and financial resources to ensure that American interests are not subjugated at ITU conferences. Most of the American discontent following the 1982 Plenipotentiary centered as much on alleged US ill-preparedness as on perceived flaws within the ITU itself. In fact, a similar sense of disenchantment followed the 1973 Plenipotentiary, when several countries were accused by the United States of "politicizing" the Union by proposing the expulsion of both Israel and South Africa from the Union. These proposals were unsuccessful, but were seen by many observers as a "dangerous precedent."[94] In the mid-1970s, just as ten years later, the calls for a US departure from the ITU became fainter as the Plenipotentiary became a more distant memory. Nevertheless, non-telecommunications issues will remain an incongruous component of ITU activity, particularly within the Plenipotentiary Conferences and the Administrative Council. These issues become increasingly difficult to justify given the restrictive budgetary constraints within which the ITU must work.

* * *

Over the past 120 years, the ITU has undergone substantial changes in the nature and scope of its functions as well as in the structure of its institutions. While subsequent chapters focus on those issues that constitute the areas of greatest political salience, issues such as technical assistance, major non-telecommunication political conflicts, and attempts to alter the legal status of the Union have all greatly influenced the shape—and hence the politics—of the international telecommunications regulatory regime.

Notes

1. Karl Deutsch, *The Nerves of Government* (New York: 1963).

2. International Telecommunication Union (ITU), *International Telecommunication Convention (Nairobi, 1982)* (Geneva: ITU, 1982), p. 3.

3. Jacques Ellul in Wilson Dizard, *The Coming Information Age* (New York: Longman, 1982), p. 13.

4. Most noteworthy is George Codding, Jr. and Anthony Rutkowski, *The International Telecommunication Union in a Changing World* (Dedham, MA: Artech House Inc, 1982).

5. Jean-Luc Renaud, "The ITU as Agent of Compromise," *Intermedia* 14:4 (July 1986), p. 23.

6. James Buchanan and Gordon Tullock, *The Calculus of Consent: Logical Foundations of Constitutional Democracy* (Ann Arbor, MI: University of Michigan Press, 1965).

7. Interviews and D. M. Cerni, *The CCITT: Organization, US Participation, and Studies Toward the ISDN* (Washington, D.C.: National Telecommunication and Information Administration, US Department of Commerce, 1982), p. 7.

8. Interviews.

9. Idea suggested by Doug Davis, US Federal Communications Commission, 1986.

10. Interview.

11. E. DuCharme, D. Fleming, R. Jakhu and A. Longman, "State Sovereignty and the Effective Management of a Shared Universal Resource: Observations Drawn From Examining Developments in the International Regulation of Radiocommunication," draft of article for *Annals of Air and Space Law*, Special Anniversary Volume, 1985, p. 5.

12. An example is single side broadcasting (SSB) which allows a far greater number of stations to operate on a given frequency by employing a narrower bandwidth. SSB technology is a more efficient use of spectrum space and requires much less power to transmit a quality signal.

13. Colin Legum and John Cornwell, *A Free and Balanced Flow* (Lexington, MA: D.C. Heath and Co., 1978), p. 41.

14. Interview.

15. George A. Codding, Jr., *The International Telecommunication Union: An Experiment in International Cooperation* (New York: Arno Press, 1972), p. 6.

16. Ibid., p. 15.

17. France, Belgium, Switzerland, and Sardinia met in Paris in June 1855 to create the West European Telegraphic Union (WETU). The Netherlands, Portugal, the Vatican, the Two Sicilies, and Luxembourg soon also joined WETU. Codding, op. cit. 1972, p. 16.

18. Ibid., p. 19.

19. Clark in Codding, Jr., op. cit., 1972, p. 20.

20. Ibid., p. 21.

21. Codding, Jr. and Rutkowski, op. cit., 1982, p. 6.

22. Codding, Jr., op. cit., 1972, p. 24.

23. Great Britain's accession to the conference was facilitated by the administration of telegraphs in British India by the UK Government. As a consequence, the British government would have represented India at the conference even had a delegation representing the UK not been allowed.

24. The new Italian Republic, host to the conference, was one member whose telegraphy was run by both public and private concerns. Great Britain had by this time nationalized its telegraphy, placing it under the authority of the Post Office.

25. Codding, Jr., op. cit., 1972, p. 27.

26. Ibid., p. 29.

27. Ibid., p. 30.

28. As telephony developed it soon became apparent that North American technical standards were developing along different lines than the European ITU standards. This was attributable to the geographical isolation of the North American market and the strength within that market of the Bell System monopoly.

29. These conferences were held in London (1879), Berlin (1885), Paris (1890), Budapest (1896), London (1903), and Lisbon (1908).

30. Telephony had been discussed by the ITU as early as 1885. See Codding, Jr., op. cit., 1972, pp. 32–33.

31. Ibid.

32. Ibid., p. 37.

33. Ibid.
34. Ibid.
35. Ibid., p. 83.
36. Sarrien in Codding, Jr., op. cit., 1972, p. 84.
37. Ibid., p. 86.
38. Ibid., p. 89.
39. Codding, Jr., and Rutkowski, op. cit., 1982, p. 13.
40. Harlow in Codding, Jr., op. cit., 1972, p. 98.
41. Ibid., p. 110.
42. Ibid.
43. Ibid., p. 111.
44. Codding, Jr., and Rutkowski, op. cit., 1982, p. 15.
45. Lawrence W. Lichty and Malachi C. Topping, *American Broadcasting: A Source Book on the History of Radio and Television* (New York: Hastings House, 1975).
46. Harvey J. Levin, *The Invisible Resourse* (Baltimore: John's Hopkins University Press, 1971), p. 4.
47. Codding, Jr., op. cit, 1972, p. 127.
48. Codding, Jr., and Rutkowski, op. cit., 1982, p. 16.
49. Codding, Jr., op. cit, 1972, p. 117.
50. Ibid., p. 122.
51. Ibid.
52. As at the Washington Conference, the United States and Canada would not accept any obligations with regard to telegraph and telephone regulations. In both countries such regulations continued to be set by private operators subject to governmental regulatory guidelines.
53. Codding, Jr., op. cit., 1972, p. 139.
54. Ibid., p. 179.
55. Ibid., p. 198.
56. Donald Fleming, *Report on Research into Mobile Communications* (paper prepared for Department of Communications, Ottawa, 1984), p. 25.
57. Codding, Jr., op. cit., 1972, p. 235.
58. International Telecommunication Union, *Report of the Administrative Council to the 1952 Plenipotentiary Conference, Buenos Aires* (Geneva: ITU, 1952), p. 2.
59. New Zealand, the Netherlands East Indies, and Egypt complained that the breakdown of the ITU into regions and the proposed recruitment of staff from these regions was inadequately planned and overlooked major regions such as Africa and the Pacific. The United States delegation expressed a similar view, but the plan was allowed to hold for the sake of expediency.

The decision to replace the Swiss-run Bern Bureau had been enthusiastically espoused by the "Big Five" at Moscow, but at Atlantic City some opposition was encountered. Several countries including Belgium, Canada, and Italy feared the increased expenses that would be incurred by such an expansion of ITU administration. Lebanon and Portugal claimed a strengthened Bern Bureau would provide a more practical solution, while Portugal also feared the loss of the scrupulous Swiss-run administration of the ITU. The United States, Britain, and

France prevailed, however, in convincing the majority that retention of the Bern Bureau would not be in keeping with the UN-inspired structure and internationalism of the era. Curiously, the efforts of the major powers were less successful for the Universal Postal Union (UPU), which decided to leave its General Secretariat under Swiss direction.

60. Fleming, 1984, p. 27.

61. D. M. Leive, *International Telecommunications and International Law: The Regulation of the Radio Spectrum* (Dobbs Ferry, NY: Oceana Publishing, 1970), p. 55.

62. International Telecommunication Union, *Final Acts of the Atlantic City Convention, 1947* (Geneva: ITU, 1947), p. 7.

63. ITU, op. cit., 1952, p. 3.

64. Robert J. Chapuis, "The CCIF and the Development of International Telephony 1923–1956," *CCITT Reprint Series*, 1976, p. 33.

65. Codding, Jr., 1952, p. 298.

66. Ibid., p. 317.

67. ITU, op. cit., 1947, Annex 5, Art. 3.

68. Leive, op. cit., 1970, p. 74.

69. Ibid.

70. Ibid.

71. Ibid.

72. ITU, op. cit., 1982, p. 329.

73. Diana Lady Dougan, *A Post-Analysis of Space WARC-85: A Policy Forum Convened by the Washington Program of the Annenberg School, November 1985*. Unpublished transcript.

74. International Telecommunication Union, *International Telecommunication Convention, Malaga-Torremolinos 1973* (Geneva: ITU, 1973), p. 242.

75. Brian Segal, *Preparatory Study for the 1982 ITU Plenipotentiary Conference* (Ottawa: Department of Communications, 1982), pp. 22–25.

76. International Telecommunication Union, *The Missing Link: Report of the Independent Commission for World Wide Telecommunications Development* (Geneva: ITU, 1984), p. 4.

77. Jonathan Solomon, "Comment: The Missing Link—A Political Hot Potato," *Telecommunications Policy* 9:2 (June 1985), p. 91.

78. ITU, op. cit. 1984, p. 25.

79. Interview, Washington, D.C.

80. Interview, Washington, D.C.

81. ITU, op. cit., 1973, p. 216.

82. T.V. Srirangan, "After Maitland," Discussion paper presented at the 1985 Annual Conference of the International Institute of Communications, Tokyo (London: International Institute of Communications, 1985), p. 6.

83. Interviews, Geneva and Washington, D.C.

84. Leslie Milk and Allen Weinstein, *United States Participation in the International Telecommunication Union: A Study of Policy Alternatives* (Paper prepared for US Department of State, Washington, D.C., 1984), p. 26.

85. Michael Gardner, *Hearings of the United States Senate on Bill S999* (Washington, D.C.: United States Senate, 1983), p. 59.

86. George A. Codding, Jr., "The Changing Nature of the ITU Plenipotentiary," *Telecommunications Policy* (December 1983), p. 323.

87. ITU, op. cit., 1982, p. 193.

88. S. Schmitt, *Hearings of the United States Senate on the International Telecommunications Deregulation Act of 1982* (Washington, D.C.: United States Senate, 1982), p. 200.

89. ITU, op. cit., 1982, p. 191.

90. This sentiment was reflected in Senator Goldwater's unambiguous words: "I think more than ever before . . . the politics that enter in and will enter into more and more this type of conference (the 1982 ITU Plenipotentiary) will be weighed against the United States, just as we see today the overwhelming number of countries in the United Nations who vote against the US if for no other reason than we are the US. . . ." in *Hearings of the United States Senate on Bill S999* (Washington, D.C.: United States Senate, 1983), p. 47.

91. Hon. Bob Packwood, Chairman, *Long-Range Goals in International Telecommunication and Information: An Outline for United States Policy*, Report of the Committee on Commerce, Science, and Transportation, United States Senate (Washington, D.C.: US Government Printing Office, 1983), p. 47.

92. Milk and Weinstein, op. cit., 1985, p. 24.

93. Charles Jonscher, "The UNESCO Fiasco," *Telecommunications Policy* (March 1984), p. 2.

94. Interview, Washington, D.C.

2

The ITU and the Radio Frequency Spectrum: Use and Management of a Shared Universal Resource

The radio frequency spectrum (RFS) is defined as that portion of electromagnetic waves used to transmit information through the air. It is the intangible yet limited resource that enables wireless communication to take place. The RFS is created by the technology that employs it; it is the sum total of all frequencies existing. A frequency is itself not actually an entity but merely the number of cycles of an electronic carrier wave diffuses in a second. As radio technology advances the number of cycles that can be wedged into a second steadily increases. This means the upper limit of the RFS is extended and the total amount of spectrum space available increases.

If technology enables periodic expansion of the spectrum, why then is it termed a limited resource, and why are such small bits of it so crowded and contentious? First, the many varied services provided over the RFS—from radar to broadcasting to satellite television—can only operate at certain wavelengths. Submarine radio communications take place at very low frequencies, as this type of signal radiates best along the ground or water. Radio amateurs, ships, aircraft, and international broadcasters use high frequencies, as these allow signals to travel great distances without great power consumption. The allocation of specific services to those specific groups, known as bands, of frequencies where they best function is the role of the ITU through the World Administrative Radio Conferences and the work of the IFRB (International Frequency Registration Board) and the CCIR (International Radio Consultative Committee).

ITU members agree upon which bands will be used for what services at the WARCs based upon their own requirements and the technical advice of the IFRB and CCIR. Conflict emerges when the number of bands assigned to a specific service—e.g., high frequency international broadcasting—are deemed by a number of ITU members as insufficient or unduly restrictive. But it must be remembered that the spectrum, while growing, is nevertheless fully apportioned between services. Therefore any gain for one service is at another service's expense. This zero-sum situation was illustrated at the 1979 General WARC when those advocating growth of the high frequency broadcast bands encountered strong opposition from developing countries who feared the fixed service high frequency bands would be made smaller as a result. These bands carry radioteletype and utility services important and, largely, profitable to developing country administrations.

One of the frustrating by-products of technical progress has been the marked increase in demands made upon existing bands. For most services on the "traditional" bands—those used for the bulk of the world's radio communications—demand now greatly exceeds supply. The number of radio communication users grows exponentially every few years. The growth of the spectrum through the discovery of new technologies can potentially relieve some of this pressure. Many developed countries have transferred utility services such as radioteletype or maritime communications to satellites employing much less crowded and far more efficiently allocated bands. From a technical perspective this should free up the high frequency utility bands for greater developing country and broadcasting use. But countries, once assigned a service, will be reluctant to forfeit it. In the 1979 utility services case, the United States and other developed countries were unwilling to relinquish their IFRB-registered frequencies, as they wanted to maintain the terrestrial services as a back-up system should a satellite dysfunction.

Just as technical innovation leads to the enlargement of the spectrum, innovation also has led to means by which existing segments of the spectrum may be more efficiently used. The IFRB in particular conducts much research and policy work, as do larger administrations, in this area. The CCIR, through radio Conference Preparatory Meetings and Interim Working Parties, reviews the technical alternatives available to upcoming WARCs. But even here technical progress may be precluded by more significant political and economic concerns. Developing countries cannot afford much in the way of expensive innovations, no matter how much spectrum space may be conserved; commitment to technical principles can only go so far when there is no money around.

Marketing considerations play a surprisingly strong role in spectrum management. More efficient use of several portions of the spectrum is technically possible, but not economically feasible. For example, an innovation known as single sideband broadcasting (SSB) on high frequencies would allow several hundred more broadcasting wavelengths without any sacrifice by other services. It would also require alterations to virtually every HF broadcast transmitter in the world and would make the vast majority of the world's existing HF radio receivers useless. Therefore international radio broadcasters are not willing to switch to this new technology unless the bulk of the new radio receivers are made to receive SSB. Radio receiver manufacturers, on the other hand, will not produce such equipment unless broadcasters show unambiguous commitment to switching to SSB. Technological progress, therefore, can as easily create new problems for spectrum management as resolve old ones, and is not in itself a solution to RFS problems.

Great differences exist in the *nature* of countries' spectrum space demands. Since the late 1950s, as developing countries came to realize that international regulations were not accommodating their present or future interests, a general promotion of more equitable means of spectrum management was sought. This has generally implied some sort of *a priori* planning which reserves sufficient spectrum space for a state proportional to its need, as opposed to the needs of other countries. LDCs fear that continuation of the present *a posteriori* "first-come, first-served" regime, which allows countries to report new frequencies to the IFRB as a *fait accompli*, will perpetuate or worsen the current inequality in spectrum allocation. At present, 90 percent of the spectrum is controlled by 10 per cent of the world's population in a small number of industrialized countries.[1] Developed countries fear that reapportionment of the spectrum along the lines of developing country demands will lead to costly, inefficient use of present spectrum space as well as hinder their own future use of expanded bands or new services. While recognizing the need to improve LDC access to the spectrum, developed countries remain the greatest employers of telecommunications technology. The central dilemma thus becomes one of efficient versus equitable use of the RFS.

The solutions employed to resolve spectrum allocation difficulties in satellite broadcasting, emergent in the early 1960s, led to a renewed interest in the 1980s concerning the feasibility of efficient *a priori* allocation. This followed many years of an ITU *a posteriori* "first-come, first-served" frequency registration system which rejected a planned spectrum as either too politically difficult to achieve or undesirable in itself due to its perceived potential to hinder technological progress. It must be said, however, that this view was never shared by all ITU members, and the concept of a planned spectrum has never been completely absent from radio conferences.

It was the new technology of satellite broadcasting which first gave impetus to a new *a priori* era. The current IFRB frequency registration process evolved in the 1940s and 1950s to accommodate the needs of terrestrial radio services. Since 1959 the IFRB has employed a complex registration process which consists of recording new frequencies reported by telecommunications administrations and judging their legitimacy over a 60 to 90 day period.[2] The flaw in this procedure rests in the fact that by the time a frequency is judged "illegal" due to some contravention of the radio regulations, that frequency will have been in use for several weeks. Administrations, especially those that chronically violate the regulations, are often reluctant to change existing frequencies even if the IFRB deems their frequencies illegal.

Calls to increase the power of the IFRB must be tempered by the recognition that national administrations will always retain the final say in the assignment of frequencies. As enforcement of the Radio Regulations in the strict sense of the word is impossible, some attempts have been made to give the IFRB a more powerful role in its recommendation of assignments, capitalizing on the high esteem and respect with which even the most recalcitrant ITU members view the Board. At the 1984 High Frequency Broadcasting WARC, Canada proposed the adoption of a sizeable computer program which would revolutionize the status quo by empowering the IFRB to allocate frequencies to administrations instead of merely registering frequencies submitted by administrations. The IFRB would in such a case recommend to national administrations which frequencies they may legally use and at what times. During the inter-sessional period between the 1984 and 1987 sessions of the Conference, the IFRB conducted extensive tests judging the feasibility of such an approach. The unwillingness of member states to compromise led to an impasse at the second session. The resulting "plan" proved little better than the status quo concerning levels of interference and low signal quality. The original hope of the planning advocates—that the IFRB could, if necessary, hold states to using one demonstrably acceptable frequency instead of 5 or 10 "shotgun" frequencies—had to be scrapped early in the second session. The major HF broadcasting states left the Conference pleased, as their facilities and regulatory power would not be threatened by the specter of any IFRB *diktat*. The situation remains unresolved at least through the mid-1990s.

Even if this new order could be realized, however, it would only be applicable to high frequency (HF) broadcasting. National administrations have finally realized that HF broadcasting is the least governable aspect of ITU activities, as it remains that portion of the spectrum most plagued by deliberate interference, illegal frequency use, and excessive demands for frequencies. With this realization may come a tacit willingness to sacrifice a certain degree of domestic control simply in order to achieve some order on the airwaves. Nevertheless, ITU officials as well as those of several developed country administrations have expressed serious doubts regarding the likelihood of such a program ever being realized. Larger broadcasters, in particular, are doubtful of the IFRB's ability to accommodate their sizeable frequency demands. In broadcasting and telecommunications media of a more domestic nature, or in portions of the spectrum where the problems of spectrum management are less acute, such a subordination of sovereign control over frequency use would appear unlikely.

Some countries, including the United States, remain suspicious of a greater role for WARCs in allocation, and are fundamentally opposed to *a priori* planning. American advocacy of applying the current IFRB "first-come, first-served" status quo to satellite broadcasting or the geostationary orbit (GSO) has engendered considerable LDC opposition and has introduced a North-South dimension to the frequency management issue.

The growing LDC voice in the ITU is increasingly expressing itself through WARCs. High frequency broadcasting, for example, was ignored as a high priority issue for the developed countries after the failure of postwar attempts to plan the HF broadcasting spectrum. Although the advanced states remain the major users of the medium, it was allowed through neglect and, occasionally, malice (see Chapter 3 below) to slide into disorder. For LDCs, however, the nature of high frequency broadcasting makes it an ideal, inexpensive way to provide national broadcasting coverage. The HF bands are also considered vital in the Third World as they provide the chief means of fixed and mobile point-to-point radio communications. Such HF radio links often provide the only communication between the central government and remote areas. Disorder on the high frequency bands consequently threatens many LDCs sense of nationhood and is politically intolerable. This is why an agreement was reached to hold a special HF-WARC and finally attempt to resolve the thorny issues within that segment of the spectrum.

Through WARCs and the IFRB, the ITU conducts what is one of the most important of its functions: frequency allocation. This aspect of the ITU's work is central to the effective use of telecommunications. The coordination and registration of frequency assignments is thus the issue area most subject to regulation and attention by the ITU. RFS management is commonly perceived as a technical domain distanced from politics. Worse, it may be viewed as a recently politicized part of the ITU's work, burdened by overt politics and undue North-South or East-West polarization.

Both views may be misleading and in part false. RFS management, as the following sections illustrate, has always featured political and economic motives behind the technical decisions. This chapter attempts to delineate the progress of the basic relationships characterizing the RFS management issue. Apart from the historical development of the institutional regime, the chapter traces the motives behind the creation of the current ITU allocations system and focuses on the current RFS management order along with certain emergent issues. Following that is an analysis of the more recent "efficient versus equitable" dispute, seeking to place that issue within the greater context of development telecommunications and the New World Information Order (NWIO). By observing who has been the chief beneficiary in recent conferences it is possible to identify which "side" is prevailing and why. Finally, the chapter looks at motives for compliance and when compliance may not occur. Clearly some parts of the RFS are more politically relevant—and hence less likely to avoid political influences—than others.

Frequency allocations and RFS management are political issues. North, South, East, and West possess different concepts concerning what the role of the ITU should be. These "politics," however, are directly related to telecommunications and are unavoidable in the distribution of a common resource among 160 members. They are not the politics of the Plenipotentiary Conferences, which often center on condemnations of South Africa and Israel, lengthy speeches, and weighty statements. The politics of RFS management relate directly to the national telecommunications objectives of each member. A corollary issue to spectrum management now deemed by many to be *the* ITU issue of the 1990s is effective coordination and assignment of geostationary orbit allotments— the orbital "parking spaces" for communications satellites and the related frequencies these satellites employ. This is a difficult and contentious issue for the ITU as it is at the heart of both developed country telecommunication priorities and developing country aspirations. The purpose of this section is to identify and clarify the political implications of RFS management and distinguish this aspect of the ITU work from that of the Plenipotentiary or technical standardization.

Evolution of Radio Frequency Spectrum Management Within the ITU

Controlling the "invisible resource" has comprised a major component of international telecommunications regulation since the earliest days of wireless telegraphy. The origin of supranational frequency allocation procedures can be traced back to the Preliminary Radio Conference of 1903. As will be recalled, this conference was convened by the German Administration and attended by most European administrations along with the United States—which was not then an ITU member—to ostensibly draft a protocol calling for a conference to establish international regulations for radiotelegraphy.

The conference, held in 1906, had been prompted by the policies of the Marconi Company which forbade users of its maritime radio equipment to communicate with radio stations not employing Marconi equipment. Marconi at that time controlled the great majority of the world's radio communications equipment, transmitters, and services. The other major radio communications users, particularly Germany and the United States, each of which had small radio equipment industries to promote, were eager to preclude the growth of the Anglo-Italian Marconi monopoly. The first radio conference was therefore "dictated not by the need to allocate frequency bands, but by the buccaneering practices of the commercial wireless companies."[3] The 1906 Convention stipulated that communication between maritime radio stations was obligatory. No one company could forbid users of its equipment from communicating with those employing another marque. Since this opened the existing radio spectrum to other companies, the Convention became in fact the first attempt to share the frequency bands between member countries.

The 1906 Conference set two noteworthy precedents. Allocations of frequency bands to specific services divided the existing spectrum into public correspondence, military, and naval bands. The second step was established in Article 4 of the Convention, which required signatories to report frequencies used to the ITU Administrative Bern Bureau.[4] The convention also limited the power of ship transmitters to one thousand watts, unless the ship was obliged to communicate at a distance of over 300 kilometers.[5]

Even in this early period of radio communication fairly specific international regulations existed governing spectrum use. While these may have been implemented due to fears of a creeping Marconi monopoly, they nonetheless provided a framework for future growth. The quality of the 1906 Regulations and Convention was such that the 1912 London Radio Conference made few substantial changes, despite dramatic growth in the use and development of radiotechnology. Some enlargement of the spectrum led to new frequency allocations. But any specific legal rights conferred by the registration of a frequency with the Bern Bureau remained unclear. At this point it appeared the Bureau's List of Frequencies was serving chiefly as a reference work for radio users.

The dynamic growth of radio communications during World War I was accompanied by a breakdown of the fragile order established by the 1906 and 1912 Conferences. Nevertheless, another international radio communications conference was not held until 1927. At least part of the reason for this delay rested with the ambitions of the victorious powers after armistice. The "Big 5" victorious powers met in Washington in 1920 to establish a new comprehensive telecommunications order which would encompass the Radio Conferences and ITU as well as domestic communications. While the fate of this "Universal Electrical-communications Union" is detailed in Chapter 1, several aspects of the unsuccessful endeavor are relevant to spectrum management. Limitations inherent in the prewar system of listing frequencies in use were recognized by 1920, particularly with the specter of sound broadcasting looming close. The draft Convention considered by the participants included a process by which the new Union would allocate specific frequencies to member states on the basis of "coefficients of distribution." These would be achieved through the consideration of "population, extent and importance of colonies, extent of commerce, and the need for international communications by the applicant country."[6] In the end the participating states did not accept this procedure nor the draft Constitution. Jakhu notes: "Had the Universal Electric-communications Union been established in 1920, it would have changed the course of development and the nature of international telecommunications law which is presently under attack in an attempt to achieve precisely what was accomplished in the 1920 draft."[7]

Sound broadcasting commenced in 1920 with experimental broadcasts in Britain and North America. The failure of the conference to establish the Universal Electric-communications Union meant the new radio services would grow in a largely unregulated environment. By the mid-1920s, Europe and North America were covered with broadcast stations using unassigned, unregulated frequencies. The level of harmful interference was serious and rapidly worsening.

The domestic and voluntary cooperative regulatory arrangements achieved during these years are described in Chapter 1. To recapitulate, European broadcasters, exasperated by the inaction of the International Radio Conferences and the high level of interference, met in London in 1925 at the behest of the British broadcasters in order to achieve a voluntary broadcast band allocation plan. Within a few years the United States had implemented federal government regulation of its broadcast band and had achieved a multilateral North American Regional Broadcasting Agreement (NARBA) with Canada and Mexico.

At this time high frequency broadcasting between countries was beginning. This largely unused band quickly became a favorite of radio amateurs who rapidly discovered that relatively limited transmitter strength would permit transoceanic communications. Again, this area was virtually devoid of any regulation and threatened to grow dangerously chaotic.

The 1927 Washington Radio Conference extended the radio regulations inherited from the prewar era in both scope and power. Moreover, it was this conference which set the approach the ITU would henceforth follow concerning the role of regulation of international uses of the RFS. The participants sought "to provide a minimum number of absolute rules and a maximum number of guides to action."[8] As so many frequencies had already been assigned or occupied in the absence of either rules or guidelines, it was decided at the conference that reallocation of existing bands would be an impossible task. Member administrations were allowed to retain frequencies then being used and to utilize additional frequencies as long as they did not interfere with existing services.

Recognition of these frequencies by the Washington Conference did not confer any sort of "priority right" of use or occupancy of a frequency. Several countries, led by Latvia, called for the introduction of such a right, which would give the first user of a frequency legal priority to keep using that frequency in any dispute. The smaller countries, then as now, were concerned with protecting their future use of the radio bands, and saw "priority rights" as one way to assert their claims over portions of the spectrum. During the discussion the American delegate stated that the United States would oppose any regulation which gave a country an absolute right to use a frequency.[9] The United States, along with several other countries, found the potential of "priority right" to imply "ownership" of a frequency. Such "ownership" contravened the Radio Regulations and Convention, which merely allowed for *use* of the spectrum by specific countries but viewed the radio frequency spectrum as the common property of all countries. Members consequently agreed to an American proposal to allow any disagreements to be submitted to arbitration.[10] A *de facto* priority right remains to this day, however, as a station operating for an established period of time on an ITU registered frequency will have more influence in a dispute with a more recent contender.

The Madrid Telegraph and Radiotelegraph Conferences of 1932, which effected the merger of the International Radiotelegraph Union and the International Telegraph Union into a new single International *Telecommunication* Union, also served to reiterate international commitment to responsible *a posteriori* "first-come, first-served" spectrum use. No major changes were made to the regime established in 1927. The Conference adopted the new Bern Bureau Frequency List, with dates of first registration, and stipulated that stations should be notified to the Bureau before commencing operation or changing transmitter power. The inclusion of registration dates was important in the List, resurrecting the issue of "priority right," but there was no accord on this issue.

It must be recalled that the Bern Bureau Frequency List, unlike its IFRB successors, did not confer any legal right to use frequencies. This seemingly basic fact was not well understood, however, by those at the

1932 Madrid Conference, and even the best prepared delegations indicated a belief that some type of "priority right" existed. Japan and Italy demanded clarification of the "priority right," and the British delegate went so far as to "assume that a right of priority, which he did not specifically define (how could he?) constituted one of the privileges resulting from notification of a frequency assignment to the Bureau."[11] The US delegate argued that the List had no legal consequences, but then contradicted himself by stating that listed frequencies could enjoy protection against new transmitters going into operation on the same frequency.[12] This latter view was reiterated by one Sub-committee Conference Chairman. No such formulation existed in the ITU regulations. Any "priority right" existed solely in the minds of delegates.

The Madrid Conference did strengthen the Frequency List, however, by making registration of frequencies obligatory. But a British proposal to enhance the Bureau's power in controlling and censuring interfering stations was rejected by the majority of delegations. Their opposition was ostensibly based on a variety of technical reasons and a belief that such activity was beyond the scope of the ITU. In fact many countries, particularly the growing telecommunications users such as the Soviet Union or countries with imperial obligations such as France, Portugal, and the Netherlands, were reluctant to accept any constraint on enlarging the number of their frequencies. The Bern Bureau continued to rely on the accuracy of information supplied to it by member administrations. Several administrations, particularly the USSR, took advantage of this "honor system" by submitting long, largely fictitious lists of frequencies in use to the Bureau. By 1938 the USSR was registered on virtually every available frequency on the Bern Bureau List. While this made life easier for domestic administrations by allowing them to disregard the Bern Bureau List and operate at will, it also made a mockery of the Bureau. More responsible members realized the British proposal, or something like it, would eventually be needed to restore the credibility and value of the List. But the British proposal was ultimately defeated. Opposing administrations voting against the proposal claimed it was not technically sound and defeated the measure on superficially technical grounds. This division over Bern Bureau power and sanction was to persist until the Bureau was replaced in 1947.

The Bern Bureau was, for all its numerous flaws, the first international center of technical expertise on spectrum management. It served as an important intermediary between conflicting administrations and was interpreter of the meaning of the Radio Regulations for specific member countries. The Bern Bureau, by refusing to acknowledge a frequency priority right, strengthened the ITU's commitment to an evolutionary *a posteriori* registration role. In the end, however, the Bureau lacked the power and personnel to resolve the growing demands and disputes which confronted spectrum management as the 1930s progressed.

It must be noted, however, that commitment to *a posteriori* registration on an international basis was not reflected by the regional or national plans developed outside of the ITU in the interwar years. The cooperative plan of 1925 for the European broadcast band (mentioned above), the NARBA Agreement of 1929 which assigned every radio station in the United States, Canada, and Mexico to a specific frequency, and the Inter-American Radio Conference of 1938 were examples of regional *a priori* plans. At the domestic level, all broadcasting countries established *a priori* allocation plans in the interwar period. The United States, strongly opposed to *a priori* planning at the international level, had itself implemented a strict system of preplanned frequency allocations for AM and later FM and television broadcast frequencies. Each frequency is assigned by the US Federal Communications Commission (FCC) according to the applicant's conformity with five social, non-technical principles: whole area service, community service, service in multiple station communities, public and education services, and commercial licensees.[13] Canada has over the years come to apply even stricter rules for domestic frequency allocation, stipulating rigorous "balanced content" and "domestic content" requirements for broadcasters. While many of the social and cultural variables considered in international frequency allocations are quite recent developments, in domestic frequency assignments such considerations have been of primary significance for over fifty years.

The substantial progress made in radio technology during World War II was accompanied by the predictable weakening of the interwar Bern Bureau order. The survival of the ITU after the war was contingent upon the decisions made by the victorious powers who met in Moscow in 1946 to determine the future of the Union. The United States and USSR each proposed extensive plans for a central frequency registration board. The Soviet plan sought to void all 1940–47 registrations and restore the interwar status quo. Subsequent registration applications would be screened for compatibility with the Radio Regulations before being accepted. The Soviets were keen to adopt the interwar list in part due to the surfeit of registrations they enjoyed under the old system—a bonus unlikely to be repeated in any new order where allocation would be determined by need. The American plan was somewhat wider in scope and more specific in detail than its Soviet counterpart. Its goal was "to work out a frequency assignment plan for all the world's stations on a technical basis without regard necessarily for any particular frequency which a nation may have registered heretofore, but rather in order that the radio stations of the World could operate in the future without causing or suffering harmful interference."[14] The time constraint on the Moscow Conference obviated detailed discussion of either plan.

The new order was to be established at the 1947 Atlantic City Conference. The need for revolutionary change and advocacy of the necessarily nihilist "clean slate" approach to frequency allocation and notification enjoyed widespread support. This apparent turnaround by the United States concerning *a priori* planning stemmed from the chaotic state of the spectrum after the war as well as a desire on the part of the American administration to remold the ITU into a more modern, scientific, international organization. A unique and unparalleled opportunity to create a "new" ITU existed, to even a greater extent than had been the case after World War I.

Widespread support for an *a priori* plan was not entirely surprising as the Bern Bureau List of Frequencies contained some 45,000 notifications for frequencies.[15] Only the Italian delegate believed the Bern Bureau could, with a modest strengthening, continue to effectively manage the RFS. His chief objection to the new IFRB concerned its cost.[16]

According to Leive, the 1947 Atlantic City Conferences made four key revisions. Primary among these was the creation of the International Frequency Registration Board (IFRB), which was "granted a range of powers such as the legal and technical examination of new notices and the issuance of findings with respect thereto, which the Bern Bureau never possessed."[17] This was evidently closest to the American plan proposed at Moscow one year earlier. The Radio Regulations would also now imply the legal right to international protection against harmful interference. In addition, several steps were taken to facilitate the achievement of a fully planned, engineered spectrum. Finally, some aspects of the former regime, chiefly the significance connoted by earlier use and notification of a frequency, were retained.

The Bern Bureau Frequency List was replaced by the IFRB Master Register. The IFRB, chartered in Article 6 of the 1947 Final Acts, was accorded two duties:

> (1) to effect an orderly recording of frequency assignments made by the different countries so as to establish, in accordance with the procedure provided for in the Radio Regulations, the date, purpose, and technical character of these assignments, with a view to ensuring formal international recognition thereof; (2) to furnish advice to members . . . with a view to the operation of a maximum predictable number of radio channels in those portions of the spectrum where harmful interference may occur.[18]

In other words, the IFRB was to be "a witness and nothing more" or "a verification board, such as Lloyd's of London."[19] This, however, did not imply the continuation of the *a posteriori* Bern Bureau registration system. It was hoped, in these early years of postwar cooperation and optimism, that a new Provisional Frequency Board (PFB) would be established to *allocate* frequencies which the IFRB would then *register*. The PFB and IFRB would have distinct and complementary goals: the PFB would design an engineered, allocated spectrum upon the advice of IFRB experts who would then judge the legitimacy of the allocation, as ultimately expressed in the Master Register.

Like so much else at the Atlantic City Conferences, this was primarily an American conception of the way the ITU should be administered. The United States dominated the conference as host, as the world's major telecommunications user, and as the strongest of the victorious powers. Nonetheless, even the American delegation was often forced to compromise. The IFRB, originally perceived by the Americans as "something of a cross between the (US) Federal Communications Commission (FCC) and the International Court of Justice,"[20] ended up resembling neither. The United States remained adamant on one point: no "priority right" would sully the registration role of the new IFRB. Britain, France, and the USSR, fearing a diminution of their many interwar Bern Bureau allocations, were keen to establish an international priority right as part of the IFRB's jurisdiction.[21] Compromise was inevitable, and eventually achieved through a watered-down version of a Mexican proposal to "give the right of international protection to that frequency assignment against a further assignment on the same frequency."[22] "International protection" remains a vague and legalistic concept, however, as the IFRB possesses no real power to stop an administration from using any frequency as it deems best. This is perhaps not surprising as member countries have been increasingly reluctant to forfeit any degree of sovereign power in an area as important as frequency use and allocation.

The goal of an engineered spectrum can be seen in hindsight as naive and overly ambitious. Even at Atlantic City some harbingers of conflict were apparent. The American proposals for a completely new *a priori* International Frequency List encountered scepticism from the USSR, which posited that the goal of the PFB might be better implemented in gradual steps, as a one-step change could be beyond the Union's ability.

There is more than a little irony in this dispute, given the later restoration of Western advocacy of *a posteriori* registration. For a few years after World War II American officials believed the scope of revision to the spectrum necessitated by the destructiveness of the war afforded an opportunity for a new order to be established. The chaos caused by a lack of regulatory foresight in the 1920s and 1930s would be precluded now by a scientifically engineered plan which could allocate and register frequencies. American faith in planning in 1947 differed little from similar developing country calls for *a priori* plans forty years later.

The United States possessed another reason to believe planning would work. The United States was, in 1947, the World's preeminent power. There was an optimism and a feeling that the old Eurocentrism of the ITU had been broken. The center of power within the Union was shifting westward. The largest conference in ITU history was taking place in Atlantic City, and the predicted rapid rise of Latin America led a sizeable number of countries to advocate moving the headquarters of the Union to Mexico City. While this did not occur, Spanish was adopted as the third official language of the ITU, equal to French and English. The IFRB and the PFB were particularly American concepts. *A priori* planning, seen before the war as impossible, was now viewed as both possible and necessary for the controlled and orderly growth of the spectrum. The US administration may have established the IFRB with greater hopes than could ever be realized, but it is worth noting that many administrations believed the new ITU was capable of achieving a planned spectrum which would exist far into the future. Modern-day disappointment with the ITU on the part of some American officials and observers may stem in part from the unbounded expectations and optimism of the immediate postwar era.

As discussion on the establishment of an engineered, planned, *a priori* spectrum continued, two camps emerged: support for one-step planning of the entire spectrum came from the United States, Britain, Canada, Latin America, and India, while gradual-step advocates included the USSR, France, Belgium, and Switzerland.[23] The Soviets were deeply fearful of losing their many prewar Bern Bureau assignments. The other opponents to the one-step plan appeared to be chiefly motivated by Gallic scepticism and the fear of relinquishing too much ITU power to the United States. The United States attempted to achieve universal support for an engineered spectrum. A vote yielded a victory of sort for the one-step method, but unanimity was not achieved. The USSR noted that as 14 administrations including their own had opposed the one-step method, they would refuse to accept the decision of the vote.[24]

A similar struggle ensued in creating the PFB, and the USSR eventually reserved the right to exempt itself from any PFB decisions. The USSR was keen to maintain the 1938 Bern Bureau List, as that list had Soviet notifications of use recorded on virtually every available frequency throughout a major part of the radio spectrum.[25] The Soviets maintained that "no sovereign state could agree to any such poorly planned attempt at interfering with decisions on its internal matters, especially in view of the fact that the question of frequency allocation touches upon the vital interests of each country. . . ."[26] France, while suspicious of one-step planning, countered that the interwar Bern Bureau List was never-theless "inaccurate . . . incomplete . . . inexplicit . . . [and included] insufficient or even erroneous details."[27] The Netherlands' delegate asserted that Soviet proposals to the PFB "deviate widely from the spirit in which the Atlantic City resolution was adopted."[28]

Within a year after the Atlantic City Conference the postwar spirit of cooperation and optimism had been irrevocably shattered. The par-titioning of Europe, the Berlin Airlift, the Truman Doctrine, and events in Czechoslovakia had all contributed to the rising tension and nascent Cold War. Only two weeks after the PFB commenced work it was clear that the USSR and the United States possessed irreconcilable differences on spectrum management which were further aggravated by an overall atmosphere of hostility. This antagonism was expressed through several conduits. Lengthy, accusatory debates took place over the admission of Spain, the handling of German and Japanese allocations, and the quantity of frequencies requested by the USSR.[29]

The original mandate for the PFB stated that the Board should complete its work on a comprehensive *a priori* plan by November 1948. The incessant disputes among member countries led to an agreement to postpone the deadline to May 1949. When at that time the PFB still had yet to complete 80 per cent of its work, the USSR and eight of its allies submitted a proposal to "break off" the work of the PFB and decide on a future plan at an Administrative Radio Conference. This proposal provoked a counter-proposal from the United States and France, among others, to continue the PFB until August 1949.[30] By August the PFB appeared to have progressed little. Despite Soviet declarations that the Board should be dissolved, the Administrative Council decided to extend the mandate of the Board into 1950. The Soviet delegation then angrily withdrew from the Board, taking in its wake Albania, Bulgaria, Czechoslovakia, Hungary, Poland, Romania, and later, the new People's Republic of China.

Was the PFB in fact a "useless holdover of naive postwar optimism?" In part it must be admitted that the task of *a priori* allocation of each and every frequency in the spectrum seems unusually ambitious and unrealistic. Nevertheless, the PFB might have enjoyed greater success had not the Socialist bloc members been so adamant and uncompromising in their demands. As it was, certain radio bands vital to maritime and aviation safety were meaningfully planned, as even the most reluctant ITU members recognized the necessity of cooperation on these bands. But these were only miniscule portions of the spectrum. By the end of 1950 a deep pessimism and sense of despair led to the postponement of the scheduled Extraordinary Administrative Radio Conference (EARC) for one year.

The failure of the PFB left the ITU in a serious quandry: The key purpose of the Union after the Atlantic City Conference was to be *a priori* allocation of the radio frequency spectrum. This objective was, only four years later, largely impossible. The ITU could thus be viewed in 1951, at least as far as radio spectrum management was concerned, as lacking a strong *raison d'être*.

It would only be a mild overstatement to say that the future of the ITU was at stake at the 1951 EARC. In light of the failure of the PFB, attention at the Conference was focused on the IFRB. While it was considered important to retain the Atlantic City commitment to the engineered spectrum goal, it was also realized that some sort of com-promise solution to allocation procedures would have to be found. This was by far the greatest difficulty confronted by the conference. The level of success achieved in the resolution of this problem was limited, but apparently adequate to ensure a modicum of tranquility within the ITU. At the EARC, two schools of thought emerged concerning the future direction of the IFRB. The United States and several Allied countries advocated "voluntary" national telecommunications administration com-pliance with the Atlantic City Allocation Table. Only stations operating on a frequency could hold and register that frequency and stations would be able to "trade" frequencies along vaguely free-market lines. Conversely, India and other incipient telecommunications powers believed this to be a departure from an engineered spectrum, and called for a planned frequency list under which, in essence, the IFRB would become a permanent PFB in that it would be entrusted with similar, and they hoped, more efficacious powers.

In four years the United States, Britain, Canada, Australia, and several other Western countries had exhausted their postwar optimism and were now ready to restore, with some modifications, the interwar status quo ante. By 1951 the Western powers were deeply disillusioned by the failure of the PFB. It appeared that the only way the Soviet bloc could be brought into a planned spectrum would be through granting them all of the frequencies they had registered on the 1939 Bern Bureau List. The growing number of newly independent and soon-to-be independent countries also indicated to more foresightful planning advocates that the technical success of *any* international plan might end up being jeopardized by a future sudden, sharp growth in the demands on spectrum space. In addition, the United States, while still the dominant actor in the ITU, could never entirely convince the more conservative French, Italian, or Swiss administrations of the merits of *a priori* planning. The continental Europeans distrusted American motives and feared a loss of influence in the Union. They were never keen supporters of US efforts in the PFB and IFRB. But it was in the end the Soviet bloc which doomed the

PFB through Soviet inability to grant the slightest compromise in its position. The Soviets refused to sacrifice any of the frequencies they had recorded on the 1938 Bern List. Once they and the Chinese withdrew from the PFB, the members of the PFB realized the futility of continuing their work. The 1951 Extraordinary Administrative Radio Conference (EARC) ratified the little progress that had been possible on the PFB. But even this conference was hindered by Soviet bloc refusal to sign the Final Acts. In the early 1950s it was clear that the Soviet Union possessed no strong desire to facilitate its communications with the outside world. Hence, it saw as advantageous a policy of destabilizing what it viewed as an American-run Union. After the EARC, the role of the IFRB was to be enhanced to gradually plan the fixed, mobile, land and tropical broadcast services, with special consideration to be given to "countries underdeveloped in the field of radio communications."[31] But "planning" in this context was, with the exception of certain aviation and maritime bands, to consist chiefly of registering frequencies already in use.

The 1950s were an evolutionary decade in which the ITU, by trial and error, developed a method of frequency coordination and registration which exists to this day. Many of the principles founded at the 1951 EARC and the High Frequency Conferences of 1949–51 remain, as does the validity of much of the technical work carried out by the IFRB and CCIR during this period. The persistence of the East-West cleavage, however, continued to threaten the credibility of the Union's work throughout the 1950s. The IFRB based much of the Master Frequency List and its technical preparation for the 1959 General WARC on the final Bern Bureau list of 1953. This list was technically inadequate, as the Soviet Union had refused to submit new frequencies to it or recognize the List. The USSR remained adamantly committed to the 1938 List. A further complication involved the inability of the ITU, as a UN specialized agency, to recognize the People's Republic of China. Taiwan had to submit frequencies for all of China, making rough estimates for mainland requirements. As a consequence, much of the IFRB's work had to be based on technical data that were either incorrect or obsolete.

The basic philosophy governing the IFRB and the ITU frequency allocation and registration regime was more or less established by 1952, even if much of it was not explicitly stated until the 1959 General WARC. The "engineered spectrum" goal survived in ever-diminishing form until the 1959 WARC. In that year several WARC decisions expanded the role of the IFRB to cover all aspects of frequency registration, including the then inchoate space services. Since that time the IFRB and Administrative Radio Conferences have pursued a complementary system of meetings and decisions which have maintained a precarious order on the bands through a registration method (discussed below). The West-East division which characterized the 1950s has been largely, but not completely, supplanted by a North-South cleavage. This new division has been exacerbated in recent years by the need to allocate the new satellite-use spectrum and geostationary orbit along lines agreed upon by the ITU with respect to the New World Information Order. This "efficient use" versus "equitable access" dispute will remain the prevalent issue facing the ITU for many years to come.

The Current Spectrum Management Order

Frequency management is commonly viewed as an apolitical activity of little interest outside the technical realm. This is not a view the ITU seeks to discourage. Even the fiasco of the 1948–50 PFB was glossed over by the Administrative Council, which merely admitted that "certain administrations considered the technical principles followed by the PFB to be incorrect. . . ."[32] Yet even the most straightforward international assignment and registration procedures will have obvious political implications. This is especially true in the modern system of states where 160 ITU members rely to an ever-increasing extent upon periodic WARCs and the IFRB to maintain a manageable spectrum.

This section will examine those institutions which shape the current RFS management order. The IFRB and the Administrative Radio Conferences remain the two key organizations responsible for revision and maintenance of the Frequency List and Radio Regulations. They are not the sole organizations involved in this task. The CCIR, through its Conference Preparatory Meetings and Interim Working Parties, provides vital technical preparation for WARCs. Non-ITU regional organizations such as the EBU or CEPT (or any group of broadcasters or administrations) may agree upon certain assignment plans or coordination procedures before a WARC and hence present a unified negotiating front at the conference. The ITU encourages regional pre-coordination and collaboration as it decreases the number of divergent opinions that then confront ITU Conferences, as well as saving time and money. The ultimate responsibility for the orderly registration of frequencies and the operational duties related to this objective rests with the IFRB.

The International Frequency Registration Board (IFRB) Since 1959

Article 10 of the ITU International Telecommunications Convention lists the IFRB's duties as effecting an orderly recording and registration of frequency assignments and geostationary orbit positions, to furnish technical advice, to perform duties concerned with the assignment and employment of frequencies and with the equitable utilization of the geostationary orbit, and to provide technical assistance in preparation for Administrative Radio Conferences.[33]

By the time of the 1952 Plenipotentiary Conference, the role of the IFRB had evolved into that of "center of advice, coordination, and assistance to administrations. . . ." Among its roles, the IFRB establishes and maintains the Master Radio Frequency Record, applies the notification and registration procedure according to the Radio Regulations, and was to prepare the new International Frequency List "including draft plans for the high frequency (HF) broadcasting service."[34]

This last function was inherited from the defunct PFB. Throughout the 1950s the IFRB attempted to reconcile its three seemingly irreconcilable roles: its role as "witness" or registrar of non-interfering frequencies in use; its role as successor to the PFB as a spectrum planner; and its role as innovator of new regulations and new approaches to regulation. These last two roles were made more difficult by strong Soviet fears that a stronger IFRB would diminish Soviet access to the spectrum guaranteed in the 1938 Bern Bureau List.

The distribution of seats on the IFRB guaranteed broad global representation. Of the eleven members, three came from the Americas, three from Western Europe and Africa, one each from Eastern Europe and northern Asia, and three from the remainder of the world. The goal of this distribution was to minimize the potential for undue strength from any one region, and to combat allegations of Eurocentrism on the part of the old Bern Bureau.[35] The 1959 WARC brought about a fundamental shift in the roles of the IFRB. While no fundamental changes were made to the 1947 regulatory regime[36] and the structure of the IFRB remained unchanged, two major steps markedly altered the future course of both the IFRB and RFS management as a whole. First, the objective of an engineered spectrum was finally laid to rest. Demand for frequencies by this time so overwhelmingly outstripped supply that acceptance of *a priori* allocation was clearly impossible to achieve. This realization led the US delegation, for one, to re-evaluate the mandate of the IFRB. This reappraisal resulted in a US proposal to compile the new frequency list solely through "evolutionary" processes. "Registration" and "notification" would be scrapped; registration dates would be de-emphasized; and the Board would be free to focus on the quality and interference levels present in employed frequencies.[37] This proposal was realized, with modifications, by the IFRB frequency registration method emergent from the 1959 WARC. This was known as the Article 10 Method, based on where it is explained in the 1959 Radio Regulations.

It is now referred to as the Article 17 Method, after the 1982 Radio Regulations.

The second substantial step involved enhancement of the IFRB's commitment to providing advice and technical expertise to developing and newly independent countries. Most LDCs did not possess the technical capability or resources required to determine the most efficient use of their telecommunications systems. By 1959 the IFRB had in several cases aided these countries through recommendations of what frequencies to use, what transmitter powers to employ, and at what times to broadcast. To LDCs the IFRB rapidly became an invaluable adviser on a variety of telecommunications issues. As will be seen, this cordial relationship with the Third World was to become mutually beneficial six years later when the LDCs were to collectively save the IFRB from an untimely death. Certain threats to the Board from advanced countries were apparent as early as 1959. The USSR, for reasons discussed above, had never much liked the IFRB. The Soviets proposed in 1959 to convert the IFRB into an "international frequency registration office" which would "dispense with unnecessary technical examination."[38] Perhaps because of the source of this proposal, it was not taken seriously.

The new IFRB Article 10 system was applied to *all* RFS services, planned or unplanned. This was a victory for American proponents of "voluntary, gradual" planning and *a posteriori* allocation. The first test for this new system emerged at the 1963 Space WARC. This conference was pioneering in several respects, not the least of which was the sense of occasion accompanying the introduction of space services into ITU jurisdiction. At the 1959 WARC certain "experimental" bands, shared with terrestrial services, were allocated for space radio communications. At that time only one commercial satellite, the American Early Bird, was in operation. Until 1963 the technical parameters determining the use of space bands remained undefined, and those set as the 1963 Space WARC were largely the result of CCIR preparatory work and extensive preconference coordination, particularly between the United States, Canada, Britain, Scandinavia, and FR Germany.

Besides being a harbinger of future growth and dynamism, the 1963 Space WARC confirmed the terrestrial "first-come, first-served" *a posteriori* system and applied it to space services. The LDCs, the Soviet Bloc, and several other countries favored a more equitable planned approach to the as yet largely unused space service allocations. Given their past opposition to the efforts of the PFB and IFRB, the Soviet position may at first glance be difficult to understand. In fact, the highly symbolic nature of this first Space WARC—the extent of actual planning was fairly limited due to the state of the technology—allowed the Soviets an opportunity to ally with the developing countries at little real cost to themselves. In addition, Soviet satellite use was limited enough at this time for the Soviets to have possibly gained from any consciously equitable assignment plan. But the United States, with the support of Western Europe, Japan, and Latin America, was still powerful enough to carry the vote in favor of applying the status quo to space services.[39] A compromise of sorts was reached in order not to completely alienate the unhappy LDCs and Eastern Bloc. Recommendation 10-A of the 1963 Conference asserts members' "right to equitable and rational use of frequency bands allocated for space communications."[40] The implications of this statement were not specified.

The IFRB was both a participant in and an object of the discussions at the 1963 Space WARC. The IFRB, along with the USSR and France, desired the global coordination of satellite use. While the Americans and others opposed this, claiming it could hinder the progress of an individual country's space plans, a separate organization, Intelsat, was established, largely under US auspices, soon after the 1963 Space WARC in order to achieve the very purpose of global coordination. It was recognized that interference among parties using the space bands would occur frequently without close coordination. The IFRB, furnished with the right information, could provide a valuable service in assessing the probability of harmful interference on a given frequency and in effecting coordination. As no new principles were established, the IFRB had to base its findings and decisions on regulatory methods that had been dismissed as unrealistic years earlier, such as that of an engineered, planned spectrum.

As the 1960s progressed, it became apparent that within the IFRB there existed a degree of inequality: only about half of the Board's members were doing their job. The cost and inefficiency of the IFRB became an increasing problem. This, when coupled with some dissatisfaction with the operation of the Board, led to calls for scrapping the IFRB.

A concerted, coordinated attempt to do away with the IFRB emerged at the 1965 Montreux Plenipotentiary Conference. In effect, it was argued by several countries, including the United States, the Soviet Union, Britain, West Germany, and Canada that the IFRB accomplished the establishment of a registration procedure and master frequency list. Having been successful, the Board should be rewarded by being disassembled. In fact, the real objection to the IFRB stemmed from its admittedly glaring inefficiency, high cost, and perceived superfluity. Since the IFRB had "outlived its usefulness," its frequency registration role could be easily incorporated into a division of the General Secretariat.[41]

One other point often overlooked or underestimated by observers was the high degree of dissension and antagonism that had developed in the early 1960s between certain members of the Board. Significant personal tension existed between several members and the American member and Board Chairman for 1963, Mr. John Gayer. Curiously, in many of these often petty yet bitter controversies the Soviet member allied with Mr. Gayer in opposing the European and Latin American members.[42]

It is unlikely the developed countries foresaw the degree of opposition their proposals to abolish the IFRB would provoke. The LDCs looked upon the IFRB as an invaluable source of technical advice which they could ill afford to lose. Moreover, the IFRB was believed by LDCs to be unbiased and objective. They were quick to rally grandiloquently to the defense of the IFRB. The vote on retention of the IFRB yielded a result of 64 for versus 39 against.[43] LDC reliance on the congested medium and high frequency parts of the spectrum, their need for assistance with complex planning, and the strong desire by LDCs to maintain this impartial voice within the ITU all gave credence—and a much needed renewal of purpose—to the continued existence of an autonomous IFRB.

Even the most strident supporters of the Board nonetheless recognized the need to streamline the Board and make it more efficient. A compromise was reached in which the Board would be reduced from eleven to five permanent members. The unpopularity of Mr. Gayer and the desire of most African delegates to expel Mr. Roberts, the South African member, may have facilitated this endeavor.

From that 1965 nadir the IFRB has steadily grown in strength and scope. Its mandate to assist developing countries and its conscious impartiality have made it a highly respected component of ITU activity. The IFRB has matured in its role as public trustee of the bands. The IFRB is now careful to undertake efforts in those areas where it knows it can achieve progress. Conflict is discouraged by the "clubby, old-boy-net atmosphere present on the Board"[44] and by a willingness to engage in positive reciprocity—in other words, horse-trading. This has led to an effective investigatory registration process and a largely consensual decision-making process. It is rare for a formal vote to be taken.[45] The IFRB works as both a semi-autonomous entity and as an integral part of the Administrative Radio Conferences. This latter role is of increasing importance given the preponderance of two session WARCs, in which the IFRB is given the bulk of intersessional technical work. A consequence of the "autonomy" of the IFRB has been the concern expressed by several administrations that the IFRB tends to occasionally "close ranks"[46] and exclude valuable input from member administrations in a belief that the IFRB knows best. Some American officials have expressed a desire to see greater involvement on the part of administrations and a decentralization of IFRB duties. The zero-growth budget under which the IFRB has had to operate since 1982 may in fact lead to developed country administrations accepting a more active role in assisting the IFRB in its duties.[47] Of course, the IFRB works largely in the context of the periodic and special WARCS, so it is that aspect of the RFS management order that is next examined.

Administrative Radio Conferences

Since 1947 periodic revisions to the Radio Regulations have taken place at Administrative Radio Conferences. These conferences vary in size and scope as much as the problems they confront. In effect, three types of Administrative Radio Conferences attempt to manage the spectrum. General non-specialized WARCs entail massive preparation and comprehensive overhauls of the entire Radio Regulations, as well as renumbering and republishing existing regulations. Two General WARCs have been held since 1947, one in 1959 and one in 1979. At a General WARC thousands of revisions are made to the Radio Regulations. The political nature of some of these "technical decisions" will be shown when particular spectrum issues are viewed.

The second type of WARC is the specialized WARC,[48] which generally looks at one section or segment of the spectrum in particular need of revision or reassignment. The Space WARCs of 1963, 1971 and 1977 are examples of such "narrow" WARCs. At WARC 1979 an important decision was taken to make more frequent use of special WARCs. In part this was an inevitable consequence of the sheer volume of decisions confronting the 1979 General WARC. Had the conferences that year attempted to tackle some of the more contentious issues on the agenda, e.g., regulation of the HF broadcast band or allocation of the geostationary orbit, it is likely the conference would have collapsed as skeptics had predicted before the conference.[49] Only by creating special WARCs for specific issues can any genuine attempt at resolution of these issues be realized. It is vital to note, however, that these specialized conferences may *not* revise the Radio Regulations, but may merely propose changes to be made at a later general WARC, at which time a complete review of the Regulations takes place.

Following the 1979 WARC, special two-session WARCs have been held to revise the Regulations concerning special services on the high frequency spectrum (1984/87) and geostationary orbit (1985/88). The dates in brackets indicate the first and second sessions of these Conferences. Second sessions are held three years after the first to ratify first-session decisions in light of specific developments, new reports, monitoring information, and technological advances. This deferral of several general WARC issues to specific, two-session WARCs may turn out to be one of the most significant ITU developments in recent years. The relative success—or at least the lack of tangible failings—of the 1984 and 1987 High Frequency (HF) WARC, which assigned services on the high frequency broadcast bands, and the 1985 and 1988 GSO-WARC (also known as ORB-85), which sought to develop an allotment plan for the geostationary orbit (GSO) and frequencies related to its use, indicates that this method of RFS management will be employed to an ever-increasing degree—particularly given the advancements in technology which can take place between general WARCs.

A third type of administrative radio conference is the Regional Administrative Radio Conference (RARC). The ITU has divided the globe into three regions: (1) Europe, Africa, the USSR, and Mongolia; (2) the Americas; and (3) Australasia and Oceania. In each region specific issues exist due to the nature of portions of the spectrum. Usually television, FM radio, and medium frequency (MW or AM) radio issues are resolved through RARCs. Even broadcasting-satellite (DBS) frequency bands may be addressed at the regional level, as evidenced by the 1983 Region 2 Satellite RARC. A high level of agreement prior to a RARC may exist, often achieved through regional broadcast organizations like the European Broadcasting Union (EBU) or the Inter-American CITEL (Conferencia Interamericana de Telecommunicaciones) through regional groups of administrations such as Europe's CEPT (Conference of European Post and Telecommunication Administrations), or through common user organizations (CUOs) like Intelsat or Eutelsat. Nevertheless, issues of keen interest to domestic telecommunications services more often arise at RARCs, making the conferences as politically and economically salient (if not more so) than the world conferences.

It is neither practical nor necessary to trace specific developments at all WARCs and RARCs. It will be of greater use to survey spectrum issues by "going up" the spectrum. Regulations for major segments of the frequency spectrum have evolved in a different way, according to the nature of the technology used, the date when employed, and the unique international implications.

Low and Medium Frequency Broadcasting
(LW/MW or AM Radio)

The political issues of the low and medium frequency (LF and MF) spectrum are largely shaped by the nature of the medium. This is the domain of longwave and mediumwave (AM) radio, the central means of radio broadcasting in the world. The longwave band may be unfamiliar to readers outside Europe. This band is used for broadcasting solely in ITU Region 1 (Europe, Africa, and the USSR). Within Europe its groundwave technical characteristics make the band ideal for national radio services to be provided from a small number of extremely high powered transmitters. The LW band is relatively limited, and most of the stations operating on it have been long established. Assignments to specific broadcasters were first made at the 1925 UIR Broadcasters Conference and ratified at the 1927 Washington Radio Conference. The higher transmitter powers required to provide national and regional LW services limited the band's users to those countries with the economic means to purchase such technology. This had the fortunate effect of reducing the number of stations and hence the level of harmful interference on the band.

The number of LW broadcasters in Europe has remained fairly static since the 1950s. The addition of several high powered LW transmitters in the USSR in recent decades has not posed a serious problem. Nevertheless, megawatt LW transmitters exist in the Asiatic and Pacific portions of the Soviet Union. Outside of Region 1 the lower frequencies are solely used for fixed, aeronautical, and maritime services. Therefore, the easternmost Soviet LW broadcasting transmitters may interfere with non-broadcasting services in the northern Pacific.

The mediumwave frequencies (MW[AM]) have not been as fortunate. Indeed, the state of lawlessness and chaos that reigns on this band in Europe has led to the first instance on the radio spectrum of what has been termed an "utter breakdown in audibility."[50] Similar dangers now confront this band in North America. The central problem, shared with much of the RFS, concerns demand for frequencies outstripping supply. A related problem entails the use of excessive transmitter power by stations wishing to circumvent crowding by "blasting" their signal through. These "air wars" have reached ridiculous proportions in Europe where, for example, the Hungarian home service employs, on one of several frequencies used for this service, a two million watt transmitter.[51] To contrast, North American MW transmitters have, by regional agreement, not exceeded a power of 50,000 watts.

While North America does not share this problem with Europe, there are other difficulties unique to the New World: a vast and rapidly growing number of low-powered stations encroaching upon one another and increasingly interfering with one another. This problem has been compounded by deregulation of the AM broadcast band in the United States. This has resulted in the relaxing of criteria distinguishing "clear" and "regional" frequency assignments provided for in the North American Regional Broadcasting Agreement (NARBA) in favor of a "marketplace" solution to frequency management assisted by only the most skeletal of regulatory frameworks.[52]

For many years the ITU perceived no need to involve itself in the medium frequency bands. The UIR European Plan of 1925 and the 1929 NARBA were seen by the ITU as evidence that broadcasters and administrations could themselves agree to control this segment of the spectrum. Since the original North American agreement seemed to guarantee a future of stable RFS management, the ITU entered the 1930s focusing its attention on the more volatile European MW band. At Madrid in 1932 it was decided to mandate the UIR, which had last effected allocations at its own conference in Prague in 1929, to employ its technical resources to establish an allocation plan which the ITU could ratify.

This plan was achieved at the ITU European Broadcasting Conference of 1933. This conference drafted the first a priori plan accepted and adopted by the Union. The larger European broadcasters, particularly Germany, France, and Italy, were wary of too restrictive a plan. Each of these countries, along with several others, intended on greatly expanding their national and international broadcasting services. As a consequence, 19 out of the 35 signatories to the plan made reservations which permitted them to disregard the plan should it hinder or interfere with their national broadcasting needs. This undermined the strength of the plan and, as broadcasting conditions degenerated as the 1930s progressed, served as a wistful reminder of how orderly the band might be if only collaboration between European countries had been possible.

The inability of administrations to achieve compromise was exacerbated by the deteriorating political and economic climate in Europe in the early 1930s. The Cairo Conference of 1938, agonizing over HF allocation demands, deferred European MW disputes to a special European Broadcasting Conference held at Montreux early in 1939. The Montreux Plan allocated 139 frequencies to 374 different stations in the LW and MW bands. Out of the 31 participants, five would not sign the Final Acts and 18 made specific reservations. Records indicate the conference was largely an exercise in frustration and obduracy.[53] The plan, which was to have come into effect on September 1, 1939, was never implemented due to the outbreak of World War II.

During the 1930s, Germany, Italy, France, and the Soviet Union were particularly reluctant to make any sacrifices or compromises on the MW band, as each had rapidly expanding home services and international propaganda services to protect. This was not an era during which much cooperation between the European powers could be expected, and MW management was no exception to this hostile status quo. During the war the few countries that had continued to respect the old 1925/33 plan succumbed to the need to protect their services against "attacks" which, from the technical perspective, involved Axis annexing of high-powered transmitters in France and the Benelux countries, the shifting of frequencies at will, jamming, and several expediencies which were in general a technician's nightmare. The ITU, on its Swiss "island," could do nothing to ameliorate this situation.

The need to restore order to the European MW band after the war led the ITU to make this objective a postwar frequency management priority. A "Committee of Eight Countries" (Belgium, France, the Netherlands, Sweden, Switzerland, UK, USSR, Yugoslavia) met shortly after the 1947 Atlantic City Conference to prepare a preliminary draft plan for MW. At the 1948 ITU European Broadcasting Conference allocations were presented to provide two sets of services—one for the population and one for the occupying forces.[54] As perhaps an indication of the turbulent and inchoate state of the IFRB at that time, many of the coordination efforts and much of the correspondence of the 1948 Conference took place through the Secretary-General's office. While the idea of an IFRB Weekly Circular to keep administrations updated was suggested in 1948, as it had been at Atlantic City one year earlier, the Secretary-General retained this role until 1961, when an IFRB Weekly Circular was instituted.[55] While 7 of the 32 participants would not sign the Final Acts, it was gratifying in light of the failure of other postwar planning attempts to witness the adherence of the USSR and its allies to the new Plan. This could only be achieved, however, by acceding to many of the sizeable Eastern bloc demands.

The ITU had by this point taken over the spectrum management role previously held by the European Broadcasters' Organization (UIR).[56] A renewed "European Broadcasting Union" (EBU) was founded by 23 Western European broadcasters in 1950. Consistent with the new bipolar nature of European politics, an association of Soviet bloc broadcasters, the Organisation Internationale de Radiodiffusion et de Television (OIRT), was soon established on similar lines to the EBU. While the spectrum allocation role of the EBU has been greatly diminished (and that of the Prague-based OIRT is minimal), the EBU maintains a Brussels-based technical section, a Belgian monitoring station, and a prestigious research facility.[57] The EBU, with its administrative base in Geneva, continues to make valuable technical contributions to both the CCIR and IFRB, but now exists chiefly as a body facilitating the exchange of radio and television programs between countries.

The administration of the MW bands in the Americas was placed under the aegis of the ITU after World War II. The NARBA of 1929 had been renegotiated through a series of Inter-American Radio Conferences. By agreeing to allocations throughout the Americas, the Inter-American Conferences allowed the countries of this region to present a largely unified force at ITU World Conferences. Periodic Region 2 conferences since that time have been relatively tranquil—at least until the 1980s.

The Region 1 (Europe-Africa-USSR) MW spectrum continued to be the chief recipient of ITU attention paid to this band in the decades following World War II. The most significant development during this time occurred at the "Regional Administrative Radio Conference for the Broadcasting Service using Frequencies in the MF Bands in Regions 1 and 3" which commenced late in 1974. The problems facing Europeans' use of the MW band outlined above were all present by the mid-1970s. The only way to attain some semblance of order was to create a new, comprehensive allocation plan. In the name of equitability the Europeans had to grudgingly make some sacrifices to reduce interference with new African allotments.[58] In all but Region 2 (the Americas) the ITU standardized 9 kHz spacing between AM frequencies. This meant that virtually all broadcasters had to retune their transmitters and all listeners had to adjust their receiving sets. This seemingly minor adjustment (say, from 1475 to 1476 kHz, etc.) in itself provoked vociferous protest from the European media and considerable dissatisfaction among listeners who soon discovered that many of these adjustments merely altered the source of interference and often did not resolve the problem. No agreement had been reached on limits to transmitter power, which compounded the problem as many European broadcasters, particularly in Eastern Europe, were using MW to transmit their external services in addition to their generally over-powered national services.

This conference provides a valuable general example of how compromise may be effected between countries at WARCs and RARCs. The 1974–75 MW Conference required extensive multilateral and regional cooperation and collaboration on the part of all European, African, Middle Eastern, and Australasian countries. Coordination of frequencies between the two Koreas and between Israel and its hostile neighbors took place within a so-called "Compassionate Committee" of the Conference established to effect coordination between countries not on speaking terms. A particular problem arose concerning South Africa, which had been barred from attending ITU Conferences since 1965 due to opposition to its apartheid racial policies, and had barely survived a concerted attempt at the 1973 Plenipotentiary to expel it from the Union. From a technical standpoint, South Africa and Rhodesia were the largest MW spectrum users in southern Africa, and it was vital to achieve a cooperative plan with their "frontline" neighbors. Zambia called for the deletion of all Rhodesian and South African assignments from the Master Frequency List. In addition, Zambia demanded the IFRB recognize the rightful status of Namibia by changing the three-letter listing code in the Register from "SWA" to "NMB." These were minor points, admittedly, but without these changes most African countries were unwilling to sign the Final Acts.

In the end, South Africa was able to achieve coordination with its neighbors. The South Africans stationed a de facto conference delegation in a hotel near the ITU headquarters and met informally, in the evenings, with delegates from black African states. South Africa agreed to change the three-letter code of Namibia, although it continued to act as Namibia's administration. Quick thinking on the part of a few IFRB members defused the crisis by allowing the scrapping of South African and Rhodesian assignments by publishing these assignments as "IFB" (unassigned) frequencies which "happened" to correspond to South Africa. This was done for Rhodesia as well prior to 1980. The success of this maneuver was confirmed in 1977 when new submissions for Rhodesia and South Africa were entered into the plan without protest.[59] Thus neither the political postures of the black African states nor the technical needs of the region were compromised. This sort of so-called politicization may have added to the length and cost of the conference, but in the end the 1975 MW Broadcasting Conference for Regions 1 and 3 proved to be an example of successful international collaboration and coordination.

In Region 2 (the Americas) the tumultuous events of Europe, Africa, and Asia were being closely observed. In the mid-1970s the countries of the Americas decided not to join Regions 1 and 3 in their switch to 9 kHz spacing. The traditional 10 kHz spacing on the band (540, 550, 560 kHz . . .) was a hopelessly inadequate means of meeting MW radio spectrum demands, but the expense and confusion expected to result from attempts to reallocate the band were considered to outweigh long-term advantages. Moreover, it must be noted that the nature of radio broadcasting in the Americas differs from that elsewhere. Outside of supplementary national radio services in Canada, Argentina, and a handful of other countries, in most Region 2 countries radio has developed along American lines: large numbers of low-powered commercial radio stations serving each population center. The United States alone possesses nearly 4,800 authorized MW broadcasters.[60] Reluctance to create long-term efficiency by forcing each and every one of these transmitters to alter its frequency was obviously based on the short-term economic and political unpopularity which would inevitably result from such change.

Pressures from a variety of interests—from minority groups to educational broadcasters to large commercial enterprises—led the United States to reappraise its commitment to the MW spectrum management status quo with the consequence that, in 1980, at the ITU Regional Administrative Broadcasting Conference for Region 2, the United States proposed the Americas switch to 9 kHz spacing on the MW Band. Such a switch would have allowed a great expansion in the number of stations able to use the limited band. A surprised Canada joined the other Region 2 members in opposing this change, due to early fears of overcrowding an already difficult band and of diminishing signal quality.[61]

After the 1980 American election, interest on the part of the new Reagan administration in regulating a shift to 9 kHz spacing quickly waned due to a deliberate policy of minimal government intervention. To compel broadcasters in such a way was considered antipathetic to the beliefs of the new leadership at the FCC. Instead, the FCC sought to disassemble the old NARBA plan which, with its distinctions between local, regional, and clear channels, was considered archaic and contrary to free market principles. The 1980–81 RARC for Region 2 established a regulatory framework to take the place of the defunct, non-ITU NARBA. The ITU plan allows countries greater discretion in how they manage domestic MW spectrum use. As a consequence, intra-regional bilateral and multilateral cooperation outside the ITU context continues in much the same way it did in the days of NARBA.

The deregulation of the MW band has deliberately led to a marked increase in the number of MW stations operating in the United States and Canada. As this growth reaches its limit, however, instances of interference will increase and the general quality of signals will decrease. Already Canadian and Mexican authorities have had to allow a de facto deregulation and similar sorts of declassification of clear and regional MW channels. The US and Canadian 50,000 watt power limitation on MW transmitters may eventually be scrapped as stations attempt to avoid a decline in their signal's coverage. Other reasons for potential transmitter power "air wars" in North America are detailed in Chapter 3.

In the late 1970s technical developments led to an agreement that the MW band could be expanded by a full 100 kHz.[62] After years of technical activity the ITU first addressed the issue in 1986 at a special two session WARC to plan this additional portion of the spectrum for Region 2. As most of this segment of the spectrum remains unused, the Conference was relatively uncontentious, with few of the North-South dimensions that have dominated other recent WARCs.

At the 1986 Conference, a division between the United States and the other countries of the Americas emerged over frequency assignment methods. Most countries assumed the new portion would be assigned in much the same way as previous MW—and other frequency—assignments had been made, employing the IFRB Article 17 Method. At the MW level, Article 17 requires submission of a station's location, frequency, transmitter power, and antenna location, with disagreements to be adjudicated at the regional level if possible. The United States delegation, reflecting contemporary FCC and administration policy concerning maintaining a minimum of regulations, proposed a unique allocation method. This allocation method reserves frequencies within 200 miles of sovereign borders. Within this limit stations on both sides of a boundary will carefully coordinate their use to avoid interference. Within the limit the assignment criteria are in fact tougher than the previously employed method. But outside of the 200 mile limit stations are, within certain broad guidelines and power limits, only subject to domestic regulation and are largely disassociated from ITU and IFRB activity.[63]

Perhaps because this portion of the spectrum remains as yet largely unused and is, due to the nature of the MW band, of little use to the equatorial or tropical areas of Region 2, the US proposal was accepted without dissent and, as one US official stated, "the US achieved 100 percent of its objectives at the conference."[64] Expansion on this band will not be rapid as few MW radio sets can receive these new frequencies. Until a large number of such sets exist, exploitation of this band will remain minimal. Despite sniping between the United States and Cuba over the American "Radio Marti" service—a subject of discussion criticized as being unrelated to the subject of the conference—the Report of the First Session is now being held up as "a fine example of harmonious, positive cooperation in this hemisphere. The conference was a real success for the ITU."[65]

With the implementation of new spacing in Regions 1 and 3 and the technical challenge resulting from deregulation and expansion of the band in Region 2, the future of MW management remains difficult. Demand will continue to far exceed supply on most of the band. Areas of contention within the MW band remain, by nature of the technology, chiefly regional in scope. Within Europe excessive transmitter powers and a lack of coordinated policies, both within the CEPT countries and between Western and Eastern Europe, lead to problems of overcrowding and inaudibility which are largely beyond resolution. Portions of Asia are facing similar constraints, caused by a steady growth of demand and a painfully limited supply. Extending the spectrum by a small margin, as is being done in the Americas, may provide some short-run improvement. Within the Americas, however, philosophical differences concerning how domestic broadcasting should evolve have led regional and international conferences to increasingly reflect this "deregulation versus regulation" division. These nevertheless remain minor planes of contention, given the importance of this band to world broadcasting. While the state of the MW band cannot be called ideal, particularly given its anarchic state in Europe, it has not been an area of major worry to the ITU. To a large extent international problems on this band are outside the ITU's bailiwick. If solutions cannot be found at the regional level, there is little the ITU can do to ameliorate the situation.

High Frequency Broadcasting (HF) (Shortwave)

By a substantial margin the high frequency (HF) bands have been one of the most difficult portions of the spectrum to regulate. In despair the IFRB has recently adopted several revolutionary measures to "stop the rot." Yet the ITU, having attempted in vain to impose order on the "zoo" of HF assignments,[66] has been hindered in achieving any degree of success by several factors endogenous to the medium: (1) the international nature of HF use; (2) certain technical characteristics of HF; and (3) characteristics of HF users (LDCs, poorest members, etc.).

First, HF is by nature an international medium—unlike its siblings on the low, medium, and FM-VHF frequencies. Relatively low-powered HF transmitters allow a signal to reach entire continents. Higher-powered transmitters may give a radio station a virtually global scope. From the late 1920s, then, HF has been employed chiefly as a means of transmitting international radio services. Only certain segments of the HF band were allocated to radio broadcasters, however, as the band was also soon employed by international fixed services (e.g., international news services, diplomatic communications, maritime services, radiotelegraphs, etc.), by international aviation, and by radio amateurs. Even in the early years much concern was expressed over the volume of frequency demand consistently exceeding the limited supply.

Yet it was not until World War II that HF came to flourish as an international broadcasting—and propaganda—medium. Just as the BBC Empire Service attracted thousands of news-starved listeners in Axis-occupied countries, the Deutschlandsender and Radio Tokyo established massive transmitting systems to attract listeners and promote their cause (see Chapter 3 below).

Since that time the scope of HF broadcasting and the worldwide number of listeners to HF stations has grown several-fold. There now exist hundreds of broadcasters vying for the still limited amount of HF spectrum space reserved for international broadcasting. The greatest users are the major international broadcasters such as the Voice of America (VOA), BBC World Service, and Radio Moscow. The largest broadcasters transmit from several sites, often with the aid of overseas relay stations, in order to ensure global coverage.[67] For example, a VOA transmission in Polish to Europe may employ as many as 12 frequencies from four transmitter sites in three countries.[68]

The desire to transmit abroad may stem from any number of motives—to improve the tarnished image of a country (e.g., Taiwan, South Africa), to provide home news and information to expatriates and travellers (e.g., Norway, New Zealand), to promote a certain political or social point of view (e.g., Soviet bloc stations, US-based religious broadcasters), or some mix of the above and other reasons. The HF audience certainly exists. The BBC estimates well over 100 million daily listeners worldwide to its World Service. While the vast majority of HF listeners are in the Third World, inexpensive yet sophisticated receiving equipment is making HF broadcasting better known in the developed countries—after a forty year hiatus. It is now estimated that the BBC World Service has an audience of over two million listeners in North America, where a decade ago that audience only numbered in the tens of thousands.[69]

In addition, certain technical characteristics of HF have both promoted its use and hindered the effectiveness of its regulation. In tropical zones medium frequency (MW) broadcasting is greatly restricted by high levels of ionospheric static. Thus HF becomes the only cost-effective way for many LDCs to provide a basic national broadcasting service.

HF consists of far more than broadcasting services. It has traditionally been the key medium for all international radio communication services. In recent years, however, developed countries have been moving their news services, radiotelexes, and maritime services from HF to more advanced satellite and microwave systems. As this continues, developing countries are becoming increasingly defensive about their right to use the inexpensive HF bands for these fixed services—which, unlike broadcasting, are usually profitable enterprises. In addition, some developing states institute elaborate international broadcasting operations, which are perceived as a sign of development, adding to the competition and crowding of the HF bands.

It has been suggested that part of the difficulty in achieving HF regulation is the low priority assigned to it by the developed countries. Despite recent growth, few HF listeners outside of hobbyists, expatriates, and travellers exist in the Western developed countries. Conversely, the millions of HF listeners in the Soviet bloc are actively discouraged from doing so, limiting the medium's potential in those countries. Nevertheless, HF listenership is far higher in the Eastern bloc than in the West. Despite jamming and censure, upwards of 70 percent of the population of most Eastern European countries and the USSR tune in to Western broadcasts at least once a month.[70] But most HF listeners are found in developing countries. Despite LDC complaints, since the development of the New World Information Order (NWIO), of "neo-colonial" dependence on Northern broadcasters as a negative force in development, their citizens rely on the major broadcasters for reliable news and quality entertainment, often tailored, in the case of several Northern broadcasters, to appeal to its target audience in Africa or Asia.

Northern neglect and Southern demands have rendered the ITU's spectrum management role more difficult. In major developed countries, however, the expenditure on external radio services is not always accompanied by an equal commitment to HF spectrum order. Through jamming and an often indiscriminate use of frequencies, Eastern bloc countries have in the past actively promoted disorder. Western countries have become somewhat ambivalent in their search for a solution, often looking more closely at satellite and DBS technologies which, admittedly, will have a much greater domestic impact for developed countries.

Managing this difficult band has never been an easy task for the ITU. The 1927 Washington Radio Conference was the first seriously to attempt HF coordination and allocation of services to bands. The HF band had been first employed for voice broadcasting in the early 1920s by radio amateurs. At the time of the Washington Conference these amateurs remained the chief users of the HF band—there were over 16,000 licensed amateurs in the United States alone as of 1927.[71] The Washington Conference successfully limited the amateurs to specific bands within the HF spectrum.

By the 1932 Madrid ITU Conference broadcasters were starting to use the HF band for beaming broadcasts to other countries. Demands for space on the HF band grew rapidly as the 1930s progressed, with Britain, France, Germany, and the USSR, all establishing major external services in the years between 1932 and 1938. At the 1938 ITU Cairo Radiocommunications Conference, the European Broadcasters' Organization (UIR) immediately pressed for a major expansion of the international HF broadcasting allocations which, the British delegate retorted, would dislocate 1,100 existing fixed and utility service stations.[72] Britain, while possibly the world's largest HF broadcasting system at that time, feared that expansion of the broadcasting bands would impinge upon vital HF military and maritime communication services. The United States delegation, citing reasons similar to Britain's, opposed any HF broadcasting expansion. In addition, the United States did not consider HF broadcasting that important, as their own pre–World War II services were relatively modest. The strength of Europe in the interwar Union guaranteed some expansion, despite the opposition of these large maritime and military users. Noteworthy in this expansion was the creation of certain HF "tropical" bands which remain to this day an important means of radio broadcasting in the equatorial regions of Latin America, Africa, and Asia.

The great era of growth for HF radio broadcasting took place during World War II. Germany possessed a network of twenty transmitters operating a 15-language foreign service, and the BBC Empire Service became a 24 hour World Service. In addition, military uses of the HF band had predictably sustained marked growth. This enhanced employment of the band did not cease with the ending of wartime hostilities. In fact, HF use and demand continued to grow after the war, and began to accelerate with the inception of the Cold War.

At the time of the 1947 Atlantic City Conference the HF bands remained virtually the sole source of international radio communications. The new IFRB, consequently, centered its attention on the HF spectrum. The *a posteriori* planning method and IFRB principles discussed above were in fact largely shaped by the Board's attempts to cope with demands on the HF spectrum. Even 18 years after Atlantic City the Board judged that "out of a total of about 4000 notices per month, an average of about 950 notices per month still relate to new HF assignments or to changes of . . . existing HF assignments."[73]

Most of the activity which led to the ultimately irreconcilable problems of the 1948–50 Provisional Frequency Board (PFB) centered on HF management disputes. It is certainly significant that the only successes achieved by the PFB occurred on those higher broadcast and utility HF bands which were not high priority items for either the USSR or the United States. Some of the *a priori* plans worked out by the PFB were rendered ineffective by the fact that they exceeded spectrum space available by as much as 180 per cent.[74] By 1950 the Chairman of the PFB virtually conceded defeat in the quest to achieve an engineered HF spectrum. Mr. Gracie summarized the failure of the PFB as a consequence of frequency demands far beyond the expectations of the Atlantic City Conference, and the coexistence of "two radically different and apparently incompatible technical approaches": the American and Allied desire to achieve a one step *a priori* plan versus Soviet bloc wishes to plan gradually and not depart radically from the pre-1939 Bern Bureau system. Combined with the general recalcitrance of the Soviet bloc, this led to excessively rhetorical political debates.[75]

Two conferences took place during the postwar period which attempted to form an allocation plan for HF broadcasting. The first was the Mexico City HF Broadcasting Conference of 1948–49. This conference began, like the PFB, in an atmosphere of optimism and hope. It soon became apparent, however, that virtually every country present was submitting excessive "requirements." Coordination quickly became impossible. Despite preparatory work by administrations and the CCIR, the conference lacked sufficient technical data and expertise to reach the ambitious objectives it had set for itself.

Through extensive compromise and "horse-trading" a provisional plan for one season (four months) was hammered out.[76] The United States delegation, still deeply discouraged by the failure of the PFB, approached the Mexico City Conference with a jaundiced, cynical view of its potential.

There was a conviction on the part of some American—and other—participants that the Soviets wished to lock the ITU into a rigid plan which the USSR could then violate at will. The American delegation also believed too many sacrifices had been made by the Europeans in order to cajole the Soviets into signing the Final Acts. One consequence of this was that the Soviet Union received a much larger overall allocation than the United States.[77] Citing inequitable distribution of frequencies, Soviet reluctance to discuss jamming, the inordinately large "requirements" submitted by several countries, and the technical failings of the proposed plan, the United States refused to sign the Final Acts of the Mexico City Conference. The absence of the United States from the plan in effect invalidated the entire effort. While the United States had several legitimate complaints—in all likelihood the ITU plan would not have worked—the atmosphere of ill will with which the conference concluded served to jeopardize future attempts by the ITU to deal with HF usage issues.[78]

The ITU formed a Technical Planning Committee after the Mexico City Conference in order to expand and improve the frequency plan proposed at the conference as well as devise plans for the three other annual broadcast seasons. This Committee could not even begin to fulfil its immense mandate. Compounding the problem, by 1950 most administrations were submitting new HF frequency requirements that were markedly larger than those they had considered sufficient three years earlier.

What ultimately doomed these early HF planning attempts, however, was not the technical impossibility of the task as much as the overt hostility and antagonism between the American and Soviet delegations. A few days after the Second International HF Broadcasting Conference commenced at Florence-Rapallo early in 1950, the Soviet delegation withdrew, accusing the American delegation of, *inter alia*, attempting to manipulate the conference in its favor.[79] This, combined with the impossibly large "requirements" submitted by most countries and the disappointing report from the preparatory Technical Planning Committee, led to an unsuccessful conclusion to the Conference.

The legacy of the Mexico City and Florence Conferences was an aversion on the part of the ITU and the IFRB to become too deeply involved in HF management issues. If countries were not willing to collaborate to coordinate their services, and if the largest ITU members did not believe in the merits of planning the HF bands, then there would be little the ITU could do to improve upon an unsatisfactory status quo. Even 34 years later, at the 1984 HF-WARC First Session, the "ghosts" of these early failures haunted attempts to establish a frequency allotment plan for HF broadcasting services.

The evolutionary *a posteriori*, or first-come, first-served approach became the IFRB norm at the 1959 WARC. This system, established by the "Article 10 Method" (see above) was far from perfect. Countries would submit, every three months, the HF frequencies they proposed to use or had commenced using. Unless the frequencies selected by the user caused interference to another transmitter within a 90 day period, the employed frequencies would be registered and accorded full legal protection against harmful interference. In many cases cooperation and compliance are forthcoming. Part of the IFRB's mandate entails aiding developing countries in the selection of optimal frequencies, transmitter powers, etc. These countries usually recognize that it is in their best interest to comply with IFRB suggestions. Perception of the IFRB as a Third World ally in fact facilitates compliance.

The system largely relies on the goodwill of ITU members. Should abuses occur the IFRB has only the recourse of "notifying" a frequency, which strips the user of legal protection rights against harmful interference or new operators on the same frequency. The level of crowding on the HF bands has led several broadcasters to consider the risk worthwhile. The Soviet bloc and, to a lesser—and declining—extent, PR China, have been guilty of the chronic illegal use of frequencies. The IFRB has traditionally been reluctant to name names and explicitly censure those countries abusing the spectrum. This derives from a natural reluctance to alienate Eastern bloc participants in the ITU and the technician's innate aversion to becoming involved in an overtly political dispute.

By the late 1970s the levels of unregistered frequencies, out-of-band broadcasters (broadcasters using frequencies reserved for fixed or amateur services and vice versa), and deliberate interference led to a re-evaluation of the Article 10 Method. Other abuses included the registration of excessive numbers of frequencies by certain countries and the increasing use of higher-powered transmitters. Of these latter sins many, if not most, countries are guilty. Most major and mid-size HF broadcasters register many more frequencies than they use or need. Some countries in the past have registered large numbers of frequencies for ambitious external services that exist solely in the pages of the Master Frequency List.[80] Virtually every major HF broadcaster consumes more power and occupies a larger number of frequencies than is necessary.

The 1979 WARC was expected to confront some of the fundamental problems which by this point characterized HF use. Major HF broadcasting countries, led by the United States, called for a much needed expansion of HF broadcast service bands. As Glen Robinson, head of the US delegation to WARC 1979, stated: "It quickly became apparent that the increases sought by the US and a few other countries were unrealistically ambitious. . . . Such increases could only, as a practical matter, be accommodated by the displacement of the fixed service which is used extensively, especially in developing countries, for basic telecommunication relay service."[81] Strong pressure was nevertheless maintained to expand the most crowded of the HF broadcast bands (6 and 7 mHz).

The Conference, by a fairly narrow vote, decided not to expand the HF bands. The LDCs opposed expansion of HF broadcast bands as it would diminish the scope of their fixed services. Some of the strongest opposition to the developed country proposals to expand the HF broadcast bands came from the Latin American countries. Ulterior political motives were not as apparent as sincere concerns on the part of Latin American delegations that they could lose access to their important fixed HF utility services. As a consequence Brazil and Costa Rica were more influential as Latin American spokesmen than was Cuba.[82] Conversely, several developing countries, including Zambia and Sri Lanka, also reserved the right to abrogate the Radio Regulations in order to guarantee the maintenance of their HF broadcasting services.

In other words, many LDCs attempted to have it both ways. Should crowding become too severe, they reserve the right to broadcast out-of-band. As Menzel asserts, the LDCs obviously acted against their own long-term interests, as the expansion plans proposed would have carefully shared and reapportioned fixed services through an orderly expansion of broadcast bands, while retention of the status quo could only "very seriously restrict the conditions of world broadcasting for many years to come."[83]

The inability to expand the HF broadcast bands occurred due to LDC strength and resolve in maintaining their fixed service assignments. Yet the problem of an allocation *plan* or how to allocate those frequencies already assigned to specific international HF services, had not been addressed at the conference until Algeria brought forward a proposal to give LDCs priority use of 70 percent of HF spectrum space allocated for fixed services.[84] While it would not have been a great sacrifice on the part of the developed countries to grant this proposal, it was believed that its acceptance could set a potentially dangerous precedent "only a short step from . . . schemes to set aside certain fixed-satellite frequencies and orbital positions for developing countries."[85] Even though developed countries had by this time largely shifted their utility services from HF radio to satellites, many countries feared setting a precedent that could later be applied against them at, say, a satellite bands planning conference. Moreover, the large military communication users such as the United States, Britain, and France, did not want to sacrifice even unused HF fixed utility service bands as they desired keeping these bands as a reserve should a communications satellite dysfunction. The Algerian priority-use resolutions received little support, even from LDCs. But the

1979 WARC did empower the IFRB to enhance its LDC assistance role and "give special recognition to HF fixed service allocations where alternative communications facilities (e.g., microwave, satellite) are not available."[86]

In order to complete the objectives of the 1979 WARC, many of the HF issues were deferred to a special, two session "WARC for the Planning of the HF Bands Allocated to the Broadcasting Service (HF-WARC)," held in 1984 and early 1987. The 1979 WARC mandated the IFRB and CCIR to investigate all potential options and alternatives to attempt to create some plan that would be an improvement to the "Article 10" status quo, since 1982 known as the Article 17 method, and also be politically acceptable to most ITU members. The results of the IFRB and CCIR endeavors were released in 1983.[87] The IFRB report turned out to be somewhat disappointing, failing to include the "necessary engineering studies and preparation" called for at the 1979 WARC. The IFRB stated that permanent use of frequency assignments, the heart of any *a priori* plan, would contradict the agenda of the first session of the Conference.[88]

The more serious of the two reports was prepared by the CCIR Interim Working Party 10/5. This report sought to illustrate alternatives in HF spectrum planning through the incorporation of the following objectives: "to guarantee all administrations free and equal rights in the use of the bands; to provide a quality of broadcast services in accordance with agreed technical standards; and to assure the efficient use of the bands."[89] Seven distinct methods were proposed, all including a degree of *a priori* planning but varying in the magnitude of control and revision.[90]

The 1984 HF-WARC represented the ITU's first real attempt in over 30 years to establish firm order on the HF broadcast bands. Termed a "considerable achievement,"[91] the report of the First Session incorporated some remarkable and revolutionary proposals. Canada submitted a proposal which proposed a central, automated procedure for assigning frequencies in such a way to ensure the rights of all countries to equitable use of the HF bands. While "there was a feeling in Geneva that the role of the computer was being exaggerated,"[92] the incorporation of such a program at the second session could have resolved much of the crowding and harmful interference burdening the HF spectrum by empowering the IFRB to recommend assignments *to* administrations, not just register assignments received *from* administrations. This could have at least diminished some of the overuse of the HF broadcast bands. It also would have removed any vestiges of legitimacy from jammers, and would have permitted greater ITU control over HF spectrum management.

It was the role of the Second Session of the HF-WARC in 1987 to take the initiative concerning adoption of such a plan. However, even before the Second Session it was apparent that the likelihood of national telecommunications administrations and government ministries to willingly defer their sovereign right to select HF frequencies and their hours of operation to the supranational authority of the IFRB seemed doubtful. At the 1987 Conference opposition arose from the largest broadcasters and HF spectrum users, particularly the United States and the Soviet Union.[93] Nevertheless compelling evidence exists to suggest that if users do *not* adopt hard-hitting solutions, the future of HF could be jeopardized.

Perhaps the aims of the 1987 Second Session of the HF WARC were too ambitious. As the Chairman, K. Bjornso of Sweden, remarked: "Delegations had come to the Second Session with widely differing views ranging from the view that the planning system should be implemented with only minor improvements to the view that no planning system should be implemented at all."[94] The main points of concern to delegations were the following:

1. The need to improve the HFBC (HF broadcasting) planning system.
2. The need to widen the bands allocated HF broadcasting.
3. The need to find an appropriate solution for both national and international uses.
4. The need to guarantee all countries a minimum service with satisfactory protection.
5. The need to improve Article 17.
6. The need to allow countries to continue operating these existing systems without disruption.
7. The need to take all the requisite precautions to ensure the successful implementation of the HFBC Planning System.[95]

These concerns were neither surprising nor melodramatic. The severity of the problem was illustrated to the conference by a series of documents showing that delegations' requests for frequencies added up to over five times the available spectrum space.[96] The only way to accommodate even a portion of these requirements was through expansion of the bands. This could only be accomplished, as has been noted, through forfeiting existing fixed service bands. For the first time, developed countries surmounted their desire to have these bands as a safety net against malfunctioning communication satellites. They were willing to turn over these bands to high frequency broadcasting. A compromise was reached, but only against the strong opposition of Chile, Argentina, and a handful of other countries that still maintain some HF fixed services.

The third point listed above is that of accommodating national broadcasters. Most Latin American countries use HF for domestic broadcasting, as do large countries such as India, China, Indonesia and, to a limited extent, even Australia and Canada. This has been a point of contention since the 1950 Florence-Rapallo HF Conference at which time it was hoped the issue could be resolved by apportioning most national services to the so-called "Tropical" bands. The concern expressed in both 1950 and 1987 focused on the priority given to national broadcasters on HF. Since HF is largely seen as an international medium, some delegations complained that the IFRB gives a higher priority to frequencies allocated by administrations to international services.

In 1950 the Florence conference sought to circumvent the priority issue by having administrations rank their own requests for frequencies in some sort of hierarchy. For example, Canada might place its external "Radio Canada International" service first, the Northern CBC shortwave service second, CBC low-powered relay stations third, and so forth. Unfortunately, most countries ranked all of their requests within the highest priority category, so the plan failed.

In 1987 the Latin American and Arabic-speaking states (which employ high-powered, ostensibly "national" services for pan-Arabic broadcasting) spearheaded accusations that the IFRB might, under a computer plan, give priority to the major international broadcasters. This dispute sank in a morass of semantic arguments over what constituted national, regional, and international broadcasting.[97]

In order for the 1987 Conference to produce anything meaningful, priority was given to addressing the fourth point listed above, that of "minimum service with satisfactory protection." The United States issued a lengthy (112 page) document detailing the sacrifices each ITU member state would have to make in order to achieve a technically feasible compromise.[98] No country, including the United States, was willing to make these sacrifices. Some of the compromises being discussed were, in fact, from a technical perspective, delivering a worse signal than the "unacceptable" status quo. The inability of countries to reduce their requirements made the launch of a computer-based planning system impossible.

Yet the Arab countries in particular were adamant that computer-based *a priori* planning had a future. Most countries believed that, at best, the Conference might make the best of a bad lot by modifying the Article 17 method. The United States was strongly opposed to the computer plan and, by the end of the Conference, most countries recognized that, given current HF requirements, no mere computer plan could guide them out of the chaos. The subsaharan African states, which had been quiet on this topic for the first few weeks of the Conference, finally sided with the Americans.

The Second Session of the HFBC WARC failed to fulfil its objective of developing a new HF frequency management system. But this failure was not disappointing to many of the delegations. The major HF broadcasters viewed proposed changes to the system as a threat, particularly since many countries are in the process of rapidly expanding their SW services. As one US delegate stated about the conclusion of the conference, "We can heave a big sigh of relief. The computer-based planning system was a threat hanging over US international broadcasting for four years. . . . We just fobbed it off for at least five years."[99]

The late 1980s did not therefore witness a breakthrough in ITU's ability to act with resolve and determination in creating HF order. The adoption of an acceptable and successful HF planning method would have greatly enhanced the credibility and prestige of the ITU and ensured a more stable future for the Union. Unfortunately, many telecommunications experts, including some within the ITU and IFRB, seriously doubt the ability of any method to plan the HF spectrum; the nature of the HF medium, they argue, is simply not amenable to planning.[100] Conversely, an inability resolutely to handle the HF issue could lead to a loss of confidence in the ITU's ability to deal with conflicts arising over satellite services and allotment of the geostationary orbit.

That a part of the spectrum as difficult and frustrating to govern as HF should become a test of the ITU's will is unfortunate but perhaps inevitable given past neglect of this important band. The HF broadcast and geostationary orbit WARCs had been consciously planned to complete their work before the 1989 Plenipotentiary. The 1989 Plenipotentiary will now have to confront the failures of the 1984 and 1987 HF WARCs. A general HF WARC (for broadcast and fixed services) is expected to be called for 1992. Given the dramatic expansion of HF broadcasting in the late 1980s and the declining ability of the Article 17 method to realistically accommodate that expansion, some change in the method of managing the HF spectrum is inevitable. Conversely, the poor track record of the ITU, not to mention the unyielding stubbornness of member states, does not augur well for future regulation of this difficult portion of the spectrum. What is beyond doubt is that the failure of the HF WARCs makes the challenges confronting the 1989 Plenipotentiary that much more daunting.

FM/VHF and Broadcast Television

The technical characteristics of FM and television signals are such that, unlike MF or HF signals, which are propagated and literally bounce off the ionosphere, FM and television signals follow a direct "line-of-sight" path. Therefore, with the exception of transmitter sites near international boundaries, these broadcasts are solely domestic in nature and thus of only limited concern to the ITU. In regions where FM and television signals become international, e.g., along the US-Canadian border or in the Benelux countries, any emergent conflicts tend to be resolved through bilateral or multilateral (regional) negotiation.

Despite the increasing importance of these higher bands, their largely domestic use precludes extensive ITU involvement in their management. The ITU convenes periodic RARCs to draft basic use plans for the very high (and higher) frequency bands. These plans apportion segments of the VHF and UFH bands to specific services, e.g., FM radio broadcasting, television, mobile radio telephone, or aviation services. Cooperation at the regional level through regional broadcasting organizations such as the EBU or through multilateral agreement has led to many of these bands being apportioned or planned on *a priori* lines. A consequence of this regional evolution has been differing uses for different bands. Seventeen sets of allocated television broadcast bands exist and three FM broadcast bands exist. What is used in Region 1 for mobile radio-telephone may be used for broadcasting in Region 2, and in Region 3 for maritime communication. The local nature of these services precludes interference, so the cost of such incompatibility tends to be economic; equipment manufacturers must make specific equipment to meet local reception requirements.

The ITU Regional VHF-FM Conferences thus tend to be largely quiet affairs consisting of technical discussion and consensus. A greater role for the ITU exists where cooperation at the regional level is difficult. The ITU, particularly through the IFRB, can then play a vital role as arbiter. An illustration of this occurred at the 1984 ITU Region 1 African VHF-FM Radio Conference. FM broadcast use is not extensive in Africa, and is limited chiefly to Arab North Africa and southern Africa.[101] Not surprisingly, there could not be a lot of communication before the 1984 conference between the South African representatives and other African delegations. In addition, South Africa could not send a delegation to the conference as it has been banned from all ITU meetings since 1965 due to its domestic apartheid racial policies. The South Africans and other southern African delegations were apprehensive about this conference, as several North African delegations were proposing changes to FM standards and use patterns, with potential adverse effects on the southern African status quo.

As there was no communication between northern and southern Africa, some members of the IFRB informally advised the South African administration to provide its neighbors with technical assistance and attempt to coordinate a draft plan before the conference. In this way, the southern African delegations could at least defend their interests at the conference. The South African administration was, despite its persona non grata status in the ITU, the only administration in the region that had the technical expertise necessary to form a cogent draft plan. A unique, informal preparatory meeting took place early in 1984 at Gaberone, Botswana, between the South African administration and five of its immediate "frontline" neighbors. A sole member of the IFRB was present in an "advisory capacity"; but it was the IFRB that was largely responsible for the conference. The preconference meeting was successful and was able to form a draft plan within, enabling southern Africa to present a unified front at the Regional Conference.[102] The IFRB in this case enabled international cooperation and coordination to take place where it otherwise would not have. Even in portions of the spectrum used for chiefly domestic services, and over which national administrations exert near total control in assignment and allocation, the ITU can prove itself indispensable as international arbiter and counsel.

Space Radiocommunication Services and the Geostationary Orbit (GSO)

In late 1957 the Soviet Union launched a primitive orbiting satellite named Sputnik. This event represented the commencement of a new era in science and technology. The "space age" had formally begun and it would revolutionize telecommunications along with every other technology-related field. The hype and hyperbole which surrounded Sputnik and the early years of the space race were at least in part related to the Cold War. America was caught unaware by Sputnik and it became widely believed that the control of space would determine the future balance of power. Both superpowers and Europe rapidly commenced development of fixed satellite services for military and commercial use.

The ITU was a neutral observer of the frantic activity surrounding the early years of satellite development. But the Union clearly recognized the need to reserve some portion of the spectrum for satellite use. National telecommunications administrations, however, would soon be requiring spectrum space for uplink and downlink services, although technologies such as direct broadcasting by satellite (DBS) were at least two decades away.

When the 1959 General WARC met satellite use was quite limited, but the radio spectrum was expanded to include allocations for "experimental space services."[103] Though debate on this issue did not comprise a great deal of time at the conference, some controversy was raised by the implication of some speakers that new satellite services would be subject to the same first-come, first served *a posteriori* allocation norms as terrestrial radio services. The US administration was particularly keen to have the status quo applied to space services, as they felt any set plan could hinder their progress in developing and exploiting satellite communications. The developing countries, who even at that early date foresaw the potential of satellite radio services for their development, were wary of applying the imperfect *a posteriori* system to space services. Pakistan proposed that "measures to neutralize the advantages of earlier recorded assignments" be used,[104] and other countries voiced a desire to see the IFRB promote more equitable use of this new band. The Conference decided to defer discussion of this important but time-consuming issue to a special Space WARC in 1963.

Shortly before the 1963 Space WARC commenced the IFRB clearly sided with the aspirations of the LDCs, with the then Secretary-General of the ITU declaring: "I remember clearly the haphazard way in which uses of radio generally developed, with all the ensuing confusion and difficulties in the allocation of frequencies. If this were to happen in outer space, the situation would be even more chaotic and damaging."[105] The ITU recognized that both the Union and telecommunications administrations would have to show greater care in planning these bands than had taken place with terrestrial services. Not only was this necessary to avoid chaos on these vital bands, but also to show developing countries that the ITU and its branches were there to serve the interests of *world* telecommunciations, not just those of the Northern developed countries. The ITU was compelled to clearly state its own commitment to equitable distribution of access to telecommunications services. The UN had reinforced the equitable use doctrine in its first resolution on "International Cooperation on the Peaceful Uses of Outer Space" in 1961, in which the UN General Assembly declared that "space communications should be available to the nations of the world on a global and nondiscriminatory basis."[106]

At the 1963 Space WARC the two opposing camps set the battle lines which remain firmly entrenched to this day. The LDCs feared American and "Northern" domination over frequencies available for space communication. As the Israeli delegate stated, "the duty sine qua non of the Space Conference is to abandon or at least modify the present practice of "first-come, first-served" frequency assignments. . . . The present system . . . fails to ensure *later* the national interests of LDCs. . . ."[107] Soviet and Cuban proposals did more than merely object to the status quo: Cuba advocated "principles guaranteeing equitable participation by all countries."[108] The USSR proposed a Special Conference to draft *a priori* plans and a permanent registration procedure. These proposals were defeated.

The Soviets did not seem to share the American concern that other countries might reserve segments of the spectrum irrespective of ability to use them and thus hinder development in satellite communications by those who did possess the requisite technology. The Soviets, despite being at that time virtually the only other sizeable user of space communications services, appeared to fear the rapidity of American technological growth. They may have felt that they would, over time, lose substantial access to the spectrum if the status quo was applied to space services. In addition there may have been recognition by the Eastern bloc delegations that the Western voting bloc would dominate this conference—as it did—and that they might as well use this opportunity to ally publicly with the Third World and engage in some potentially productive anti-Western posturing.

The American proposal to apply the *a posteriori* procedure to space services was supported by Western Europe, Latin America, and Japan. Western Europe and Japan were at this early stage inexorably tied to American space services. Their latitude for independent action at the Space WARC was limited. Moreover, it seems Western Europe and Japan did largely support American goals at the conference. They viewed future development of their own systems as being linked with US collaboration, e.g., through the then embryonic Intelsat commercial satellite cooperative. Latin America, not having much at stake at this conference, appeared to support the United States for the more traditional reasons of maintaining Region 2 bloc unity, American pressure, and an aversion toward voting with the Soviet Union, even if that meant voting against fellow developing countries. This was long before the era of Third World "Group of 77" solidarity. The American position was ultimately victorious, but contained a proviso which required the resultant procedures to be viewed as interim in nature. A Soviet proposal to explicitly state the registration procedure to be interim by specifying a future conference date did not receive much support. The Soviets tried again to achieve their goal indirectly through proposing that the new revisions be considered "complementary" to the Radio Regulations and not an integral part of them. This proposal was soundly defeated.[109]

The LDCs could not achieve their objectives in 1963 due to a lack of technological capabilities and an inability to field delegations to the CCIR, which had spent the years before the Conference formulating space service recommendations. The CCIR decisions were almost exclusively shaped by the United States.[110] Some placating of the dissatisfied LDCs was attempted at the 1963 Space WARC by the passage of Recommendation 10A, which recognized ITU members' "interest in and right to an equitable and rational use of frequency bands allocated for space communications." The recommendation also advised "utilization and exploitation of the frequency spectrum for space communication be subject to international agreements based on principles of justice and equity."[111]

The ITU avoided directly addressing these issues until the convening of a special Space WARC in 1971. Much had occurred in the years following 1963 to remold the policies and attitudes of many countries regarding space services. The 1967 UN Committee on the Peaceful Uses of Outer Space (UNCOPUOS) had established several widely accepted platforms concerning general, non-technical principles of spectrum use, including an explicitly stated doctrine of prior consent in the international use of satellite broadcast frequencies.[112] In addition, the years between the first 1963 WARC and the 1971 Space WARC witnessed a dramatic degree of growth in communication technology. The coordination of earth stations and satellites, which had been discussed in 1963, was in part accomplished in 1964 with the creation of Intelsat, the international satellite consortium. Intelsat was first established as a cooperative body on commercial lines, owned and operated by the private satellite companies and national telecommunications administrations of member countries. Because Intelsat was established by a United States initiative and, in its early years, was heavily influenced by American interests and trends, the Soviet bloc countries (which were not major satellite users anyway) refused to join the organization, preferring instead to form their own similar consortium, Intersputnik, in 1968.

While these organizations, along with later regional bodies such as Eutelsat and Arabsat, owned and operated virtually all international civilian communication satellites on behalf of the numerous national telecommunication administrations, the ITU did not and does not recognize this ownership. Neither Intelsat nor any similar common user organization (CUO) has been granted even associate member status in the ITU.[113] This creates some curious and politically uncomfortable situations. All Intelsat frequencies must be registered by the United States as US frequencies. Similarly, all Intersputnik frequencies are registered as USSR allocations. This is not a satisfactory arrangement, particularly to Intelsat and Intersputnik which continue to experience difficulty in being recognized as legitimate international organizations. Only in the mid-1980s did the ITU begin to recognize the distinctions between national users and multi-national CUOs (see below). The status of CUOs within the ITU remains a controversial and unresolved issue.

The technological developments of the 1960s centered on improvements in geostationary satellite technology, which was to rapidly supplant the weak and inconvenient tracking systems which had been used previously. As satellite technology improved, the number of users increased markedly. By the early 1970s several countries were developing national satellite systems exclusive of Intelsat,[114] and several regional projects, such as the Franco-German Symphonie, had been instituted. This quantitative increase in satellite communications was promoted by qualitative im-

provements in the technology. While the 1963 WARC had made some
minimal provisions concerning broadcast satellite services (DBS), it was
considered premature to allocate any spectrum space before the CCIR
thoroughly investigated the feasibility of this medium for broadcasting.
Developments in the late 1960s, particularly in the transmission of
television signals, clearly indicated that a future conference would have
to accommodate both the increased demand and improved technology
of the satellite bands.

Preparation for the 1971 Space WARC was, not surprisingly, extensive.
The United States believed several areas of reform would be needed to
render the ITU effective in satellite management. But the American
administration remained committed to applying the terrestrial first-come,
first-served registration system to space services. The position of the
Western European administrations was a modified version of this status
quo. While France and Britain believed it was unnecessary to distinguish
terrestrial from space services, they were at that time increasingly
advocating *a priori* planning for certain bands. The motives behind this
advocacy stemmed less from the need to reserve a portion of the
spectrum for space services than from the Europeans' desire to apportion
selected space bands which would be shared with terrestrial microwave
services used for telephony and other services. Incipient European support
for *a priori* in 1971 therefore stemmed from the short-run need to maintain
and guarantee microwave telephone service and to guarantee that such
service did not take over the bands, precluding space service access.
This was a fundamentally different motive than that of the developing
countries, who were truly concerned with long-term satellite needs—as
well as greater political principles of justice and equitability.[115]

The Soviet Union submitted a ten-page document which stressed the
need to scrap the *a posteriori* status quo which could confer de facto
priority rights and hinder future use of the band by developing countries.
Soviet use of the satellite spectrum was increasing rapidly at this time,
so it is likely they shared many of the concerns of developing countries
and Western Europe regarding a desire to reach an agreement to limit
the dominance by any one country of the spectrum, particularly if that
country was the United States. Argentina, representative of the LDCs,
submitted a rather detailed *a priori* plan for all space services.[116] Latin
America had undergone a marked change in attitude after 1963. By the
early 1970s the Latin American countries worried that satellites would
be used by the United States to expand its own economic and cultural
dominance over the region. Latin Americans feared a regional US
monopoly on satellite construction, use, and equipment, as well as the
content of what the satellites would transmit. Without an *a priori* plan
allocating specific frequencies, the Latin American countries feared they

would find it difficult to ever obtain access to what would inevitably become, under the status quo, a satellite frequency spectrum dominated by the United States.

The emergence of DBS technology raised a range of questions which were analogous to some problems facing international HF radio services. DBS was potentially a medium for international communications and difficult to restrain at a domestic level. (The debates centering on DBS issues at the 1971 Space WARC are considered in Chapter 3.) "At the heart of the DBS issue was the question of signal spillover (broadcasting radiation that cannot technically be prevented from covering a territory adjacent to the intended coverage area)."[117] Fears of unwanted "spillover" broadcasts led France, Argentina, and Brazil to adamantly emphasize that no ITU plan could or should be implemented prior to the formulation of consensually acceptable draft plans. A majority of developing countries agreed that future conferences must pursue the goal of *a priori* registration on the broadcasting satellite bands in order to realize equitable and fair use of the spectrum among sovereign states.

For other space service allocations the "first-come, first-served" approach adopted by the 1963 Space WARC was maintained by the 1971 conference, albeit with difficulty. Developing countries remained highly dissatisfied with this system. Some delegates asserted that both the satellite spectrum and the geostationary orbit should be apportioned to all countries expecting to eventually employ satellite services.[118] The system employed by the IFRB was not under any obligation to change or accommodate WARC opinion. Nevertheless, the 1971 Space WARC sought to placate the LDCs through Resolution Spa2-1, which stated that "all countries have equal rights in the use of both the radio frequencies allocated to various space radio communication services and the GSO for these services" and "the registration with the ITU of frequency assignments for space radio communication services and their use *should not* create an obstacle to the establishment of space systems by other countries."[119] This resolution originated with the USSR and expressed general principles which were acceptable to all administrations.[120] Again the Soviets were consciously seeking to ally themselves with the aspirations of the Third World. Through the succinct and popular phrasing of Resolution Spa2-1, they succeeded in firmly placing themselves with the developing countries in the *a priori* camp. Still, no legally binding obligations to members were created. Yet Recommendation Spa2-1 remains the most notable produce of the 1971 Space WARC, as it indicated ITU recognition of the space service RFS and the GSO as limited but necessarily shared universal natural resources.

This recognition was reiterated at the 1973 ITU Plenipotentiary Conference at Malaga-Torremolinos, where, besides establishing the date for the next Space WARC and granting additional powers to the IFRB regarding the GSO, a revision was made to Article 33 of the Convention so that it would read: "In using frequency bands for space radio services members shall bear in mind that radio frequencies and the geostationary orbit are limited natural resources, that they must be used efficiently and economically so that countries or groups of countries may have equitable access to both . . ."[121]

The most contentious aspect of the management of the satellite bands remained direct broadcasting by satellite (DBS). Fifteen European ITU members requested that the Administrative Council call a special WARC to consider the issue. The request stipulated that if a world wide conference was not possible, it would be their intention to convene a European regional conference as soon as possible to plan the shared broadcast satellite and terrestrial service bands.[122] The American delegates, with support from other Region 2 members, firmly believed the time for such a conference was still several years off. While the WARC would remain a world conference, Region 2 members decided to delay implementation of a plan and develop a set of interim procedures instead.

The ITU acceded to the European request for a Space WARC, and the 1977 Broadcasting Satellite WARC for Regions 1 and 3 (Europe, the USSR, Africa, and Australasia) attempted to redress the difficult political problems implicit in any DBS plan, particularly in Europe, as well as the need to accommodate technical progress in the field. The perceived threat to national sovereignty and the spectre of controls on DBS information flows are discussed in Chapter 3. In the field of frequency coordination, the concern to limit satellite signals to "footprints" corresponding as closely as possible to national boundaries and the conflicting need to accommodate all members led to a degree of compromise which, from a technical standpoint, resulted in a final plan that was surprisingly unrealistic and short-sighted. Compromise and haste in the creation of an *a priori* plan was not motivated by any pressing demand, as the DBS band was then largely unused, but was inspired by the fear expressed by several Western European administrations and, to a lesser extent, developing countries, that if they did not assert themselves at this early stage they would lose out to the major early DBS users, chiefly the United States, which would come to dominate the band if the *a posteriori* system continued.

This view was based on some valid concerns. During the conference, however, acceptance of a universal *a priori* plan was not amenable to all members. Not surprisingly, the United States vehemently opposed any type of planning of DBS services and advocated retention of the status quo. This opposition was merely a reiteration of what had been the American position regarding space services since 1959: that *a priori* planning hinders technical development and efficient use of the spectrum by denying the dynamism inherent in the development of satellite technology. As the United States was far and away the greatest user of satellite spectrum space, it was also concerned with losing existing claims enabling American use of sizeable chunks of the satellite spectrum.

The majority of the countries of Region 1 and Region 3, however, as well as several members in Latin America, were committed to the creation at the Conference of an *a priori* plan. The US view that the imposition of a plan at this time would hinder and restrict technological progress led to the American delegation adamantly refusing to accede to a plan. Canada attempted to effect a compromise middle ground through a proposal to defer a Region 2 Conference to a later date. The launching of the Canadian Hermes satellite at about that time proved to be a valuable face-saving device for the delegations of Region 2. This satellite tested several frequencies and services on the bands Regions 1 and 3 were pressing to allocate.[123] Canada and the other Region 2 members were able to legitimately express a desire to postpone their region's apportioning of DBS channels pending the return of technical data from the Hermes satellite. While this compromise appeared sufficiently based on valid technical grounds to placate most members, lengthy debates and heated discussions still ensued. The Region 2 countries did eventually accept the Canadian proposal and postponed their DBS planning conference for another six years. During those intervening years it is worth noting that no broadcast satellite system was implemented in any Region,[124] giving credence to those who believed the 1977 Plan was too ambitious at too early a date.

The countries of Regions 1 and 3 therefore circumvented American opposition to planning through allowing Region 2 to postpone its planning for six years and by applying the 1977 WARC solely to Regions 1 and 3. The plan adopted at the 1977 Space WARC was to remain in effect for 15 years. Virtually every ITU member adhering to the plan received an equal number of DBS channels, regardless of audience size or geography,[125] although larger single allotments went to the USSR and China. The arrangements achieved were far from ideal, particularly concerning allocation of the geostationary orbit. Work began immediately after the Conference within the CCIR and IFRB in an attempt to satisfy the growing requirements from both fixed and DBS service users.

In preparation for the 1983 Region 2 Conference to plan satellite DBS services, the United States and Canada made proposals at the 1979 General WARC to extend the satellite use spectrum in Region 2. The Canadian proposal advocated shared use on all the new frequencies while the US proposal preferred the new band be divided into DBS and fixed portions. American concerns over the protection of what the

ITU terms "government services"—military communications—motivated the United States to attempt to distance these fixed utility bands from the "civilian" broadcast bands. Other Region 2 countries were divided over which proposal to support. Several South American delegations questioned the US proposal's ability to provide sufficient channels for their future DBS needs. In the end a compromise was reached incorporating some of the specific assignments of the American proposal and some of the shared-use aspects of the Canadian proposal. Potential Latin American opposition was quelled by certain technical advancements made in the years following 1977 which allowed even the smallest and least likely Region 2 member a minimum allocation of eight DBS channels. This compromise package drew some criticism from some Region 1 members, notably France and the USSR, who were concerned with the potential for inter-Regional interference.[126] This opposition was fueled more by annoyance at having to admit that Region 2 had probably been wise in postponing its planning of DBS bands, as it had allowed them to come up with a plan technically far superior to the restrictive Region 1 and 3 Plan of 1977.[127]

The success of the 1983 Region 2 RARC, in comparison to the 1977 Plan for Regions 1 and 3, is attributable to several key factors. Primary among these is the marked advances in DBS technology which allowed Region 2 and the IFRB to develop a far more flexible plan which served to guarantee access to both the smallest and largest members. The technical merits of the Region 2 plan facilitate agreement by guaranteeing a minimum of 16 channels to each and every regional ITU member—as opposed to the 5 channels allocated to even major countries by the 1977 Plan. Canada, for example, is allocated 190 channels over several orbital beams in several blocks of 16 and 32 channels. Secondly, a high degree of regional cooperation existed prior to the conference between delegations and administrations. While the United States, Canada, Brazil, and Mexico have divergent policy approaches, they tend to be more amenable to compromise at least at the regional level, than their European counterparts. This is not, as it once was, due to the overwhelming dominance of the United States in Region 2 matters. Such dominance is questionable now that Canada and Brazil, in particular, have risen as major international telecommunications powers while having policies often at odds with those of the United States. It would appear that Region 2 compromise, at least in the 1983 DBS agreement, was more a product of the complementary interests of the different countries of the region, as well as the benefit of vast geography which allows countries to largely stay out of each others' way in the distribution of telecommunications services.

For Latin America, the kinship of language and, to lesser extent, culture, as well as common concerns about US policies, assists Latin American efforts to present an often surprisingly unified posture in ITU negotiation. The conference itself was cited as a model of how efficient and effective the ITU can be.[128] Countries as politically divergent as Argentina and Cuba presented common drafts and proposals. A further catalyst of Latin American unity was distrust of American motives at the conference and a fear that too much "flexibility" in the plan might allow the United States as much freedom to act as had been provided by the status quo. Efforts by the United States to convince Latin America that it was pursuing objectives beneficial to all countries in the region, along with strong intermediary efforts by Canada, allowed the establishment of a Final Plan with which all countries were satisfied. This plan incorporated regulatory procedures proposed by Canada for interim or first generation broadcasting satellite systems, a step which was first viewed with suspicion by some Latin American delegations which believed the "interim use" clauses might undermine the strengths of the Final Plan.

To summarize, the allocation regime for space services on the RFS existed first as a first-come, first-served system, in parallel to that for terrestrial services, until the late 1970s. The longevity of the old order may be attributable to the strength of American wishes regarding satellite services within the ITU, a power itself based on the marked US dominance in space service technology.

As early as the 1960s, however, it was feared that retention of an *a posteriori* system could result in either the dominance of a very few countries over the bands with the consequent monopoly/oligopoly over content therein and exclusion of all other countries from the benefits of satellite services, or a chaotic scramble for satellite channels analogous to the sorry state of the HF bands. By the 1970s, and particularly after the UN and UNESCO declarations regarding the New World Information Order (NWIO) (see Chapter 3), it was recognized that some sort of organized *a priori* plan would have to be drafted to ensure the equitable allocation of frequencies to all users and potential users of space radio communication services. Equitable allocation was firmly established as an ITU norm for space services by the mid-1970s.[129] The first *a priori* plan was achieved for DBS services in Regions 1 and 3 in 1977. An improved plan for Region 2 was adopted six years later due to American hesitancy to undertake any sort of planning on these bands.

An issue of major importance to the ITU in the late 1980s is the equitable coordination of space services and the geostationary orbit (GSO). This has been identified as the paramount issue confronting the Union as it enters the 1990s.[130] In 1985 the first session of a two session

Space WARC was convened to develop an allotment plan for communication satellite "parking spaces" in the GSO as well as coordinate frequencies and bands using space services. The need for such a conference stemmed from LDC concerns expressed as early as the 1968 UNCOPUOS that equitability of access to space services can only be guaranteed if a strong international regulatory framework exists to explicitly assign both frequencies and orbital allotments to each country. Only through such measures do developing countries believe they can ensure long-term access to space services.[131] The CCIR Conference Preparatory Meeting (CPM) held in preparation for the 1985 Space WARC (ORB-85) concluded, after extensive investigation, that "most space services, other than fixed, broadcast, and mobile satellite services, make little use of the GSO. Access . . . by ITU members is not likely to be a problem. . . ." The CPM reported that, in its opinion, the need for planning was questionable.[132]

Conversely, a European Space Agency report published in 1981 considered the potential for physical congestion of the GSO. The report states that "at present the chance of a collision is rather small . . . [but] it certainly will increase considerably over the next 15 or 20 years."[133]

Coordination of orbit arc allocations and cooperation between satellite users is believed to be vital if physical collisions are to be avoided in the future. The need for urgent action to resolve this matter remains questionable. One expert in the field has argued that the chance of two satellites allocated to the same orbital position colliding is comparable to that of a collision between two ping-pong balls thrown from opposite ends of a football stadium.[134] Nevertheless, the ITU could facilitate cooperation in this area through greater recognition of Common User Organizations (CUOs) like Intelsat. Currently, the ITU convention is based on principles of national sovereignty, and CUOs, being supranational, have no substantial role in the ITU. Some observers believe this must change, as Dr. Ram Jakhu states, "any future plan or other approach based purely on the concept of national access without recognizing the needs of CUOs would seem to defeat the purpose of efficient, economic, and equitable use of the orbit spectrum resource."[135]

While Intelsat and other CUOs are ostensibly owned and operated by all their members (in Intelsat's case over 110 countries), satellite technology remains the domain of a handful of developed countries. The 1977 and 1983 Plans guaranteed LDC access to DBS channels, and the 1985 GSO-WARC achieved an orbital allotment plan for all countries. But the fact remains that most LDCs possess neither the means nor the resources to take advantage of these allocations. This was recognized by the 1984 ITU Independent Commission for World Wide Telecommunications Development (the Maitland Commission), which concluded that an annual investment of US$12 billion will be required if LDCs are to achieve the requisite improvement and expansion of their tele-communications networks.[136] An integral part of this redistribution of resources includes a guarantee of universal access to satellite use.[137] In the short run, however, it is universally agreed that it is more important to develop basic terrestrial services such as telephone and radio com-munication networks. Until this is achieved, the chance of most LDCs ever employing their orbital allotments remains distant and unlikely.

ITU involvement in the GSO must recognize the significance of the CUOs as well as the distinction between the current norms of international law and some of the principles of space law,[138] in that space law, while a branch of international law, concerns the management of a common resource. Governing the GSO thus is closely analogous to RFS man-agement, and allocation goals concerning the GSO also must seek to achieve an efficient and equitable allocation of a limited common resource.

The 1985 GSO-WARC (ORB-85) sought to address developing country concerns. The Northern countries, and the United States in particular, were not convinced of the necessity of such a conference, citing many of the same sentiments expressed by the CCIR Conference Preparatory Meeting noted above. But the Maitland Commission eliminated any remaining doubts concerning the role of telecommunications in Third World development. Nevertheless, ORB-85 demonstrated that consensus regarding the means by which equitable access might be secured remains an elusive objective. The LDCs, particularly Algeria, India, and Costa Rica, among several others, pursued a policy of active "democratization" of geostationary orbit allocation. Their goal resembled that of the 1977 and 1983 broadcasting satellite RARCs: to allocate a minimum number of positions to each and every ITU member administration.

As with the allocation of broadcast satellite channels to countries which have little hope of ever employing them, to many countries it appeared ludicrous to assign orbital "parking spaces" to Third and Fourth World countries that possess neither the ability nor the need to have their own satellites. While developing countries lauded "democratization" of the orbit, the major telecommunication powers, particularly in the West, termed the same process "politicization."[139] As one American observer stated, "it appeared that the amount of rhetoric was inversely proportional to a nation's requirement for a commitment to procuring its own satellite."[140]

ORB-85 illustrated several paradoxical problems confronting any at-tempt at satisfactory resolution of the GSO issue. The same developing countries that were lobbying the hardest for national orbital allocations for each member were also among the strongest proponents of ITU recognition of the supranational Intelsat. Several countries claimed they could not ensure guaranteed access unless they acquired orbital slots. Conversely, these same countries, as members of Intelsat, enjoy *ensured, guaranteed* access to communications satellite services, both international and national. Currently, no country is denied access to satellite services.

The Third World position can only be understood within the context of recent events affecting the future of Intelsat. Deregulatory legislation in the United States has authorized new international satellite services to be established by private American corporations. These new services will compete directly against Intelsat on its most profitable traffic routes such as the North Atlantic—the routes used to cross-subsidize the costly, loss-making services to and from the Third World. By establishing ITU recognition of Intelsat it would, proponents argue, be possible to ensure operational stability and continuity in services to LDCs. Several documents were proposed at ORB-85 seeking to ensure recognition of the international nature of CUOs and take this into account in any allocation plan[141] and, in fact, the ITU did, in Document 324 of the Conference, formally recognize that any planning method "shall take into account the requirements of administrations using multi-administration systems (common-user organisations) created by inter-governmental agreement."[142]

This phrasing permitted a compromise acceptable to all. The United States remained cautious and reluctant to support ITU recognition of CUOs. There was a strong feeling within the American delegation that guaranteed access was not the *actual* issue under debate but that, behind the rhetoric, the developing and some developed countries were attempting to undermine the American "separate (private) satellite systems" policy. This conference illustrated some of the basic philosophical differences between American, European, and Third World policies mentioned in Chapter 1. The ITU, with the support of Europe and the LDCs, recognized inter-governmental CUOs. The American administration has authorized *national, private* communications satellite operators to provide *international* service. This service is achieved through bilateral agreement with other countries. At the WARC a considerable amount of discussion took place in an attempt to define "national" and "international" services. The Algerian delegate finally ended the discussion by stating that "nationally authorized international service" was an international service, and that "national" means domestic (difficulties also came about in attempting to translate these semantic nuances into French and Spanish).

The United States actively promoted an enhanced role for the private sector at the 1985 conference. Most other countries were cool to this idea. Private organizations have an important role in the composition of national delegations, particularly in the technical work of the CCIs (see Chapter 4), but the ITU will only recognize private operating agencies as being under the greater aegis of their national delegations. The ITU is an inter-governmental organization encompassing an important but limited role for private users. The Union will not be willing to allow a greater political role for private companies, as that is seen to potentially imperil the carefully constructed universality and reputation of the ITU.

Likewise, ITU recognition of Intelsat will probably not lead to "associate membership" or any special status for it or any other CUO. While it seems to make little sense to continue allocating CUO frequencies and allotments through one country, e.g., the United States for Intelsat or the Soviet Union for Intersputnik, to give associate or quasi-membership to Intelsat would serve to introduce an element of "second-class citizenship" which runs contrary to both the spirit of the International Telecommunications Convention and the philosophy of the UN system. In addition, delegates are largely hesitant to recognize Intelsat as an "equal." When delegates go to an ITU conference, such as the 1985 GSO-WARC First Session, they are representing *all* the relevant telecommunications interests of their country, including their needs as a member of Intelsat. They do not wish to see Intelsat speaking, even indirectly, on their behalf.[143]

It would also introduce a hierarchy of priorities in assigning allocations or allotments to satellite services. Proposals made at the 1985 WARC would confer a priority to national systems which would leave Intelsat and other CUOs at a marked disadvantage. A senior British delegate reported his surprise and dismay when LDC members wholly reliant upon Intelsat demanded priority for national systems they would probably never possess. Fortunately, the advocates of priority were somewhat placated by the Document 324 compromise, but this issue will undoubtedly re-emerge at the Second Session of the Conference.

The nature of the GSO "allotment plan" devised by the First Session remains vague and unclear. Bands and assignments of importance to the developed countries or in use at the time were, for the most part, excluded from the plan. The adoption by the conference of such an indistinct proposal could be seen as an attempt to work out a politically acceptable compromise: to allow a plan with *a priori* characteristics,[144] but only in completely non-controversial segments of the spectrum. Many key decisions could not be made at the First Session. Most of the work that was accomplished occurred in the final week of the conference, much of it on the last day—when a quorum for a legal vote did not exist.[145]

The First Session of the GSO-WARC was nevertheless viewed, even by some of the ITU's harshest critics, as a moderately successful enterprise. The developing countries emerged optimistic as they received certain guarantees of orbit allotment equitability, including a minimum of one allotment per country and ensured access to space services. Several developing countries were at the forefront in obtaining ITU recognition of CUO needs in conference Document 324. Noteworthy in this regard was the Algerian delegate, Mr. Bouharied, who has been one of the pre-eminent "Group of 77" spokesmen within the ITU over many past conferences. Despite the acknowledgement of the need for cooperative ventures and multi-administration collaboration to guarantee access, Document 324 encapsulates some of the paradoxical aspirations of the LDCs. The general Third World perspective was to view the First Session of the Conference as a vital component within the greater "democratization" of the ITU.[146] This implies pursuing a greater goal of equitable redistribution and "justice" beyond the specific technical requirements of each administration. A community of equal, sovereign nations should have equality of access to the spectrum and to the GSO. It is up to the IFRB and CCIR, in their intersessional work before the Second Session of the conference in 1988, to devise some sort of plan that will allow specific allotments in certain bands for every ITU member country as well as be flexible enough to accommodate the CUOs, who remain the actual users of international civil communication satellite services.

The intersessional mandate handed by the First Session to the IFRB and CCIR is virtually impossible to fulfill. This has led to speculation that a Third Session of the GSO-WARC may become necessary if the Second Session cannot resolve these thorny issues. The first issue is one that emerges in some form at virtually every ITU conference, but is of particular concern at a conference devoted to the GSO. That issue is the claims by several equatorial countries to sovereignty over portions the geostationary orbit.[147] Traditionally, the ITU has attempted to push this issue over to UNCOPUOS. Unfortunately, UNCOPUOS is equally keen to have the ITU handle the GSO sovereignty issue. At ORB-85 several developed countries made formal attempts to forward the issue to UNCOPUOS. Kenya, Colombia, and Ecuador were adamant, however, in insisting that WARC recognize and discuss the issue. The majority view remains that claims of sovereignty over the GSO, like those over spectrum space or any other common resource, are illegitimate. Conference Document 324 clearly reiterates this view: "(A) planning approach must be consistent with the universally accepted principle that administrations or groups of administrations are not entitled to permanent priority in the use of particular frequencies and GSO portions. . . ."[148] The country with perhaps the most to gain from "sovereignty over the GSO, Brazil, unconditionally opposed any claim to GSO sovereignty and has repeatedly denounced such claims as illegitimate.

Nevertheless, in order to placate Kenya, Colombia, and Ecuador, as well as other countries which half-heartedly raise the issue but do not actively pursue it, such as Indonesia, Document 324 states that "the planning method should take into account the relevant technical aspects of the special geographical situation of particular countries."[149]

The IFRB was thus asked to devise an allotment plan which does not recognize CUOs but takes their "needs" into account and firmly rejects priority rights over the GSO while not fully denying the claims of the equatorial countries. In addition, the Report of the Second Session left the bulk of technical work for the IFRB to complete in the intersessional period before the second session in 1988 (ORB-88).

Strict confines on the IFRB budget served to limit the amount of work the Board could handle in the short intersessional period. As a consequence the likelihood of an acceptable plan being devised in time for the Second Session was fairly remote. At the 1982 ITU Plenipotentiary, the United States, along with the majority of Western developed countries, supported a Canadian proposal to commit the ITU to a zero-growth budget policy.[150] There was some validity to Western arguments in the late 1970s and early 1980s that several branches of the ITU were overfunded, inefficient, and wasteful of resources. What particularly alarmed the United States was the potential emergence of direct ITU funding of telecommunications programs traditionally funded through the UNESCO International Programme for the Development of Communication (IPDC).[151] Yet in the realm of frequency management, accusations of wastefulness or inefficiency were not entirely accurate. Since the shrinking and near destruction of the IFRB in 1965, the Board has been consciously circumspect in its spending. Many would argue the IFRB consumes remarkably little money given the scope and importance of its work.

The rise of two-session WARCs gives the IRFB a greater intersessional role than that envisaged by the 1982 Plenipotentiary Conference. This is particularly true of the 1985/88-WARC. Yet the IFRB will not receive an increase in funding. As Mahindra Naraine states, "The IFRB is constrained in all this (intersessional) work by lack of time and resources. It is unable to conduct the number of planning exercises that administrations would like and its approach will take the conservative stance of indicating what it not possible rather than suggesting solutions or avenues of compromise."[152] The United States has stated repeatedly that it will not sign or adhere to any plan that does not come under budget. The ironic consequence of this policy, in this instance, is that the IFRB may be unable to successfully prepare for the Second Session of the Conference and it appears the United States will propose at the 1989 plenipotentiary a costly Third Session to take place in the early 1990s.

The IFRB would like to avoid this scenario. The Board has proposed four different possible planning approaches to the Administrative Council. Three of these plans would be significantly over budget and are hence unacceptable to several Western administrations. The fourth plan has serious technical flaws and will require much work to be rendered effective. The Canadian delegate to the relevant CCIR Interim Working Party studying this issue has suggested that this plan, largely based on work done by the Japanese administration, will require a major technological power to volunteer to program the plan if it is to come in under budget. As of early 1988 no volunteers had come forward, nor were any likely.[153]

The budgetary issue, the role of CUOs, the ever-present issue of GSO sovereignty, and the definition of an acceptable "allotment plan" combined to make ORB-85 contentious. Yet delegates were largely satisfied with the outcome, perhaps because most of the substantive "outcome" has been deferred to the Second Session. The difficulties of resolving GSO issues will influence the tone and proceeding of the 1989 ITU Plenipotentiary. Along with the HF Broadcasting WARC, these two mid-1980s WARCs have brought the ITU out of the disillusionment which followed the 1982 Plenipotentiary. Despite the looming difficulties remaining for the 1990s, they have proved the necessity and vitality of the ITU in an era of rapid technological change.

Conclusion

Spectrum management is an indispensable task. Given the fairly diminutive size of the IFRB, the recalcitrance of several larger administrations, and the hostility which exists between several others, it often seems miraculous that international registration and coordination of frequencies takes place at all. The Board has evolved into far more than just a registrar of frequencies: it is at the center of global frequency use and management. Developing countries rely on its advice and, as was seen in the southern African case, its impartiality in accommodating the needs of all spectrum users. Developed countries rely upon its skill in supervising the intersessional work between two-session WARCs as well as maintaining the Master Frequency List employed by all countries.

The IFRB faces new challenges—of increased burdens and decreased resources—but challenges are not new to the Board. From its earliest gloomy prospects as the compromise-ridden successor in the prewar Bern Bureau List, it has slowly evolved from an overly ambitious planner to a careful registrar of frequencies in use to a technical center of information and advice. It has had to confront early Eastern bloc accusations of American dominance, personality conflicts, later American attempts to do away with the Board, new technological challenges such as DBS and the GSO, and recent budget constraints.

It is traditionally argued that the ITU could not fulfill its spectrum management role without the Conference Preparatory Meetings (CPMs) and Interim Working Parties (IWPs) of the CCIR. The CCIR is deeply involved in pre-WARC planning and the exploration of policy alternatives. Some observers believe the CCIR could have even greater influence. The administrations at ORB-85 and the 1987 HF WARC second session made far less use of the CCIR material than they could have. Likewise, the burdensome intersessional activities delegated to the popular IFRB illustrate an aversion—chiefly on the part of developing countries—to allowing too great a role for the CCIR. This imbalance will continue to exist as long as the CCIR is so heavily weighted toward developed country representation. Increased LDC input in the CCIR, particularly if that input seeks social or political redistribution goals, could result in an equally unattractive diminishing of the CCIR's technical ability. For the first time, the directors of the CCIR and CCITT will be elected at the 1989 ITU Plenipotentiary instead of being elected at a CCI Plenary Meeting. This could alter the nature and direction of the CCIR and could, by the turn of the century, greatly remold the way in which the CCIR takes part in spectrum management.

It is the WARCs and RARCs, however, which are the ultimate expression of ITU activity in the field of spectrum management. From the earliest days of radio technology it has been these periodic international conferences which have enabled national administrations to coordinate and plan the use of new radio services, from primitive radiotelegraphy to direct broadcasting by satellite. General WARCs, such as those held in 1932, 1947, 1959, and 1979 are immense affairs which make thousands of highly technical decisions encompassing all aspects of radio communications. The 1979 WARC was expected, as the major telecommunications event of the era, to reflect the tension between *a posteriori* and *a priori* planning methods as well as the conflicts emerging from the New World Information Order, the rise of jamming, and questions of differing political principles. These greater issues were, surprisingly, not dealt with at the 1979 WARC.[154]

While the 1979 Conference was successful in minimizing political tension, this was accomplished at a cost. Many important issues were not adequately covered or were deferred to later Special WARCs. The 74 days of the conference were difficult, and the Final Acts consisted of 1,150 pages.[155] It was believed by some that the advanced state of telecommunications precluded the ability of any one conference to adequately accommodate new requirements for *all* broadcast telecommunication services. The decision to make increased use of Special two-session WARCs such as the HF-WARC and the GSO-WARC, has had significant implications for the direction of the ITU in the 1980s and 1990s. These conferences are more specialized and hence more able to achieve satisfactory technical outcomes, despite the non-technical implications of many of the issues discussed. In addition, regional Administrative Conferences (RARCs), particularly those related to portion of the spectrum that are national or regional by nature, such as MW or DBS, are increasingly providing a vital forum for multilateral coordination and cooperation. A greater role for regional conferences enables the ITU to act as a supervisor and arbiter in the setting of disputes or resolution of differences within regions.

Radio conferences may find their work occasionally hindered by rhetorical posturing or irrelevant discussion. These hindrances lead some observers to consequently level accusations of "politicization" at the entire ITU spectrum management process. Such accusations are unfair and erroneous. Political posturing occurs and may, in fact, be a significant reflection of important concerns expressed by entire groups of countries.

Equitability of access, the need to establish orbital allotments, the dominance by a few countries of certain bands, and the chronic violations by some countries of specific ITU radio regulations are all difficult issues that will continue to test the ITU's ability to facilitate international telecommunications. Nor can the greater issues of justice and equality and of development and equitable distribution of services be ignored under the guise of a "purely technical" spectrum management process. The balkanized balance of WARCs, RARCs, the IFRB, and the CCIR, imperfect as they are, has evolved into a system of spectrum and orbital management which can accommodate the technical needs of all ITU member countries without precluding the greater social, cultural, and political aspirations of these countries.

Notes

1. Interview, Geneva.
2. Known as the "Article 10 Method," based upon the 1959 ITU Radio Regulations. Since 1982 known as the "Article 17 Method," based upon the revised Radio Regulations of that year.
3. Glazer in Ram S. Jakhu, "The Evolution of the ITU's Regulatory Regime Governing Space Radiocommunication Services and the Geostationary Orbit," *Annals of Air and Space Law* (Vol. 8, 1983), p. 383.
4. Ibid.
5. George A. Codding, Jr., *The International Telecommunication Union: An Experiment in International Cooperation* (New York: Arno Press, 1972), p. 96.
6. Jakhu, op. cit., 1983, p. 385.

7. Jakhu, op. cit., 1983, p. 386.

8. Tomlinson in David M. Leive, *International Telecommunications and International Law: The Regulation of the Radio Spectrum* (Dobbs Ferry, NY: Oceana Press, 1970), p. 44.

9. Ibid., p. 46.

10. Codding, op. cit., 1972, p. 126.

11. Leive, op. cit., 1970, p. 49.

12. Ibid.

13. Harvey J. Levin, "Foreign and Domestic US Policies: Spectrum Reservation and Media Balance," *Telecommunications Policy* (June 1982), p. 123.

14. Codding, op. cit., 1972, p. 199.

15. This figure denotes frequencies below 20 MegaHertz.

16. Codding, op. cit., 1972, p. 242.

17. Leive, op. cit., 1970, p. 57.

18. ITU, *International Telecommunication Convention (Atlantic City, 1947)* (Geneva: ITU, 1947), p. 7.

19. Codding, op. cit., 1972, p. 245.

20. George A. Codding, Jr. and Anthony M. Rutkowski, *The International Telecommunication Union in a Changing World* (Dedham, MA: Artech House, 1982), p. 119.

21. Leive, op. cit., 1970, p. 58.

22. Ibid., p. 60.

23. Codding, op. cit., 1972, p. 259.

24. Ibid., p. 260.

25. Leive, op. cit., 1970, p. 65.

26. Ibid.

27. Codding, op. cit., 1972, p. 345.

28. Ibid.

29. Ibid., p. 352.

30. Ibid., p. 360.

31. Ibid., p. 375.

32. ITU, *Report of the Administrative Council to the 1952 Plenipotentiary Conference (Buenos Aires, 1952)* (Geneva: ITU, 1952), p. 37.

33. ITU, *International Telecommunication Convention (Nairobi, 1982)* (Geneva: ITU, 1982), p. 9.

34. ITU, op. cit., 1952, p. 42.

35. Brian Segal, *Preparatory Study for the 1982 ITU Plenipotentiary Conference* (Ottawa: Department of Communications, 1982), p. 26.

36. Leive, op. cit., 1970, p. 69.

37. Ibid.

38. ITU, *Book of Proposals to the 1959 ITU Plenipotentiary Conference* (Geneva: ITU, 1959), pp. 30–31.

39. Leive, op. cit., 1970, p. 209.

40. Ibid., p. 213.

41. Codding and Rutkowski, op. cit., 1982, p. 121.

42. Leive, op. cit., 1970, p. 79.

43. Ibid., p. 77.

44. Interview.

45. Interview.

46. Interview.

47. Interview.

48. Such conferences were also known in the past as "Extraordinary Administrative Radio Conferences" (EARC). The last Conference to employ this title was the 1963 Space WARC, occasionally referred to in the literature (but not herein) as the 1963 Space EARC.

49. Ann Branscomb, "Waves of the Future: Making WARC Work," *Foreign Policy* 34 (Spring 1979), p. 140.

50. Donald R. Browne, *International Radio Broadcasting: Limits of the Limitless Medium* (New York: Praeger Publishing, 1982), p. 22.

51. Jens Frost, ed., *World Radio TV Handbook 1984* (Hvidovre: Billboard AG, 1984), p. 100.

52. The ITU Regional Administrative Medium Frequency Broadcasting Conference for Region 2, held in 1980–81, devised a plan which supercedes the NARBA while retaining a similar classification system. This system does not carry much weight, however, as it merely sets some basic principles concerning coordination between the countries of the region. An *a priori* plan could not have accommodated the rapid growth in the number of MW(AM) radio stations during the 1980s. This expansion was particularly acute in North America due to deregulatory policies in the United States intended to liberalize the band. The deregulation of the AM band in the US was a hotly debated issue in the early part of the 1980s, with the old NARBA finding some unusual defenders among American long-distance truck drivers and country-and-western music personalities (who feared the loss of "Grand Old Opry" broadcasts over a Nashville clear channel station).

53. ITU, *Documents de la Conference Europeene de la Radiodiffusion (Montreux, 1939)* (Berne: ITU, 1939).

54. Codding, op. cit., 1972, p. 382.

55. Interview.

56. Interview, EBU.

57. Interview, EBU.

58. Codding and Rutkowski, op. cit., 1982., p. 48.

59. Interview.

60. Frost, ed., op. cit., 1984, p. 271.

61. Canada, *Discussion Paper on the Regional Administrative Radio Conference for Medium Frequency Broadcasting in Region 2 (RABC-2 1981)* (Ottawa: Department of Communications, 1980), p. 42.

62. Ibid., p. 50.

63. This meant moving the upper limit of the MW (AM) broadcasting band from 1605 to 1705 kHz.

64. S. Stuart, "Talks Set on How to Expand AM Spectrum," *New York Times* (April 19, 1986), p. 18.

65. Broadcasting, "US Satisfied with AM Conference Results," *Broadcasting* (May 12, 1986), p. 82.

The ITU and the Radio Frequency Spectrum   125

66. Interview, Montreal.

67. The need for such "overkill" is motivated by the relatively poor quality of high frequency (HF) signals and by rapidly changing ionospheric conditions which make some transmitting bands more useful than others at a given time.

68. Frost, ed., op. cit., 1984, p. 282.

69. Interview, London.

70. East European Area Audience and Opinion Research Section, *Listening to Western Radio in Eastern Europe 1985–Early 1986* (Washington, D.C.: Radio Free Europe–Radio Liberty, 1986), p. 1.

71. Codding, op. cit., 1972, p. 24.

72. Codding, op. cit., 1972, p. 181.

73. Leive, op. cit., 1970, p. 57.

74. Codding, op. cit., 1972, p. 364.

75. Ibid., p. 365.

76. Interview. As noted above, the effectiveness of HF broadcasting is greatly influenced by solar cycles and ionospheric interference. Unlike other broadcast services, HF broadcasters may periodically change frequencies in order to provide continuous reception quality in a given region. The ITU has divided the HF broadcasting periods into four seasons beginning in March, June, September, and December. In addition, annual charts and forecasts are made to help broadcasters and listeners determine the least disruptive frequencies. See for example George Jacobs, "World Broadcast Reception Conditions Expected During 1988," in Andrew Sennitt, ed., *World Radio TV Handbook 1988* (Amsterdam: Billboard AG, 1988), p. 32.

77. Telecommunications Policy Staff, U.S. Department of State, *Report of the Delegation of the United States Concerning the International High Frequency Broadcasting Conference, Mexico City, October 22, 1948–April 9, 1949* (Washington, D.C.: US Department of State, 1949), p. 71.

78. Interview.

79. Interview.

80. In the mid-1970s, Ghana and Mexico registered extensive international services which were largely expressions of wishful thinking on the part of their administrations.

81. Glen O. Robinson, "Regulating International Airwaves: The 1979 WARC," *Virginia Journal of International Law* (Vol. 21, 1980), p. 29.

82. Office of Technology Assessment, United States Congress, *Radiofrequency Use and Management: Impacts of the World Administrative Radio Conference of 1979* (Washington, D.C.: United States Congress, Office of Technology Assessment, 1982), p. 80.

83. Willi Menzel in Jens Frost, ed., *World Radio TV Handbook 1981* (Hvidovre: Billboard AG, 1981), p. 37.

84. Robinson, loc. cit., 1980, p. 31.

85. Ibid.

86. Ibid., p. 33.

87. In the years after the 1979 WARC the technical broadcast quality of the HF spectrum further degenerated, in part due to worsening ionospheric conditions.

These conditions work with solar sunspot cycles to enhance or impair the propagation of signals and the amount of spectrum space that may be used. For example, in the late 1970s much publicity surrounded the expanded use of the 21 and 26 MHz bands for HF radio broadcasting and how these new bands could relieve pressure on the other, greatly crowded bands. An experimental very low-powered station in Ecuador, on 26 MHz, was heard during the course of 1980 by listeners from Scandinavia to New Zealand. By the mid-1980s a particularly severe solar cycle and negative ionospheric conditions rendered further use of these new bands virtually impossible . . . at least until the early 1990s.

88. George A. Codding, et al., *ITU World Administrative Radio Conference for the Planning of HF Bands Allocated to the Broadcasting Service: A Pre-Conference Briefing Paper* (London: International Institute of Communications, 1983), p. 18.

89. Ibid., p. 19.

90. Ibid.

91. Intermedia, "ITU-HF: Planning a New Order," *Intermedia* 12:2 (March 1984), p. 8.

92. Ibid.

93. Interview.

94. ITU, *World Administrative Radio Conference for the Planning of the HF Bands Allocated to the Broadcasting Sevice, Second Session (Geneva, 1987)* (Geneva: ITU, 1987), Document Plenary 6, Attachment 1.

95. ITU, *World Administrative Radio Conference for the Planning of the HF Bands Allocated to the Broadcasting Sevice, Second Session (Geneva, 1987)* (Geneva: ITU, 1987), Document DT-41, 16 February 1987.

96. ITU, *World Administrative Radio Conference for the Planning of the HF Bands Allocated to the Broadcasting Sevice, Second Session (Geneva, 1987)* (Geneva: ITU, 1987), Document DT-50, 20 February 1987.

97. ITU, *World Administrative Radio Conference for the Planning of the HF Bands Allocated to the Broadcasting Sevice, Second Session (Geneva, 1987)* (Geneva: ITU, 1987), Document 82-E.

98. ITU, *World Administrative Radio Conference for the Planning of the HF Bands Allocated to the Broadcasting Sevice, Second Session (Geneva, 1987)* (Geneva: ITU, 1987), Document 120-E.

99. Broadcasting, "Shortwave WARC: Limited Victories for US Delegates," *Broadcasting* (March 16, 1987), p. 81.

100. Interview.

101. On why FM radio came to prevail in Southern Africa, see chapter 3.

102. Interview. The IFRB member strongly recommended to South Africa that it submit long term requirements for Namibia. After December 31, 1984 the ITU would no longer allow South Africa to submit Namibian requirements. From a technical standpoint this policy was untenable, as once Namibia was recognized as independent the SWAPO forces could not realistically field a competent delegation to the ITU nor accurately estimate the country's frequency requirements. What proved politically astute in the UN General Assembly, or what might have even worked in the "high politics" atmosphere of an ITU

Plenipotentiary Conference, appeared fairly ludicrous in the spectrum management context of the WARC.

103. E.D. DuCharme, R. Bowen and M.J.R. Irwin, "The Genesis of the 1985–87 ITU World Administrative Radio Conference on the Use of the Geostationary Satellite Orbit and the Planning of Space Services Utilizing It," *Annals of Air and Space Law* (Vol. 7, 1982), p. 264.

104. Jakhu, loc. cit., 1983, p. 398.

105. Ibid., p. 399.

106. Leive, op. cit., 1970, p. 211.

107. Ibid.

108. DuCharme, et al., loc. cit., 1982, p. 265.

109. Leive, op. cit., 1970, p. 213.

110. Jakhu, loc. cit., 1983, p. 400.

111. Donna A. Demac, et al., *Equity in Orbit: The 1985 ITU Space WARC* (London: Institute of International Communications, 1985), p. 10.

112. E.D. DuCharme, M.J.R. Irwin and R. Zeitoun, "Direct Broadcasting by Satellite: The Development of the International Technical and Administrative Regulatory Regime," *Annals of Air and Space Law* (Vol. 9, 1984), p. 270.

113. The term "Common User Ogranization" (CUO) is gradually becoming obsolete. The preferred term is now "Multi-Administration System" (MAS).

114. Among these were Brazil, Canada, India, Indonesia, Mexico, Pakistan, Saudi Arabia, and the United States.

115. Interview.

116. Jacques Garmier, *L'UIT et les Telecommunications par Satellites* (Brussels: Etablissement Emile Bruyant, 1975), p. 142.

117. DuCharme, et al., loc. cit., 1984, p. 270.

118. Demac, et al., op. cit., p. 10.

119. ITU, *Final Acts of the World Administrative Radio Conference for Space Telecommunications (Geneva, 1971)* (Geneva: ITU, 1971), Resolution Spa 2–1.

120. DuCharme, et al., loc. cit., 1982, p. 267.

121. ITU, *International Telecommunication Convention (Malaga-Torremolinos, 1973)* (Geneva: ITU, 1973), Article 33(2).

122. DuCharme, et al., loc. cit., 1984, p. 271.

123. The 12 GigaHertz (GHz) Direct Broadcasting by Satellite (DBS) band.

124. DuCharme, et al., loc. cit., 1984, p. 275.

125. For example, Andorra received the same number of channels (five) as the United Kingdom.

126. DuCharme, et al., loc. cit., 1984, p. 277.

127. The 1977 Plan for Regions 1 and 3 was to be firmly in place for fifteen years. By the early 1980s, however, there were many calls to scrap or heavily modify the plan as it was rapidly becoming technologically obsolete. Throughout the 1980s there was pressure on the ITU to address the issue before 1993 (the end of the fifteen year period).

128. Interview.

129. As documented by Resolution Spa-2 of the 1971 Space WARC and by Article 33(2) of the 1973 *International Telecommunication Convention*.

130. Interview.

131. Twelve services currently employ the GSO: 1. Fixed satellite service; 2. Broadcasting satellite service; 3. Mobile satellite service; 4. Radio-determination satellite service; 5. Space operation service; 6. Space research service; 7. Earth exploration satellite service; 8. Meteorological satellite service; 9. Intersatellite service; 10. Amateur satellite service; 11. Radio-astronomy service; 12. Standard frequency and time signal satellite service. See Demac, et al., op. cit., 1985, p. 13.

132. Ibid.

133. Ram S. Jakhu, "Legal Aspects of the 1985 Space WARC," *Intermedia* 13:3 (May 1985), p. 16.

134. Interview, Washington D.C.

135. Jakhu, loc. cit., 1985, p. 18.

136. Demac, et al., op. cit., p. 16.

137. Sir Donald Maitland, Chairman, *Report of the Independent Commission for World Wide Telecommunications Development* (Geneva: ITU, 1984), p. 27.

138. Jakhu, loc. cit., 1985, p. 18.

139. Interview.

140. Heather Hudson, "Comment: Mixed Planning Approach at Geneva," *Telecommunications Policy* (December 1985), p. 271.

141. ITU, *World Administrative Radio Conference on the Use of the Geostationary Satellite Orbit and the Planning of Space Services Utilising It, First Session (Geneva, 1985)* (Geneva: ITU, 1985), Documents 146, 166, 216, 324.

142. ITU, *Addendum to the Report to the Second Session of the Conference: World Administrative Radio Conference on the Use of the Geostationary Satellite Orbit and the Planning of Space Services Utilising It, First Session (Geneva, 1985)* (Geneva: ITU, 1985), p. 4.

143. Interview.

144. US Department of State, *Executive Summary of the Report of the United States Delegation to the ITU World Administrative Radio Conference on the Planning of the Geostationary Orbit and the Space Services Using It, Held at Geneva, August 8 to September 16, 1985* (Washington, D.C.: US Department of State, 1986), p. 2.

145. Interview.

146. E. Vargas, *A Post-Analysis of Space WARC-85: A Policy Forum Convened by the Washington Program of the Annenberg School, November 1985*, Unpublished transcript.

147. Orbital allotments are usually placed directly over the equator in order to give optimal signal beam arrays.

148. ITU, *Addendum to the Report to the Second Session of the Conference: World Administrative Radio Conference on the Use of the Geostationary Satellite Orbit and the Planning of Space Services Utilising It, First Session (Geneva, 1985)* (Geneva: ITU, 1985), p. 3.

149. Ibid.

150. ITU, *International Telecommunication Convention (Nairobi, 1982)* (Geneva: ITU, 1982), p. 85.

151. Ibid., p. 285.

152. Mahindra Naraine in G. Clarke, J. Savage and G. Staple, *ORB-88: A Pre-Conference Bulletin* (London: International Institute of Communications, 1987), p. 13.

153. Interview, Washington, D.C.

154. Canada, *Summary Report of the Canadian Delegation to the World Administrative Radio Conference, Geneva, September 24–December 6, 1979* (Ottawa: Department of Communications, 1980), p. 1.

155. Ibid.

3

Free Flow Versus Prior Consent: The Right to Communicate and International Control of Deliberate Interference

All stations, whatever their purpose, must be established and operated in such a manner as not to cause harmful interference to the radio services or communications of other Members or of recognized private operating agencies, or of other duly authorized operating agencies which carry on radio service, and which operate in accordance with the provisions of the Radio Regulations.
—Article 35, 1982 Nairobi ITU Convention, p. 24

The ITU exists to coordinate and facilitate international telecommunications. When member states undertake actions which hinder international communication, they do more than merely violate the Radio Regulations. By intentionally restricting international communications an ITU member contravenes the basic principles of the Union with regard to interference-free telecommunications services and jeopardizes both the effectiveness and credibility of the ITU.

The ITU will remain unable to successfully ensure efficient or equitable use of the radio frequency spectrum as long as the spectre of deliberate interference remains unresolved. But because this issue is by nature political, the ITU has been notably reluctant until recently to tackle the deliberate interference problem. Because the ITU rarely addresses the issue, many observers have come to view the problem of deliberate interference as less important than spectrum management or standard-setting. Since the late 1970s, however, the realization that several countries have reserved the right to block unauthorized DBS-TV (direct television broadcasting by satellite) signals, along with a sudden and dramatic increase in the level and severity of signal jamming on the high frequency (HF) international shortwave broadcast bands, has driven the ITU into

131

recognizing deliberate interference as an integral problem of international telecommunications. That recognition of deliberate interference by the ITU took so long to occur—jamming of international radio signals dates back to the early 1930s—is an indication of the distaste with which the technically minded personnel of the Union have traditionally regarded this thoroughly political issue.

The problem at the heart of any discussion of the issue remains agreement upon what exactly constitutes deliberate interference. Any definition must recognize the ambiguous and amorphous nature of the problem and the essentially jurisdictional matters surrounding it. It is these complexities which preclude resolution of the problem, particularly by the ITU. If deliberate interference is to be defined as any measure that prevents international communication or intentionally contravenes Recommendation Number 1 of the 1982 International Telecommunication Convention,[1] then the definition of deliberate interference may become so vague and encompassing as to render any attempts by the ITU to resolve it impossible.

Definitions of deliberate interference may be ambiguous. What one country calls jamming another may call "protection against subversive psychological warfare" or "protection against threats to sovereign national security." Whatever the nomenclature, when countries employ technical means to restrict the free flow of information from abroad as a defensive tactic, it immediately becomes an international telecommunications issue under the jurisdiction of ITU Radio Regulations and the International Telecommunication Convention. The most obvious and best known example of deliberate interference is hence the jamming of international radio broadcasts.

It is nevertheless important before proceeding to recognize that deliberate interference occurs through other, more subtle, means which do not necessarily contravene the ITU Radio Regulations *per se*—and are thus not subject to ITU action or censure—but nonetheless violate the principles of the ITU in that they act as disincentives to international communication as well as going against the spirit of Article 4 of the International Telecommunication Convention.[2]

The most draconian of such means is to make the reception of "unauthorized" foreign broadcasts a violation of national law. This method was first employed in Nazi Germany and extended during World War II to all Axis-occupied territories. Listening to foreign broadcasts was made a capital offence. Today, listening to international broadcasts is a violation of domestic legislation in Albania and North Korea, among several other countries. In South Korea mere possession of a shortwave radio receiver capable of receiving international broadcasts is strictly illegal. This method can only work in the most xenophobic of countries.

It did not work for the Nazis in either the countries they occupied or in Germany itself.[3]

New technologies create new means of deliberate interference. The most successful are domestic means of blocking foreign broadcasts which do not adversely affect third parties or listeners outside the jammer's borders. Such jamming still violates ITU principles—but not specific Radio Regulations. One popular method of subtly keeping out the foreign hordes is through wired (cable, or rediffusion) broadcasting. This method has been widely employed in the past in the Soviet Union and People's Republic of China where expansive wired networks carry home service signals.[4] Since the widespread dissemination of transistor radios this means of broadcasting has experienced a notable and not unwelcome decline, but its presence remains widespread, particularly in PR China, Vietnam, North Korea, and Albania. A kindred technique is the manufacture of cheap receiving sets which are permanently set to fixed frequencies. Nazi Germany pioneered this method with a "People's Receiving Set" that was much cheaper to buy, and hence far more popular, than its tunable rivals.[5] During the Vietnam War the United States military dropped behind enemy lines approximately 10,000 fixed frequency transistor radios tuned to Saigon. During the 1960s and 1970s Taiwan sent thousands of "propaganda balloons" into PR China containing leaflets, candy, and a cheap transistor radio fixed to Taipei's Mainland service.[6]

A more recent technique involves the establishment and promotion of domestic radio systems on FM. This was the deliberate policy of the South African Broadcasting Corporation from the early 1960s and its Rhodesian counterpart from the late 1960s. The nature of the FM signal is such that even with high transmitter powers the signal does not travel very far and then only in a line-of-sight pattern. Reception of foreign FM signals in any country is limited to those living within a very few miles of another country's border, and is then contingent upon the existence of foreign FM stations being located relatively close to the border. The establishment of the several FM networks in South Africa was not done for reasons of economy, as providing nationwide radio coverage through FM radio is notably expensive; nor was it done because of FM's deservedly good reputation for sound quality, as the popular music service "Radio 5" remained on medium wave (AM). The switch to FM in southern Africa was intended to dissuade African listeners from tuning in external signals hostile to Pretoria and Salisbury.[7]

One somewhat desperate non-technical method of interfering with foreign radio broadcasts is to attempt to discredit foreign broadcasters in the home media. In 1968 Isvestia attempted to link the BBC with the British Secret Intelligence Service (SIS). The Isvestia report claimed

"The BBC, the mouthpiece of naked anti-Communism in the British
Isles, has been taking a very active part in several extremely ugly SIS
operations . . . an agreement exists with the BBC to turn over to the
SIS all letters sent to the BBC from listeners in the socialist countries.
. . ."[8] On February 7, 1980 the Pionerskaya Pravda, journal of the Soviet
Young Pioneers (ages 11 to 15) charged the "enemy voices" of the BBC,
Radio Liberty, the Voice of America, and West Germany's Deutsche Welle
with being "generally controlled by the CIA."[9] These two examples are
illustrative of a type of interference which, while non-technical and well
outside ITU jurisdiction, remains contrary to the spirit and intent of the
ITU Convention.

There is not a great deal the ITU can do about wired radio networks,
fixed coverage receivers, or active efforts to discredit signals from abroad.
While these techniques all restrict the free flow of information, they do
not cause specific harmful interference to radio signals travelling from
point A to point B. Such methods merely attempt to minimize or control
reception of A's signal within B's territory. The ITU must respect each
country's sovereign right to regulate its own telecommunications services.
This much is noted in the Preamble to the ITU Convention.

The prevailing type of deliberate interference remains the jamming
of international radio broadcasting through the transmitting of irritating
noise on the same frequency as the unwanted broadcast. The goal is to
render reception impossible or at least inordinately difficult. Since jamming
is undertaken against foreign broadcasts, it is not surprising that the
greatest impact of jammers is felt on the international high frequency
(HF) broadcast bands.

Radio jamming may occur on other bands, however, if those bands
are bringing in unwelcome foreign broadcasts. After the 1965 Rhodesian
Unilateral Declaration of Independence, the Rhodesian government erected
a 400,000 watt medium wave (AM) transmitter, nicknamed "Big Bertha,"
to jam the BBC World Service relay station at Francistown, Botswana.
The Rhodesian gambit was successful—from the Rhodesian perspective—
as the BBC closed down the transmitter and handed it over to the
Botswana government in 1968.[10] For a few years prior to 1973, Soviet
authorities jammed the Voice of America's West German–based relay for
Eastern Europe and the Soviet Union on 173 kHz long-wave.[11]

Jamming, as it is described above, remains largely limited to the
international high frequency (HF) broadcast bands. Before tracing attempts
at regulatory and cooperative resolution of the problem, it is necessary
to review the jamming situation at present, who jams, and how jamming
takes place. Recent international regulatory arrangements, incorporating
the popular tenets of the New World Information Order, may have the
unforeseen result of extending the scope of jamming to space and satellite

communications. Finally, the most important aspect to be observed is *why* countries jam and what this signifies about the ITU.

Jamming of the International Broadcasting Bands

As has been mentioned, deliberate interference of international tele-communications entails far more than merely the jamming of radio broadcasts. It is jamming, however, which is the most conspicuous manifestation of deliberate interference, and the only one which is at least potentially controllable through international collaboration and regulation. Jamming is also the most pervasive and serious of all means of deliberate interference. Jamming has a serious and adverse impact on all parts of the HF broadcast spectrum. Monitoring efforts conducted by the IFRB in the early 1980s showed the impact of jamming to be widespread and growing. Heavy and continuous jamming has been employed by the Soviet Union against the Voice of America, BBC, Deutsche Welle, Kol Israel, the American-financed Radio Free Europe/ Radio Liberty, and Radio Beijing. During the course of 1987 jamming of many of these stations declined as part of the Soviet "Perestroika" policy of increasing openness. PR China jams Radio Moscow, Taiwan, and the Voice of Vietnam, but discontinued jamming of the Voice of America in 1979.[12]

As jamming is a far from perfected technique and is often quite sloppy in its application, one of the most serious consequences of jamming is interference with adjacent broadcast channels. In such a case, the jammer blocks both his target as well as stations to either side of the target. As a consequence the IFRB discovered jamming could render entire broadcast bands useless:

> For example, in the evening hours, 86% of the 17 MHZ band is affected by jamming in Europe, 79% of the same band is affected in Africa, 54% in South Asia and 56% in the Far East. . . . One of the surprising observations in the study was the impact of jamming in the 7 MHZ band in Washington, DC (according to monitoring reports submitted by the US administration) since this band is not allocated for broadcast use in Region 2 (the Americas). Obviously, jamming signals propagate well beyond their intended targets.[13]

Jamming grew as a consequence of the political turbulence of the early and mid-1980s, and particularly due to the cooling of relations between the superpowers. In 1982 alone jamming increased by about 10 percent.[14] Technical innovations reducing the level of adjacent channel interference have been more than offset by this general increase in the number of HF frequencies directly jammed.

Jamming is a crude and often ineffective method of stopping the reception of an unwelcome signal. Countries that employ jamming believe they have no option, however, and are willing to ensure the considerable costs of jamming. When Poland ceased direct jamming in 1956, the Polish government admitted their limited jamming efforts had cost them $17.5 million a year (in 1956 dollars). At the time that figure equalled the annual budget for the worldwide operations of the Voice of America.[15] All estimates since that time are little more than vague conjectures that are put forward from time to time. At the United Nations Special Political Committee which met in December 1958, the American delegate, George Harrison, estimated that the USSR spent $100 million annually to maintain a network of 2,500 jamming transmitters representing a capital investment of $250 million (1958 dollars).[16] These estimates are roughly accurate and have been repeated periodically.[17] The Economist noted in 1973 that annual operating costs for Soviet jammers were then approximately $185 million. Electricity costs alone for 25,000 kiloWatts of transmitting power were estimated in 1980 to run $43 million annually, a figure which escalated rapidly in the 1980s as Soviet power costs rose. Moreover, at least 10,000 technicians and engineers are believed to be employed solely to maintain the jamming network. Out of 76 emitters of deliberate interference identified on the HF broadcast bands by monitors during 1984–85, 43 were located in the USSR. The remainder were located in Eastern Europe.[18] Even by the most conservative estimates,[19] the monetary, energy, and manpower costs of jamming are staggering. Edward Barrett, a former official of the US Information Agency, has estimated that it costs five times as much to jam a given program than to transmit it.[20]

Most jamming takes place on the HF international shortwave broadcast bands. The nature of the HF signal is such that the emitted "sky-wave" signal is reflected off the ionosphere and can thus travel great distances and serve audiences in large geographical areas irrespective of political boundaries. A 500 kiloWatt transmitter—currently one of the most powerful of types of shortwave broadcast transmitter—has a virtually global reach. As the HF signal relies on ionospheric conditions which are in turn dependent upon levels of solar activity as well as the 11-year sunspot cycle, reception of HF signals is subject to diurnal and annual variation.[21] This is why jamming can so easily affect adjacent channels or non-targetted stations thousands of miles away. The global effects of jamming, even in corners of the world farthest from the centers of jamming activity, indicate that the jammers themselves employ high powered HF transmitters.

How is deliberate interference distinguished from unintentional harmful interference? Because jamming is such a crude means of hindering the free flow of international broadcasts it is painfully obvious when a broadcast is being intentionally jammed. Julian Hale has summarized the prevalent type of HF jamming as follows:

> Deliberate interference usually takes the form of a loud noise. It can be like a petrol engine or a rotary whine. . . . The effect can also imitate static. . . . In any case, jamming makes a horrible noise, demanding extraordinary powers of perseverance on the part of the listener hoping to pick up some of the original message beneath it.[22]

Radio wave jamming stations may be grouped into two categories: (1) sky-wave jammers which transmit a jamming signal on HF frequencies, effectively blocking reception over a potentially large geographical region; and (2) local jamming installations which are intended to provide saturation jamming to population centers. As our focus is on the former category, a few words on the latter may be warranted. Local jammers, often termed "ground-wave" jammers, employ networks of low-powered short-range transmitters located atop hills, tall buildings, and church steeples. Evidence exists to suggest most major Soviet cities have local jamming networks employing on average an array of 15 transmitters, with cities like Moscow or Leningrad having three or four times that number.[23] These transmitters emit a broad white-noise signal which effectively ruins *all* HF reception in a given area on all HF broadcast bands. Soviet city dwellers can and do circumvent local jamming, however, by taking radios with them to the countryside on weekends, to areas around major airports and airfields which are free of local jamming, and by circulating cassette recordings of broadcasts.[24]

Sky-wave jamming achieves national and international coverage, and remains at the core of the deliberate interference problem. A method of jamming less obvious than the traditional "shucks, whistles, roars, screeches, howls, and walls"[25] emerged in the Soviet Union in the early 1970s. This type of jamming has come to be called "Mayak jamming." It consists of relays of the Soviet second home service, Radio Mayak (Beacon), on the same frequencies as incoming stations.[26] Mayak jamming seems to enjoy cyclical popularity among Soviet authorities. It was fairly common in the late 1970s but in the early 1980s a reversion to the stronger noise jamming was noted, particularly against Beijing, Radio Liberty, and the Voice of America.[27] Mayak jamming continues to be employed by Eastern European countries, particularly Poland. Since these are not actual "white-noise" jammers, this enables the Eastern European countries to make the dubious claim that broadcasts from abroad in their home language are not, according to their narrow technical definition, jammed. Nevertheless, Mayak jamming, like any other type of deliberate interference, distorts incoming signals with the intention of preventing reception, and thus clearly is merely another method of jamming.

As jamming enters its fifth decade of existence, the method continues to provide the greatest obstacle to rational use of certain portions of the radio frequency spectrum. Since the 1984 First Session of the WARC for the planning of the high frequency (HF) bands allocated to the broadcasting service (known as the HF-WARC), jamming has become a test of the credibility and effectiveness of the Union. While direct regulation (or even acknowledgement) of deliberate interference is somewhat new for the ITU, attempts to control jamming through international collaboration and regulation date back to the earliest days of the problem.

The Free Flow of Information Versus the Sovereign Right
of Each Country to Control Its Telecommunications:
Attempts to Regulate Deliberate Interference

Attempts to regulate jamming have been as frequent as they have been unsuccessful. The ITU has traditionally been reluctant to address the issue of jamming. This neglect stems from a certain logic, still harbored by several ITU members, which dictates that the ITU exists as a technical forum to address technical means of facilitating international telecommunications. The ITU, so the view proceeds, must be apolitical if it is to be effective. Jamming is by nature a political issue. Therefore, the ITU would jeopardize its effectiveness and credibility by tackling this issue.

Conversely, many others believe that the ITU places itself in jeopardy by ignoring the jamming problem, particularly on HF radio. While jamming is politically motivated, it is nevertheless a technical process which directly violates Articles 4 and 35 of the 1982 ITU International Telecommunication Convention and several provisions of the Radio Regulations. For the ITU to ignore HF jamming is to render meaningless any decision of the Union regarding the control or use of the HF spectrum. Past neglect is one factor in the growth of jamming in recent decades.

Jamming is, nevertheless, not a recent phenomenon. Several sources attribute the first successful use of radio jamming to, of all countries, Austria. The Dollfuss government in 1934 employed jamming against the annexationist Nazi propaganda of the Deutschlandsender.[28] Yet evidence exists tracing jamming back to the 1920s, with twelve countries attempting to block the first Vatican Radio broadcast in 1931 and several cases of French and German stations deliberately interfering with one another.[29] In 1932 Romania unsuccessfully attempted to jam Soviet radio.[30] By the late 1930s jamming was omnipresent throughout Europe. The Germans undertook a program of "Broadcast Defense" which employed fairly indiscriminate, powerful jamming. The Italians jammed Ethiopian rebel stations and the BBC. In Spain the Fascists jammed the Republican stations and, by 1938, virtually every European country except for Britain employed some type of jamming.[31] Jamming grew in the immediate prewar years as a direct consequence of rising intra-European tension.

In 1936 the first international attempt to defuse this tension and its consequences for the radio spectrum took place under the aegis of the "League of Nations International Convention Concerning the Cause of Peace." This grandiloquent title belied concerns that broadcasting was increasingly being employed as a weapon of war and aggression. The Convention, which came into force in April 1938, enjoined League members to hold to the following:

> (1) Prohibit broadcasts of such a character as to incite the population of any territory to acts incompatible with internal order or security. (2) Ensure that domestic transmissions shall not constitute an incitement either to war against another high contracting party or to acts likely to lead thereto. (3) Prohibit any transmission likely to harm good international understanding by statements the incorrectness of which is or ought to be known to the persons responsible for the broadcasts. (4) Ensure especially in time of crisis that stations . . . shall broadcast information concerning international relations the accuracy of which shall have been verified . . . by the persons responsible for broadcasting the information. . . .[32]

This Convention was as strong a statement as any that has been produced concerning how international broadcasters ought to behave. It was considerably weakened by not having Germany as one of its 37 signatories. Moreover, by 1938 the effectiveness of any action by the League of Nations, no matter how well-intended, was questionable. Within fifteen months the European powers were at war. During World War II, predictably enough, most international broadcasters were jamming one another, with some noteworthy exceptions.[33]

In the immediate postwar atmosphere of optimism, it was hoped that jamming would disappear as a result of the new peaceful internationalism that was expected to characterize postwar international relations. This is the spirit in which the 1946 ITU Moscow Preparatory Conference and, to a lesser extent, the 1947 Atlantic City ITU Conferences took place. As a consequence, Article 44 of the 1947 Atlantic City International Telecommunications Convention, which survives as Article 35 of the

1982 Convention, addresses the issue of unintentional harmful interference without once directly referring to intentional harmful interference. The third paragraph of Article 44, proposed by Italy,[34] calls on members to take "all practicable steps to prevent the operation of electrical apparatus and installations of all kinds from causing harmful interference. . . ."[35] This reinforced the notion that all future problems of this nature would be the unintentional product of new technologies and innovations.

Jamming did not, of course, disappear from the international airwaves for long. The USSR had sporadically jammed Russian language shortwave programs from Franco's Spain even prior to the 1946 ITU Moscow Preparatory Conference. It was the sudden worsening of US-Soviet relations, the partitioning of Europe, the Berlin Airlift, and the rise of the Truman Doctrine which doomed the HF broadcast bands to inevitable jamming. The establishment of the Voice of America's Russian and East European language services led Stalin and the Soviet Politburo to decide late in 1947 to commit a dozen transmitters to full-time jamming of the new VOA services. This jamming commenced in February 1948. Within a month the United States launched a formal protest to the USSR concerning the jamming of the Voice of America.[36] The Soviet Minister of Foreign Affairs, Mr. Andrei Vishinsky, replied by denying the existence of Soviet jammers.

In June 1948 the ITU European Broadcasting Conference meeting at Copenhagen assigned European mediumwave frequencies to European broadcasters in an attempt to restore order to European broadcasting and salvage as much as possible from the 1939 ITU Montreux Plan, which was never implemented due to the outbreak of World War II. The USSR was signatory to the Conference but reserved the right "to take necessary technical measures to eliminate interference in the work of its stations"[37] if other signatories did not abide by the plan. This provided the Soviets with a legal loophole to continue jamming. As soon as the plan came into effect, the Soviets accused the West of violating the plan and intensified their jamming efforts in response.

The year 1948 also witnessed the first actions of the United Nations General Assembly and the ITU with regard to jamming. The Universal Declaration of Human Rights, while not concentrating on freedom of information *per se*, stated in Article 19:

> Everyone has the right to freedom of opinion and expression; this right includes freedom to hold opinions without interference and to seek, receive and import information and ideas through any media regardless of frontiers.[38]

Article 19 provided the first explicit manifestation of what later became known as the free flow of information norm of international telecommunications. The ITU International HF Broadcasting Conference which met at Mexico City late in 1948 adopted a resolution stating that "frequencies assigned by the Conference should not be used for purposes contrary to mutual understanding and tolerance. . . ."[39] Nevertheless, the apparent circumvention of this issue by the Conference led the American delegation to refuse to sign the Final Acts of the Conference. The United States delegation feared the Western Europeans, in particular, had given undue concessions to the USSR in order to bring them into the plan and that, as a consequence, jamming would be "condemned to the back burner" for several years hence.[40]

As Cold War tensions escalated, the level of jamming rose accordingly. By 1950 the Soviets were employing a network of 450 jamming transmitters blocking the Voice of America as well as Russian broadcasts from the BBC, Deutsche Welle, and the new CIA-financed émigré station Radio Free Europe, broadcasting out of Munich. The Soviets did not admit to the existence of USSR-based jammers until November 1949, when, in a speech to the UN General Assembly, Mr. Vishinsky defended his country's considerable jamming efforts by declaring that "the Russian people had to be prevented in the name of world peace from rising up in wrath to attack the United States, as they assuredly would if they were to hear the American broadcasts. . . ."[41]

It was in this sort of rarified oratorical atmosphere that the UN Sub-Commission on Freedom of Information and the Press of the Commission on Human Rights met at Montevideo in May 1950. Debate on the jamming issue was vociferous, heated, and hostile. The United States delegate, Mr. Binder, submitted a proposal explicitly condemning the jamming of radio broadcasts and accusing the Soviet Union of deliberately interfering with foreign radio transmissions directed to that country.[42] The Polish delegate, arguing the Soviet case, claimed jamming was necessary to defend its citizenry against psychological warfare and that "each country has . . . the sovereign right to defend itself against this form of aggression, just as it had the right to prevent opium smuggling, the sale of pornographic literature, or the traffic in persons. . . ."[43]

The Sub-Commission nevertheless adopted the American resolution which was then forwarded to the UN Economic and Social Council. The Council recommended the General Assembly call upon member governments to refrain from interfering with their people's right to freedom of information. Direct references to the Soviet Union, however, were deleted. When this modified resolution was debated in the Third Committee (Social, Humanitarian, Cultural) of the UN General Assembly, the Soviet and Eastern bloc delegates remained strongly opposed to it. The Soviet delegate argued that his government had "the right and duty to paralyze the aggressor in this radio war."[44] The Soviet arguments did not convince many, however. Few would agree at this point that the free flow of information could be a genuine infringement upon sovereignty. Most countries believed the listener had the right to judge the value of a given program. The General Assembly proposed a resolution in December 1950, which condemned "measures of this nature (i.e., jamming) as a denial of the right of all persons to be fully informed concerning news, opinions, and ideas regardless of frontiers. . . ."[45] The Resolution passed by a vote of 49 to 5.[46]

A harbinger of future regulatory trends also appeared in 1950 to accompany the strong words of the UN. The Council of Europe met that year to pass a European Convention for Human Rights and Fundamental Freedoms. Article 10 of that Convention essentially reiterated the UN Universal Declaration of Human Rights of two years earlier. A clause was added, however, allowing that freedom of information flows may be subject to restrictions "necessary in a democratic society . . . (e.g.,) for the protection of health and morals."[47] Presumably it would be each country's sovereign prerogative to determine the degree of restriction it considered necessary. This 1950 resolution therefore established the defense of sovereignty as a justification for government control over the dissemination of information within domestic boundaries. This of course included information flowing in from outside national boundaries, but this was not in fact the objective of the clause. The restrictions envisaged by the Europeans seemed to concern the threat to the state monopoly radio networks posed by private commercial "pirate" broadcasters. For most of the signatories of the Convention, incoming information from foreign sources could not be seriously viewed as a political threat.

Up to this point most discussion and debates had centered on Western support for a virtually unrestricted flow of information across borders versus Eastern bloc support for the need to defend one's country against externally sourced subversion. Like the Cold War itself, the "players" in the jamming issue, as it existed in the early 1950s, were relatively easy to identify and the issue merely one component within the greater East-West struggle. At the Foreign Ministers Conference at Geneva, in October 1955, the French delegate submitted a tripartite proposal on the development of East-West contacts in which the Western position was encapsulated:

> The systematic jamming of broadcasts of news and information is a practice to be deplored. It is incompatible with the directive from the Four Heads of Government and should be discontinued.[48]

The rise of Khruschev and the de-Stalinization campaign of 1956 led to the temporary cessation of virtually all Soviet jamming.[49] For a short while it appeared that the problem had been solved and that jamming would join the long list of unsavory methods of repression characteristic of the Stalin years now to be repudiated. Several East European countries also publicly stated that jamming had been "a method which has brought us no credit" and that stopping it "is a victory for the principle, correct in our opinion, that the foreign radio stations should be countered by factual arguments."[50] Polish authorities also released cost figures for their jamming efforts (see above) and decried the methods as "dirty work," the cessation of which "would save enough electric power to supply a town of several thousand people."[51]

Unfortunately, the Suez and Hungarian crises of October 1956 led to a rapid restoration and intensification of all prior jamming efforts. The jammers had been off for less than six months. Jamming was by now beginning to interfere with other HF services. The ITU, which had been observing the escalation, cessation, and intensified restoration of HF jamming with quiet despair for ten years, now found itself thrust into the center of a specific harmful interference dispute.

In 1957, the United States notified the IFRB that Soviet jamming operations directed against the Voice of America were interfering with European aeromobile radio services. The USSR acknowledged that it was using the frequency specified and insisted that the frequency had been brought into use by the USSR in 1933 and that the old ITU Bern Bureau had been notified at that time. As the USSR was not signatory to the 1952 EARC or the subsequent regulations (see Chapter 2 above), its use of the frequency was, according to Soviet interpretations, legitimate. The Soviet delegate stated that the USSR was nevertheless willing to cease jamming *if* the United States ceased all Voice of America transmissions directed to the Soviet Union. In response the American administration rejected any connection between Soviet interference with European utility services and the content of Voice of America Russian-language transmissions. The US administration conveyed its disappointment with the IFRB's reprinting of the Soviet "swap" proposal without any objection or comment.[52]

The situation was never resolved, confirming a belief within the ITU that the deliberate interference issue was simply too innately political for ITU activity to be of any assistance. The 1957 IFRB wrangle only served to harm the Board's reputation, particularly with the American administration.

By 1958 hope of international cooperation regarding the jamming issue was rapidly diminishing. This did not stop attempts to convince the Soviet Union that jamming was in *no one's* interest. In the summer

of 1958 the Voice of America announced it would broadcast a special
session of the UN General Assembly concerning the Middle East crisis.
These broadcasts would be simulcast in all five official UN languages.
The American Ambassador to the UN, Henry Cabot Lodge, made an
appeal to the Soviet Union not to jam these broadcasts and allow the
Soviet people to listen to the UN proceedings. While the French, English,
and Spanish services were not jammed, the Chinese and Russian-language
broadcasts were heavily jammed, even when the Soviet Ambassador,
Mr. Gromyko, was speaking.[53]

As 1958 progressed, Edward R. Murrow, the Director of the Voice
of America, decided that the sole effective means for dealing with
jamming would be by fighting the jammers through saturation broadcasting. An early example of this was the VOA "Sunday Punch" broadcast
of November 5, 1958, criticizing the Soviet decision to resume nuclear
testing. Fifty-two Voice of America transmitters on 80 frequencies were
directed at the Soviet Union in an eight-hour barrage.[54] It was later
estimated that about half of the signals reached their target—a victory
for the VOA.

At the international level, however, American diplomats and negotiators
remained hopeful that the Soviets could be persuaded through the UN
to cease jamming. The UN Special Political Committee, which met in
December 1958, seemed an ideal forum for such persuasion. The American
delegate appealed to the Soviet Union to cease jamming of foreign
broadcasts as a sign of goodwill and to encourage communication with
the West. The American delegate, George Harrison, attempted to convince
the Soviets that from an economic perspective—by 1958 jammers were
costing the Soviets about $100 million each year—jamming served no
one, including the USSR. The Soviet delegate, Arkady Sobolev, immediately retorted by accusing the US delegate of having "used this tribunal
for a cheap propaganda statement such as we have not heard in many
years in this General Assembly."[55] Mr. Sobolev asserted that the United
States would not be able to conquer the Soviet Union by force or by
subversion, as "Moscow had atomic bombs to reply to aggression, and
jamming transmitters to handle subversive broadcasts beamed to
Moscow."[56]

The level of jamming largely parallels the level of general tension
between the two superpowers. However, jamming between the Soviet
Union and PR China has been constant since the mid-1960s, as has
Soviet jamming of the US-backed, émigré-operated Radio Liberty and
Radio Free Europe. Periods of amicability and detente between the USSR
and USA bring about reductions in the overall level of Soviet jamming.
One such occasion was the suspension of most Soviet jamming during
Nikita Khrushchev's visit to the United States in 1959. Unfortunately,

these rhapsodic intervals never endured. The Soviet jammers were back on the air the moment Mr. Khrushchev was back in Moscow.[57] Another suspension brought about by British Prime Minister Harold Macmillan was undone by the 1960 U2 spy-plane scandal. Yet another suspension accompanied the 1963 Test-Ban agreement.[58]

Some progress was made in the early 1960s toward achieving a reduction in the overall level of jamming. When jamming resumed after the U2 crisis, monitors noted that jammers were focusing their efforts only on certain programs and time periods. Partial jamming "let in those parts of Western broadcasts which, in the interests of 'balance', revealed the seamy side of 'Free World' life. The ruse was too obvious . . . it made listening to the censored bits that much more attractive."[59] The level of Soviet jamming was further reduced after the 1963 Test-Ban Treaty. One achievement which helped reduce the cacophony, particularly in Europe, was the cessation of all jamming by Romania in 1963 and Hungary in 1964.[60]

The Americas received a taste of what was occurring in Europe and Asia when Cuba commenced limited jamming of the Voice of America and of Miami medium wave (AM) stations in 1962. Actual jamming by Cuba has never been more than limited and half-hearted, but the potential for Cuba to wreak havoc on the airwaves of the Western Hemisphere has been of concern to the United States for over 25 years.[61]

While the 1960s proved to be a period of relative tranquility and cooperation in the control of jamming, neither the UN nor the ITU could claim any credit for this achievement. The extent to which jamming ceased or declined was determined by the general state of relations between the USSR and the United States. The Eastern European countries were permitted to scale down or scrap their jamming efforts. This was reflective of an overall improvement in East-West relations, particularly within Europe, after 1962 and also a recognition on the part of the Politburos of Eastern Europe that Western radio signals were far too omnipresent to be effectively blocked.[62]

The international organizations wrestling with the legality and morality of jamming were confronted with a more complex situation in the 1960s as a result of the granting of independence to many Third World states. In the 1950s, as has been mentioned, the situation was relatively clear for the majority of non-Communist states: jamming was indefensible. But as the 1960s progressed, new factors were introduced which had not heretofore been considered. On the one hand, the human rights of the individual—including the right to communicate, be informed, and determine one's own destiny—had never been stronger. The most powerful manifestation of this principle was the utter discrediting of colonialism and the rapid accession to independence of dozens of former colonies.

The new era of independence, however, also brought about an unprecedented reaffirmation of the concept of sovereignty.

Self-determination quickly asserted itself as each *state's* sovereign right to determine the destiny of its citizenry. Central to the operation of the state was the need for media to encourage cooperation and foster development. The concept of a free, critical press, like that of opposition political parties, was often deemed irrelevant and possibly contrary to the needs and aspirations of newly independent countries. Radio stations from abroad, particularly the HF shortwave voices of the BBC, Radio France, and the Voice of America, along with the large Northern wire news services, came to be seen as neo-colonial perpetuators of a repressive one-way media flow that was seriously jeopardizing Third World development.[63] While most developing countries did not have the resources to actually jam incoming HF broadcasts, such broadcasts were not popular among Third World governments. Commitment in the "South" to the free flow of information norm was at best equivocal and more often distrustful of developed country motives.[64]

When the UN General Assembly adopted a Covenant on Civil and Political Rights in 1966, Article 19 of that Covenant provided, at first glance, a strong reiteration of the 1948 UN Declaration of Human Rights in its denunciation of restrictions on information flow. The 1966 Covenant asserts the right to hold opinions without interference, the right of freedom of expression, and the right to impart or receive information "regardless of frontiers, either orally, in writing, or in print, in the form of art, or through the media of his choice." But a third paragraph was introduced subjecting the above rights to certain conditions under which "special restrictions" may be permitted. These include the "protection of national security, public order, or public health or morals."[65] These restrictions were in fact indicative of a new era in which the country's sovereign right to determine information flows and control telecommunications media within its boundaries take precedence over any commitment to a vague free flow of information principle. In the late 1960s a North-South conflict over deliberate interference did not emerge, as the developing countries had yet to perceive their interests clearly within the issue. Jamming remained an East-West problem.

The period of equivocation over jamming which had commenced with Khrushchev's de-Stalinization of 1956 did not really end until the Czechoslovakian crisis of 1968. The failed experiment of "socialism with a human face" led to a high-level review of toleration of outside influences, and subsequently a tougher policy toward "interference":

> Efforts were . . . directed toward reinforcing the ideological battle-front
> and protecting the socialist community from evil influences . . . without

too seriously inhibiting the proposed collaboration with the West. . . .
Detente needed to be strictly contained on the societal plane; accordingly,
the campaign against the penetration by Western influences became indispensable.[66]

The Warsaw Pact countries discussed an "umbrella" policy of coordinated counter-measures against "revisionist forces" and "psychological
warfare." Unlike pre-1956 jamming efforts, which were quite unambiguous in their hostility toward all and any incoming foreign broadcasts,
jamming in the 1970s—to the extent that it would be acknowledged at
all—would have to be more strongly legitimized in order to be made
saleable to the international community and, in particular, the Third
World. The Soviet strategy was motivated by two objectives, the first
of which had essentially remained unchanged from the start; that of
excluding viewpoints seen as subversive and a threat to the well-being
of the state (explained below). The second objective was cooperation of
the West and especially the South without unduly compromising domestic
controls on information flows or the existence of the jamming network.

Of particular concern to the Soviets was preparation for the Conference
for Security and Cooperation in Europe (CSCE). The first preparatory
talks were held at Helsinki in late 1972. Western and neutral participants
wished this Conference to address more than merely inter-state coexistence; they believed inter-societal issues such as human contact and
the dissemination of information between East and West needed to be
addressed.

The Soviets at first refused to consider matters such as information
flows and aspects of inter-state relations. But the fear of jeopardizing
detente and links with the Third World led to a solution which, much
to the Soviets' pleasure, did not involve any real compromise on their
part. This solution was expressed by Soviet Secretary-General Brezhnev
in December 1972:

> a plea for cooperation in the realm of culture . . . the exchange of ideas
> and spread of information along with contacts between the peoples which
> must . . . come about on the condition that there is respect for the
> sovereignty, the laws, and the customs of each country. . . . [Cooperation
> must] serve the reciprocal spiritual enrichment of the peoples, the growth
> of trust among them and the reinforcement of the concepts of peace and
> good neighborliness.[67]

Contact between societies, as the Soviets envisioned it, required the
approval of the state, whatever form this contact might take. This

encompassed all aspects of inter-social exchange, from travel and tourism to news and information over the airwaves.

The Soviets won another important victory during 1972, this time with the full support of most developing countries. The technology of satellite television first appeared in the late 1960s, and was soon followed by research into direct-to-receiver broadcasting by satellite, known as DBS. By the time of the 1971 ITU WARC for space telecommunications, many countries believed it was imperative to plan the DBS bands before the major technological powers commenced widespread use of the bands. A priori planning would ensure equitability of access for all members (see Chapter 2 above). While such planning was not forthcoming from the 1971 Space WARC, the majority of members did indicate at the conference where they stood on the issue of DBS as a potential medium for international broadcasting. The fear of international television signals, unlicensed and uncontrolled by national administrations, led to the establishment of a "doctrine of prior agreement" whereby, according to the 1971 Space WARC Final Acts, "all technical means available shall be used to reduce, to the maximum extent possible, the radiation over the territory of other countries (i.e., spillover) unless an agreement has been previously reached with such countries."[68]

Unlike HF Broadcasting, DBS television is not by nature international. It is, however, impossible for a DBS signal "footprint" to correspond strictly to national boundaries, as the 1971 Space WARC advises. Some spillover is inevitable.[69] Developing countries, particularly those physically closer to developed countries (e.g., Mexico, the Caribbean, North Africa) or those bordering major LDC broadcasters (e.g., countries contiguous to Brazil or India), fear that if DBS receiving dishes become inexpensive and pervasive, domestic telecommunication administrations will suffer a serious loss of control over the domestic television services as viewers become accustomed to an inundation of attractive foreign signals.

The fear within the Eastern bloc is similar but perhaps more stark. The USSR and other Eastern European countries can already look to the example of the German Democratic Republic (GDR), where terrestrial television and radio signals from West Berlin and the Federal Republic cover most of the country. East Germany is the wealthiest country in the Soviet bloc and enjoys the highest standard of living of any Warsaw Pact country. While East Germans are aware of their relative wealth, they nevertheless continue to view themselves as drab, poorer cousins to the dynamic West Germany viewed on their television screens. The demoralizing effects that omnipresent Western television signals would have on the less satisfied, less politically stable populations of Poland, Hungary, or Czechoslovakia cause great concern to the Soviet leadership.

Even politicians in Western Europe and other OECD countries remain fearful of losing sovereign control over television. American terrestrial television signals have been viewed as a threat to Canadian sovereignty for over three decades. In the Netherlands cable television operators were not permitted to boost foreign TV signals from one region to another.[70] In Switzerland, legislation hindered for several years the satellite-master antenna TV distribution of Italy's RAI-1 network.[71]

By 1972 the ITU had established two norms for the operation of DBS television: the obligation to limit signal spillover and the doctrine of prior consent for international operation. The Soviets were anxious to reaffirm these principles in a more visible, more binding forum than the ITU. Also, the LDCs were concerned that a free flow of information would, in a DBS-TV context, quickly devolve into a one-way North to South flow. Both groups sought pre-emptive action through the forum of the UN General Assembly.

On August 8, 1972, Soviet Foreign Minister Andrei Gromyko proposed to the UN General Assembly a convention, according to which

the relaying of television programmes by means of artificial earth satellites to other sovereign states without the clearly expressed agreement of these states . . . would be regarded as illegal. . . . [Each state may] take every means at its disposal to prevent illegal television transmissions from entering its territory . . . not only within its own territories but also in space and in other domains situated outside the national jurisdiction of any state.[72]

The chief justification of this strongly worded proposal was, as Gromyko put it, "the need to protect state sovereignty from every form of external interference."[73] The Soviet proponents of this draft proposal deliberately co-opted Third World support by emphasizing DBS' potential as a means of "information imperialism" or "electronic neo-colonialism." The Soviet line to the Third World is summarized by Wettig as follows:

The Western conception of free circulation of information among nations is tantamount to discrimination against the former colonial territories and a bestowing of privilege upon the colonial powers—hence an extremely dangerous, if veiled, form of neo-colonialism.[74]

Several Western developed countries opposed the proposal. They were able to effect a degree of compromise and remove some of the stridency from the proposal. They were not able to effect substantive change. The United States remained opposed to the resolution, arguing that it did not place sufficient emphasis on the free flow of information principle. In the end, even some of the Western countries were convinced that the Soviet resolution, while not perfect, served to introduce a necessary avowal of the sovereign right of national discretion over domestic telecommunications. The Soviet resolution, with full developing country support, gained approval by a vote of 102 to 1 (the USA) with only seven abstentions.[75]

UN General Assembly Resolution 2916 (1972) came to be known as the "Jammer's Charter" with its warning that "the introduction of direct television broadcasting by means of satellites could raise significant problems connected with the need to ensure the free flow of communications on a basis of strict respect for the sovereign rights of States."[76] It also clearly set out the rules of the road for international DBS services: transmitting agencies must acquire prior agreement from the target country, or else that country is fully within its legal rights to deliberately interfere with the incoming signal. The debate on the "Jammer's Charter" made explicit the opposing Soviet and Western viewpoints on the role of international broadcasting. The LDCs, having their own reasons for distrusting the "free flow" principle, could more easily support Soviet pronouncements on the nobility of the principle of sovereignty and the need to defend against external cultural imperialism than support American calls for the absolute liberalization of information exchanges. Several Western countries, particularly France, West Germany, Canada, and the Scandinavian countries, added an element of division within the Western bloc. Their own fears over losing sovereign control over telecommunications in a complete "free flow" scenario led to guarded support of American positions, with calls for greater consideration of the motives and concerns of developing countries.

The high frequency broadcast bands continued to be the sole effective means of international broadcast communications. The "detente" of the early 1970s led to hopes that jamming would disappear. Jamming did in fact decline as an issue. But it did not diminish on the airwaves. The Soviet Union continued to jam Radio Liberty, Radio Free Europe, and Kol Israel, and resumed jamming of the Deutsche Welle in 1974.[77] For a few years the Voice of America and the BBC were spared from the sort of intensive jamming they had known in the past.

Jamming and the free flow of information between East and West was to be a major topic of discussion at the Conference on Security and Cooperation in Europe (CSCE). As has been mentioned the Soviets delineated their position early on in the preparations for the Conference. This was reaffirmed in July 1973 by a Polish-Bulgarian draft proposal on cultural cooperation, contacts, and information exchanges which warned of the duty "to respect basic political, economic, and cultural principles of other states. . . ."[78] In effect, the Soviets proposed that international broadcasting must be subject to the jurisdiction of the governments of the receiving countries involved.

This position was not well received by Western delegates to the CSCE Preparatory Conferences. In October 1973, the Western countries attempted to reaffirm their commitment to free flow with an Italian proposal for "unrestricted circulation of news among nations" akin to Recommendation Number 1 in the 1973 ITU International Telecommunication Convention.[79] The Soviets and Eastern bloc countries accused the Western delegates of using this resolution as justification for the deliberately interventionist policies of their external radio broadcasts to the East. The Soviet delegation stated—repeatedly—that the principle of *inter-state* relations, in other words contact between representative governments, not between undefined "individuals" or "societies," and the principle of non-intervention in the internal affairs of other states must take precedence at the Conference and that these principles should be clearly expressed in any Convention, preferably in the Preamble.[80]

The Western countries were striving for a guarantee of a freer exchange of information and cooperation over the airwaves. The United States delegation sought an explicit prohibition—or at least a denunciation—of jamming. Not surprisingly the Soviets were wary of renouncing a telecommunications policy they had championed for 40 years. While expounding on the virtues of enhanced information exchanges as promoting "peace and mutual understanding," the Soviets successfully introduced enough ambiguity into the discussion to permit—without contravening the norms of the Conference—the jamming of radio broadcasts or the censorship of incoming information the moment such action is deemed "necessary" by the domestic authorities.

The Basket Three accords of the CSCE Final Acts, signed at Helsinki on August 1, 1975, involved 35 heads of state agreeing to the wider exchange of information, freedom of communications, and a renewed commitment to human rights. Integral to Soviet and Eastern European support of CSCE was the equality of the principle of individual state sovereignty, along with a right to restrict free flows of information "when this is necessary in order to safeguard the rights and reputations of other persons, and to protect state security, the social system, health and morals."[81]

The GDR introduced the notion that CSCE commitment to state sovereignty and the inviolability of frontiers would be interpreted by Warsaw Pact countries as license to legally block unwanted information: ". . . the freedom of information referred to in the resolution of the CSCE could not . . . be interpreted as an obligation (for Wasaw Pact signatories) to throw their doors wide open to subversive anti-Soviet propaganda."[82] Just as the Americans unsuccessfully attempted to use

CSCE to halt Soviet jamming, the Soviets used CSCE to propose that the Americans take Radio Free Europe/Radio Liberty off the air in order to "wind up the inheritance of the 'Cold War' in all its facets, including propaganda."[83] Soviet recalcitrance concerning the removal of jammers, however, did not make the Americans particularly amenable to sacrificing the US-backed émigré stations. Even at the height of "detente," American commitment to Radio Free Europe/Radio Liberty was unequivocal, and it remains difficult to envisage a negotiating context in which an American administration would be willing to take these stations off the air.

The CSCE accord, with its reaffirmation of both the free flow of information principle and the principle of state sovereignty over the domestic dissemination of information, did not serve to diminish the level of jamming. Nor did it introduce any legal constraint that would provide leverage against countries that jam. That progress was not possible at the height of "detente" is illustrative of the importance attached to jamming—and the right to jam—by the Eastern bloc.

The specter of satellite television at this time acted as a catalyst for Third World support for constraints on the free flow principle. Real concerns about cultural sovereignty and the development of nationhood led LDCs to commence international actions on their own part to guard their nascent media. The Soviet Union was acting from different motives than the developing states when it championed state sovereignty as a preeminent principle to be respected in international communications. The LDCs generally sympathized with Soviet statements concerning the UN General Assembly "Jammer's Charter" or CSCE. Few were convinced, however, that the USSR was benignly pursuing the interests of developing countries. The non-aligned G77 countries realized that they should develop their own distinct approaches in telecommunications policy.

The traditional UN forum for discussion of North-South issues relating to international social and cultural issues has been UNESCO, the UN Educational, Scientific, and Cultural Organization. The "information issue" was introduced to the Organization at the 16th UNESCO General Assembly in 1970. At that conference the Soviets and socialist bloc countries vociferously allied themselves with LDCs in their calls for development of national telecommunications systems to lessen and eventually end technological dependence on the Western metropoles. One year later, at the 17th UNESCO General Assembly, a vote of 100 to 1 confirmed the ITU-established principle of prior consent governing any international DBS operation. Not surprisingly, the United States was the sole obstacle to a unanimous vote, as the US delegation found both the wording and spirit of the prior consent draft anathema to the free flow norm. The USSR successfully introduced a resolution concerning the "fundamental principles governing the use of the mass media with a view to strengthening peace and international understanding and combatting war propaganda, racialism, and apartheid."[84]

It was not until the 1973 meeting of Non-aligned Foreign Ministers at Algiers that several developing countries began actively pursuing a policy regarding the control of information flows that was neither American nor Soviet in inspiration. As a corollary of the New International Economic Order which sought to free the Third World from economic dependence on the North, the New World Information Order (NWIO) attacked the status quo of international broadcasting, wire services, international publishing, and potential satellite television flows. Its assumption was that the current state of affairs allowed the promulgation of cultural imperialism and the perpetuation of neo-colonial dependence on the former colonial metropoles, to the detriment of indigenous cultural media development. The LDCs were also tired of getting a "bad press" from the developed world. Many LDCs believed that under the status quo stories of Third World development and progress were subordinate in the minds of news editors and broadcasters to sensational stories of Third World oppression, failure, or violence. Racine Sy, director of Senegalese Radio, put the LDC position succinctly:

This *de facto* situation . . . concretizes [sic] a form of domination—not to say colonisation—on all fronts: political, economic, social and cultural. The point is that information given [over the radio] by these agencies, whether government run or private is very often, no doubt not deliberately, tendentious and subjective in the eyes of their Third World users. . . . [85]

An indication of LDC equivocation over the unrestricted transmission of news is discussed by Monsieur Sy:

I have spoken of a value system and I shall give you an example: During the Falklands War (1982), the British authorities accused the BBC of undermining the morale of the British troops at the front by broadcasting information from Argentinian sources. To which the BBC's deputy Director-General retorted: "If that's all it takes to undermine our men's morale, they have no business being there." Do not ask me if I share this view. The Director of Senegal Radio would have been more inclined to stick with the troops whatever the circumstances. I confess that I studied this statement for days in the privacy of my office, torn between the feelings of the professional broadcaster and the responsible servant. In other words, between the concern to provide objective information and to ensure that the information that we should like to be objective is not a source of unrest in the country. My patriotism won. I am not suggesting that journalists in the South are more patriotic than journalists in the North, far from it. But I think that . . . there is a difference in the way people think and that this should on no account prompt the North to minimize, through a superiority complex or cultural disdain, the development and treatment of information in the Third World.[86]

Monsieur Sy then directs his comments to international radio broadcasting:

The radio broadcasters in the developed countries daily practice a full-blown piracy of the air, aiming their high-powered transmitters directly at the Third World. Programmes are devised and produced by Europeans and Americans for peoples of whose tastes and concerns they are sometimes quite ignorant. . . . [87]

Support for the NWIO gathered quickly in the early 1970s. By the middle of the decade appearances suggested that the objectives of the New International Economic Order (NIEO) were not only possible but, with the success of OPEC and the rise in commodity prices, were actually being realized. Many observers believed that a fundamental shift of economic power to the resource-rich LDCs would accelerate as the 1970s and 1980s progressed. The exchange of information was seen as an integral element of this development. Indeed, a domestically controlled telecommunications infrastructure was viewed as requisite to advancement.

The newly rich OPEC states spent vast sums in the 1970s building elaborate broadcasting networks. Virtually all major OPEC members quickly established large international broadcasting stations. The number of international HF broadcasts in Arabic increased dramatically. By the mid-1980s the Middle East and Persian Gulf regions possessed some of the most advanced telecommunications systems in the world, albeit without exception using fully imported technology. The point, nevertheless, is that the Arabic-speaking world has control of its telecommunications services and programming to an extent that other regions of the Third World might envy and, if they had the money, might follow.

The Arabic-speaking world is exceptional, however. The circumstances which permitted countries like Saudi Arabia, Kuwait, or even Oman to establish telecommunications networks are not likely to emerge in Zambia, Peru, or Bangladesh. Moreover, pan-Arab culture and the strength of the Islamic faith provide an insularity from "attacks" on home cultures. Most Arabic-speaking countries nevertheless are loath to take any unnecessary chances, and thus fully support the aims and restrictions prescribed by NWIO. Some, notably Algeria, Egypt, and Pakistan, have been leaders within the NWIO movement.

Third World promotion of NWIO objectives has continued and grown in the years since its appearance. UNESCO stated these aims boldly in the 1976 Conference agenda paper:

> The old notion of the free flow of information must now be extended to include that of the balanced flow of information. . . . A national communications policy is necessary to safeguard national sovereignty.[88]

Calls for the establishment of a NWIO were also strongly voiced at the 20th and 21st UNESCO General Assembly Meetings of 1978 and 1979 which culminated in the MacBride Commission and the publication of its report. Other works describe the evolution and spirit of the new order established at these conferences in far more detail than space permits here. By the early 1980s it was apparent that most of the countries of the world viewed the free flow norm as distinctly subsidiary to the sovereign right to control the entry of information into a country. Without the option of restricting inflows of information smaller countries and LDCs fear inundation and subjugation by American and other developed country media.

The concept of restricting the flow of information across borders, at one time seen as just "an admission of a bad cause . . . and bad conscience,"[89] must now be viewed as a manifestation of a renewed attachment to national sovereignty and an expression of new Third World attempts to lessen "cultural" dependence on the North. The promotion of international telecommunications cannot be unconditional. Where, then, does this leave the ITU? Does the NWIO jeopardize the entire ethos of the Union? Or, at the very least, does the new reality invalidate ITU efforts to regulate jamming and other restrictions on the free flow norm?

In fact, the ITU has carefully incorporated UNESCO declarations concerning "the contribution of the mass media to strengthening peace and international understanding, to the promotion of human rights and to countering racialism, apartheid and incitement to war . . ." into Recommendation Number 1 of the 1982 ITU International Telecommunication Convention.[90] Moreover, note that the free flow principle is upheld in a Recommendation, not a Resolution or article. This leaves individual members far more discretionary power to restrict information flows.

This latitude does not extend to deliberate jamming of incoming radio or television broadcasts. The success of the "Jammer's Charter" and rise of the NWIO aided Soviet bloc attempts to legitimize jamming as a necessary safeguard to sovereignty. The ITU, if not the other UN agencies, recognized the distinction between Eastern jamming and Southern concerns about guarding indigenous cultures. In addition, by the 1980s the ITU was under considerable pressure to recognize the need to take action against deliberate interference. Despite the expectation of decisive action and strong stands at the 1979 WARC,[91] the jamming issue and, indeed many issues relating to HF, were postponed at the Conference for a variety of reasons, not the least of which was a lack of political will to confront what would inevitably be a complicated, contentious issue.[92]

Recognition of jamming as having a serious impact on HF use would have to be an integral part of the discussions at the 1984 HF-WARC First Session if the Conference, and indeed the ITU, was to have any significance at all to future HF Spectrum management. As a consequence, the Report to the Second Session of the HF-WARC (held in early 1987) incorporates a resolution instructing the IFRB to

> organize monitoring programmes in the bands allocated to the HF broad-
> casting service with a view to identifying stations causing harmful inter-
> ference [and] to seek . . . the cooperation of administrations in *identifying
> the sources of emissions which cause harmful interference and to provide this
> information to administrations.*[93]

The Second Session of the HF-WARC (1987) explicitly censured those administrations causing deliberate interference to the HF bands.[94] Some observers have accused the United States and other Western countries of "politicizing" the 1984 First Session of the HF-WARC by compelling the Union to confront the jammers, but as one technical report stated, "any frequency plan developed for the HF broadcasting service that does not expressly account for jamming activity will not come close to simulating the actual situation in the broadcasting service."[95] This is a major step for the ITU, but one that is undeniably imperative in any attempt to restore order to HF broadcasting. Such a step provides a clear warning to member countries as well: the need for sovereign control over domestic telecommunications and everyone's right to communicate is inviolable, but when attempts to ensure this valid objective involve deliberate interference to legitimate international broadcasts, adminis-trations can no longer expect the ITU to turn a blind eye. The growth of jamming during the renewed Cold War of the 1980s and the spectre of new restrictions from the Third World led the ITU to act.

Conclusion:
Jammers' Motives and Limits to ITU Power

Deliberate interference with international telecommunications takes place through a variety of means. Increasingly, these methods entail some sort of *domestic* constraint or disincentive to receiving incoming information flows. Legislation forbidding the reception of foreign radio stations, the existence of wired rediffusion networks, fixed-frequency receivers, and FM-only networks all contravene the spirit of the ITU Convention, the UN Universal Declaration of Human Rights, the CSCE Helsinki accords, and many other lofty international agreements lionizing the exchange of news and views between countries. Yet restrictions of this sort remain within the limits of what are viewed as acceptable, sovereign controls over domestic telecommunications. No country has ever been censured by the ITU for restricting the access of its citizenry to telecommunications services.

The ITU can therefore only involve itself in a deliberate harmful interference dispute when attempts to restrict incoming signals affect other countries' use of the radio frequency spectrum. Jamming of HF shortwave broadcasting stations is the most lucid manifestation of spectrum abuse, and the easiest to censure—although far from the easiest to control. But the clarity of the HF jamming problem does not exist when observing other restrictions to international telecommunications. Will the ITU be so ready to censure Third World restrictions to transborder data flows? International DBS-TV services are already subject to the ITU-sanctioned doctrine of prior consent and the "Jammer's Charter." If an international DBS broadcaster contravenes one of these principles and is subject to retaliatory jamming, how will the ITU respond? Would this "legitimate" jamming damage ITU attempts to stop "illegitimate" HF radio jamming?

From the beginnings of deliberate radio interference in the 1930s recurrent statements, charters, resolutions, and regulations have condemned jamming as morally wrong and antithetical to peaceful cooperation in international relations. Jamming contravenes specific ITU Convention articles and Radio Regulations. It leads to irrational spectrum use and impedes the free flow of information. Moreover, jamming has proven astronomically expensive. It costs five times as much to jam a broadcast as to transmit one. Countries that jam must employ complex networks of monitors and jamming transmitters. The Soviet jamming network, for example, is a technical marvel which, ironically, is largely ineffectual.

Listeners to HF broadcasts in the Western bloc countries are to a great extent limited to expatriates, travellers, newshounds, and radio hobbyists. In the Eastern bloc, despite the jammers, all indications suggest an immense and varied audience for HF broadcasts from the West. Soviet studies estimate the following percentages of segments of their population tune in to Western HF broadcasts in Russian: 56.6% of "workers," 49.3% of farmers, 72.4% of engineers and technicians, and

74.9% of students.[96] Audience research studies conducted by Radio Free Europe–Radio Liberty proposed the following percentages of radio listeners in Eastern Europe tune in to Western radio broadcasts: 78% of Czechoslovakians, 71% of Hungarians, 89% of Poles, 84% of Romanians, and 73% of Bulgarians.[97]

It would therefore appear that jamming is an ineffective, self-defeating exercise which only serves to encourage listeners to try that much harder to listen to the forbidden message. One suspects that if the Soviet authorities did not take Radio Free Europe/Radio Liberty quite so seriously neither would many Soviet listeners. The realization that jamming was not dissuading most would-be listeners led several countries in Eastern Europe to scrap jamming as early as the mid-1950s, and has led PR China to take an increasingly half-hearted approach to the jamming of Moscow, Hanoi, and Taipei. In the Soviet Union, too, jamming is rapidly losing its credibility as a consequence of the Gorbachev "Glasnost" policy, which encourages a more open, communicative relationship with the West.

If the method is so costly, ineffective, and internationally unacceptable, why do the Soviets continue to jam? The answer must be viewed within the context of Soviet attitudes toward the management of information and the place of the USSR within the world of international broadcasting.

The Soviet attitude toward the exchange of news and information has never seemed acceptable to Westerners. But the thought of competing and contradictory ideas being promoted by the media is equally unacceptable—and is indeed somewhat terrifying—to the centralized structure of the Soviet planning bureaucracy and is inimical to the singular ideology of the Soviet state. Wolfgang Kleinwachter asserts that "to exercise the right of free speech under socialism will be basically different from exercising it under capitalism . . . [based upon] the thesis of Karl Marx and Friedrich Engels, that under capitalism the ideas of the ruling class are the ruling ideas in any epoch. . . . As Lenin wrote, ' . . . freedom of the press as defined by the capitalist class is the freedom for the rich to bribe the press and the freedom to use wealth for fabricating and distorting so-called public opinion'."[98]

The reception of foreign radio signals, like the importation of books, the freedom to travel, the availability of direct international telephone dialing, and access to personal computers, harbors the potential to create a pluralism of dissonant ideas, some of which would inevitably challenge the position of the state. Political pluralism is unacceptable to the USSR, as the structure of Soviet power is dependent on the ability to make unchallenged decisions and act without constraint:

Since 1917 the Soviet Union has had to struggle against far greater odds than any Western country—this includes the self-inflicted wounds of the Stalinist excesses. But whatever the arguments, the basis of Soviet thinking on the subject remains the same. To them hostile propaganda is far more of a threat than it is to the prosperous West whose techniques of government and propaganda depend at least on the illusion of having a balance of multiple opposing forces. To the West, allowing foreign propaganda to function . . . is part of the fundamental political credo. To the countries between Berlin and Vladivostock the very opposite is true. What to one is an affirmation of a human right, to the other is an irresponsible invitation to chaos.[99]

Jamming will never completely cease. The USSR will continue to jam, no matter how cordial East-West relations become. For fifty years jamming has been the only viable means of blocking out foreign broadcasts which, if allowed in, could jeopardize the security and well-being of the Soviet state and constitute "the very recipe for setting back all the progress made so far."[100] An element of Russian xenophobia must also be considered. When this is combined with an ideology inimical to information exchanges, the result is an inability and unwillingness to give up that protective barrier, no matter how flawed and permeable that barrier may be.[101]

International broadcasting nevertheless has a far reaching importance to the USSR. While Radio Moscow and the other Soviet external services together constitute the world's largest international broadcasting organization, the influence of these extensive services—including 24 hour world services in English and French—is not significant. The West does not jam because it does not need to jam. Third World concerns about international broadcasting focus on the influence of the old metropoles or the United States. Radio Moscow, while easily received anywhere on the planet, is simply not that popular to Third World listeners, no matter how modern, upbeat, and jovial it attempts to be.[102]

But the BBC, Voice of America, and Radio Liberty have an important impact on the USSR. Soviet admissions of "negative" events—such as the shooting down of the Korean airliner in 1984 or the Chernobyl nuclear disaster in 1986—are often the result of domestic pressure generated by large numbers of listeners hearing disturbing news over the airwaves. The Western stations are viewed by Soviet authorities as maliciously anti-Soviet and subversive.[103] In fact, it must be admitted that there is an element of truth to this allegation, particularly when discussing some of the private religious broadcasters or the editorially independent Radio Liberty. Even the Voice of America and the BBC have run into difficulties curbing the anti-Communist biases and prejudicial excesses of their émigré Russian-language service staff. This, of course, fuels Soviet recalcitrance.

The LDCs have reserved the right to deliberately interfere with incoming information flows should those flows imperil their sovereignty or threaten indigenous culture. The Eastern bloc will continue to likewise reserve the right to guard against what it sees as aggressive or subversive misuse of the airwaves. While the two positions are over-simplified by the above stark statements, they do lead to one conclusion. Jamming and other forms of deliberate interference, no matter how antithetical to the spirit and word of the ITU or lofty free flow principles, will continue to exist and may, as information exchanges increase, multiply in form, severity, and technological complexity.

The ITU, and indeed any other international organization reliant upon cooperation, is helpless to actively change this situation. Censuring the USSR and other jamming countries at the 1987 HF-WARC Second Session and in the ITU Administrative Council has nevertheless illustrated the ITU's resolve to confront any member that violates the Radio Regulations, no matter how influential that member is within the Union. The ITU's past reluctance to actively involve itself has contributed to the current seriousness of the situation. The ITU could, through pressure and censure, conceivably effect a decline in the overall level of HF jamming.

To the extent that a decline in jamming has occurred, credit must be given to the gradual thawing of US-Soviet relations that has taken place since Mikhail Gorbachev's accession to power. But the spectre of LDCs and the East jamming or blocking DBS-TV signals leaves the ITU in a thorny and uncomfortable quandry. The ITU must condemn those violations of the free flow principle which contravene the Radio Regulations and/or the ITU International Telecommunication Convention. At the same time, however, the ITU must silently accept—however uncomfortable that may be—the option of legitimate DBS jamming against countries violating the principles of limiting spillover and prior consent to broadcast.

The precedence of sovereignty led observers to question the ability—or will—of the IFRB to "name names" at the 1987 Second Session of the HF-WARC. As a technical body, the IFRB and the ITU are not comfortable with censuring jamming on HF while permitting it on DBS satellite bands. The IFRB has nevertheless taken the courageous step of identifying the sources of jamming and notifying the administrations concerned that they could expect censure at Second Session. Sure enough, the Soviet Union, Poland, and Czechoslovakia were "called on the carpet" at the Conference for violations of the Convention and Radio Regulations.[104] Arguments that DBS-TV will have greater societal impact or that television plays a vital domestic cultural role rest uncomfortably with ITU technicians who prefer to apply engineering principles. By only censuring HF jammers, the IFRB would appear—to itself—to be applying a technical double standard.

Despite increased international attention, jamming and other means of deliberate interference, including those sanctioned by the New World Information Order, will continue to be the issues most likely to call into question the credibility and effectiveness of the ITU, as the sole global organization existing to facilitate international telecommunications is confronted by an increasing number of members who fear the implication of that objective.

Notes

1. Recommendation No. 1 declares "that Members of the Union facilitate the unrestricted transmission of news by telecommunications services," *International Telecommunication Convention (Nairobi, 1982)* (Geneva: ITU, 1982), p. 342.

2. Ibid., p. 3.

3. For most of World War II the BBC German-language services could estimate an audience of about one million listeners. Toward the end of the war, from 1944 on, this figure climbed to between 10 and 15 million listeners. Fouad Benhalla, *La Guerre Radiophonique* (Paris: Collection de la RPP, 1983), p. 63.

4. These systems often worked through both home receivers and public loudspeakers. A few years ago such loudspeakers were omnipresent in PR China, usually relaying the Beijing home service across fields, in villages and town squares, in city parks, and on railway trains.

5. Julian Hale, *Radio Power: Propaganda and International Broadcasting* (London: Paul Elek Ltd, 1975), p. 128.

6. Interviews.

7. In Rhodesia, all "African" services were transferred to FM and cheap FM-only receivers were promoted by the government, accompanied by a publicity campaign extolling the merits of FM sound quality and criticizing static-ridden unmodern shortwave (HF) radio. To ensure success, FM-only receivers were made exempt from the annual radio receiver license fee. But by the late 1970s, even Rhodesian Broadcasting Corporation (RBC) personnel admitted that the majority of listeners preferred tuning in the "static-ridden" clandestine ZANU and ZAPU rebel broadcasts from Zambia and Mozambique. See Julie Frederikse, *None But Ourselves* (Johannesburg: Ravan Press, 1982), pp. 96–99.

8. Abshire in Dante B. Fascell, ed., *International News: Freedom Under Attack* (Beverly Hills: Sage Publications, 1975).

9. Benhalla, op. cit., 1983, p. 131.

10. This transmitter has never been reactivated. Frederikse, op. cit., 1982, p. 97.

11. Stanley Leinwoll, "Jamming: Past, Present and Future," in Jens Frost, ed., *World Radio TV Handbook 1980* (Hvidovre: Billboard AG, 1980), p. 40.

12. Ibid.

13. In Region 2, the 7 mHz band (also known as the 41 meter band) is allocated to radio amateurs. See ITU, *Administative Council, 38th Session, Submission by the United States of America, 13 February 1984* (Geneva: ITU Administrative Council, 1984), Document No. 6036 (Rev. 1) CA38–139., p. 4.

14. C. Edwardes, *WARC '84* (London: European DX Council Annual Conference, 1983), p. 4.

15. Hale, op. cit., 1975, p. 132.

16. Ranjan Borra, "The Problem of Jamming in International Broadcasting," *Journal of Broadcasting* 11:4 (Fall 1967), p. 360.

17. See Fascell, ed., op. cit., 1975, p. 63; Hale, op. cit., 1975, p. 133; Leinwoll, loc. cit., 1980, p. 40.

18. M. Sowers, et al., *Monitoring of Harmful Interference to the HF Broadcasting Service: The Results of the October 1984 and March/April 1985 Coordinated Monitoring Periods* (Washington, D.C.: National Telecommunications and Information Administration (NTIA), US Departmenmt of Commerce, 1985), p. 56.

19. Estimates, being just that, may greatly vary. United States government estimates are usually submitted by the Voice of America, the United States Information Agency (USIA), or the Bureau of International Broadcasting, each of which may have a vested interest in dramatizing the problem, particularly at budget time. The most accurate estimates are likely to come from IFRB monitoring results or technical studies such as the NTIA report cited in the above footnote.

20. Hale, op. cit., 1975, p. 133.

21. G. Stirling, "Babel On the Air," *The Geographical Magazine* (Autumn 1985), p. 380.

22. Hale, op. cit., 1975, p. 127.

23. Sig Mickelson, *America's Other Voice* (New York: Praeger Publishers, 1983), p. 206.

24. Abshire in Fascell, ed., op. cit., 1975, p. 62.

25. Mickelson, op. cit., 1983, p. 205.

26. Moscow's Radio Mayak is described as "a musical service intended for all-Union coverage featuring all kinds of music. This service is on the air continuously." Jens Frost, ed., *World Radio TV Handbook 1985* (Hvidovre: Billboard AG, 1985), p. 140.

27. Leinwoll, loc. cit., 1980, p. 40.

28. Leinwoll, loc. cit., 1980, p. 38. Also see Hale, op. cit., 1975, p. 136.

29. Borra, loc. cit., 1967, p. 356.

30. Hale, op. cit., 1975, p. 136.

31. Jamming during the 1930s was not always a technological success. Hale cites one occasion in 1938 of a Soviet attempt to jam Hitler's Deutschlandsender: "While engineers monitoring in London thought the effect very successful, a Russian psychologist, who was unaware of his country's part in it, hailed the combination of brooding thunder in the background with the vivid cries of Hitler and his followers as one of Goebbels' masterpieces in mass terrorization. . . ." Hale, op. cit., 1975, p. 128.

32. George A. Codding, Jr., *Broadcasting Without Barriers* (Paris: UNESCO, 1959), p. 74.

33. The policy of the BBC was put succinctly in 1940: "Jamming is really an admission of a bad cause. The jammer has a bad conscience. . . . He is afraid of the influence of the truth. . . . We have no such fears, and to jam broadcasts in English by the enemy might even be bad propaganda." Hale, op. cit., 1975, p. 137.

34. George A. Codding, Jr., *The International Telecommunication Union: An Experiment in International Cooperation* (New York: Arno Press, 1972), p. 323.

35. ITU, *International Telecommunication Convention (Atlantic City, 1947)* (Geneva: ITU, 1947), p. 29.

36. Leinwoll, loc. cit., 1980, p. 38.

37. Borra, loc. cit., 1967, p. 358.

38. Donald R. Browne, *International Radio Broadcasting: The Limits of the Limitless Medium* (New York: Praeger Publishers, 1982), p. 24.

39. Codding, op. cit., 1959, p. 33.

40. Interview.

41. Borra, loc. cit., 1967, p. 358.; Hale, op. cit., 1975, p. 137.; Leinwoll, loc. cit., 1980, p. 40.

42. Borra, loc. cit., 1967, p. 359.

43. Browne, op. cit., 1982, p. 24.

44. Borra, loc. cit., 1967, p. 359.

45. Ibid.

46. Abshire in Fascell, ed., op. cit., 1975, p. 64.

47. Browne, op. cit., 1982, p. 24.

48. Borra, loc. cit., 1967, p. 359.

49. Soviet jamming of the US government-financed Radio Liberty, companion station to Radio Free Europe, has never ceased.

50. Statement by Polish delegate in Hale, op. cit., 1975, p. 139.

51. Ibid.

52. David M. Leive, *International Telecommunications and International Law: The Regulation of the Radio Spectrum* (Dobbs Ferry, NY: Oceana Publishing, 1970), p. 132.

53. Borra, loc. cit., 1967, p. 360.

54. Hale, op. cit., 1975, p. 133.

55. Borra, loc. cit., 1967, p. 360.

56. Ibid.

57. Ibid., p. 363.

58. Hale, op. cit., 1975, p. 137.

59. Ibid.

60. Borra, loc. cit., 1967, p. 360.

61. These concerns and their somewhat ignominious manifestations are chronicled in Howard H. Frederick, *Cuban American Radio Wars* (Norwood, NJ: Ablex Publishing, 1986).

62. For this reason the GDR never seriously attempted to jam broadcasts from the Federal Republic or from West Berlin (although reception of these broadcasts was nominally illegal until 1961). While other European Warsaw Pact countries are not as inundated with foreign broadcasts as the GDR, the percentage

of listeners tuning in the West remains far higher in Eastern Europe than in the Soviet Union. Mickelson, op. cit., 1983, p. 210.

63. This school of thought is reflected in W. Klienwachter, K. Nordenstreng and E.G. Manet, *New International Information and Communication Order Sourcebook* (Prague: International Organization of Journalists, 1986).

64. This may illustrate a slight hypocrisy and paternalism on the part of Third World elites. Evidence suggests that elites in many developing countries, including senior government personnel, rely on foreign HF shortwave broadcasts, particularly the BBC World Service, for information and news—often including news of developments in their own country.

65. Browne, op. cit., 1982, p. 24.

66. G. Wettig, *Broadcasting and Detente: Eastern Policies and Their Implications for East-West Relations* (New York: St Martin's Press, 1977), p. 13.

67. Ibid.

68. E.D. DuCharme, M.J.R. Irwin and R. Zeitoun, "Direct Broadcasting by Satellite: The Development of the International Technical and Administrative Regulatory Regime," *Annals of Air and Space Law* (Vol. 9, 1984), p. 270.

69. Interview. This could be a desirable development. The 1977 DBS assignment plan devised for Regions 1 and 3, and to a lesser extent the 1983 Plan for Region 2, organize national "footprints" based upon the reception qualities of a one meter diameter receiving dish. Plans to restrict the availability of larger dishes in order to make the plan work quickly became unpopular in Western Europe, as part of the attraction of the technology is the ability to receive international signals.

70. Commission of the European Communities, *Television Without Frontiers: Green Paper on the Establishment of the Common Market for Broadcasting, Especially by Satellite and Cable* (Brussels: Commission of the European Communities, 1984). For developments since 1984, see the European Television Task Force, *Europe 2000: What Kind of Television* (Manchester: European Institute for the Media Monograph Series, 1988) and the Television Fiction in Europe Project Team, *Stories Come First: Television Fiction in Europe* (London: International Institute of Communications, 1988).

71. E. Gard, "Radiodiffusion directe: Satellite Hors Orbite," *L'Hebdo (Lausanne)* (July 25, 1985).

72. Wettig, op. cit.. 1977, p. 57.

73. Ibid.

74. Ibid., p. 60.

75. Browne, op. cit., 1982, p. 25.

76. Ibid.

77. Hale, op. cit., 1975, p. 138.

78. Wettig, op. cit., 1977, p. 60.

79. ITU, *International Telecommunications Convention (Malaga—Torremolinos, 1973)* (Geneva: ITU, 1973), p. 251.

80. Wettig, op. cit., 1977, p. 60.

81. Ibid., p. 76.

82. Ibid.

83. Ibid., p. 77.

84. Thomas McPhail, *Electronic Colonialism* (Beverly Hills: Sage Publications, 1981), p. 94.

85. Racine Sy, "For A New World Information Order," *EBU Review* 34:6 (November 1983), p. 26.

86. Ibid.

87. Ibid., p. 27.

88. McPhail, op. cit., 1981, p. 97.

89. Hale, op. cit., 1975, p. 137.

90. ITU, *International Telecommunication Convention (Nairobi, 1982)* (Geneva: ITU, 1982), p. 342.

91. Francis S. Ronalds, "Voices of America," *Foreign Policy* (Spring 1979), p. 159.

92. The United States did make a protocol statement at WARC 1979 "calling attention to the fact that some of its broadcasting in the high frequency bands allocated to the broadcasting service are subject to willful, harmful interference by administrations that are signatory to these Final Acts, and that such interference is incompatible with the rational and equitable use of these bands. . . . [The United States] reserves the right . . . to take necessary and appropriate actions to protect its broadcasting interests. . . ." Neither the Soviet Union nor any other country known to jam American broadcasts responded to the statement. See Office of Technology Assessment, United States Congress, *Radiofrequency Use and Management: Impacts From the World Administrative Radio Conference of 1979* (Washington, D.C.: US Congress, Office of Technology Assessment, 1982), p. 80.

93. Emphasis added. ITU, *Report to the Second Session of the Conference, World Administrative Radio Conference for the Planning of the HF Bands Allocated to the Broadcasting Service, First Session, Geneva, 1984* (Geneva: ITU, 1984), p. 88.

94. ITU, *World Administrative Radio Conference for the Planning of the HF Bands Allocated to the Broadcasting Service, First Session, Geneva, 1984* (Geneva: ITU, 1984), Documents 9 (18 December 1986), 26 (23 January 1987).

95. Sowers, et al., op. cit., 1985, p. 99.

96. Benhalla, op. cit., 1983, p. 129.

97. East European Area Audience and Opinion Research, *Listening to Western Radio in Eastern Europe: 1985–Early 1986* (Washington, D.C.: Radio Free Europe–Radio Liberty, 1986), pp. 3, 9, 15, 21, 26.

98. Kleinwachter, Nordenstrng and Manet, op. cit., 1986, p. 79.

99. Hale, op. cit., 1975, p. 140.

100. Ibid.

101. Rex Malik, "Can the Soviet Union Survive Information Technology?" *Intermedia* 12:3 (May 1984), p. 15.

102. Graham Mytton, "Audience Research for International Broadcasting," *Intermedia* 14:2 (March 1986), p. 37.

103. Gennady Alov and Vassily Viktorov, *Aggressive Broadcasting: Evidence, Facts and Documents* (Moscow: Novosti Press Agency Publishing House, 1985).

104. Broadcasting. "Shortwave WARC: Limited Victories for US Delegates," *Broadcasting* (March 16, 1987), p. 82.

4

The Establishment
of Technical Standards in
International Telecommunications

The primary "good" provided by the ITU is the facilitating of international telecommunications. This is achieved through the cooperation of administrations, harmonization of plans, and the standardization of the technical means of transmission. Standard-setting provides a role for the ITU that is unlike frequency registration or control of deliberate interference. Standard-setting is a process more directly related to the nature, size, degree of efficiency, and modernity present in domestic telecommunications industries. Global standardization of telecommunications equipment and the means of delivering telecommunications services "ensures continuity of technique and service, cuts manufacturing costs with benefits for the customer, and provides telecommunication authorities with ensured internationally compatible equipment. [This is important] as adaptation of equipment to a multitude of techniques, rather than using one world standard, can be expensive and wasteful of resources."[1] In other words, standardization provides an integral part of the greater ITU objective "to promote actively the worldwide development of telecommunication techniques and to assist by its actions in the ever-advancing integration of human communication media."[2]

The ITU is the sole supranational body legally empowered to regulate international telecommunications. Within the ITU the consultative committees for radio communications (CCIR) and wired communications (CCITT) are the two agencies authorized to advise telecommunications administrations on telecommunications technical standards through the issuing of recommendations. These recommendations are often of a highly narrow, technical nature. The criteria employed by the CCIs in selecting a recommended standard combine optimal technical efficiency with cost-effectiveness of manufacture. CCI recommendations are only that: legally binding standards can only be set domestically by national standard-setting agencies (e.g., Canadian Standards Association [CSA], American National Standards Institute [ANSI], Deutsche Industrie Normen [DIN], etc.).

Efforts to strengthen CCI Recommendations by giving them the power of international law might be seen as one way of promoting international standardization. This would be a mistaken perception. Most CCI Recommendations are either first submitted by one of the national administrations, each of which coordinates research and development at the domestic level, or are adopted *ex post facto* by the national standard-setting body. Some countries do, in fact, adopt CCI Recommendations as national legislation as a matter of course.[3] As most CCI decisions have great effect on domestic telecommunications services and equipment procurement, it would be unacceptable to even the most diminutive ITU member to relinquish national standard-setting discretion to the international CCI level if the international process was anything stronger than recommendatory.

The CCIR studies "technical and operating questions relating specifically to radio communication. . . ."[4] These questions are selected by either the Plenipotentiary Conferences or the CCI Plenary Assemblies. An elaborate infrastructure of Working Parties, study groups and committees exist to "facilitate coordinated development of international telecommunication services."[5] Not surprisingly, the sheer volume of technical development in recent decades, the dominance of a very few countries in this development, and the economic implications of many CCI Recommendations make the fulfilment of the CCIs' mandate an enormously difficult task.

Several problems now confront international standards organizations. For the CCIs, focusing on world telecommunications development, the "age of information" which commenced in the 1970s merely exacerbated what was already becoming an overworked order. The complexity of CCI structure (see chart) and the magnitude of the committees' task leads to a languid decision-making process which may take anywhere from 18 months to eight years. The process entails work in study groups, research on the part of the Union, correspondence with the applicants, correspondence with any other relevant international standard-setting organizations, and meetings in plenary assemblies. Every four years the sum of all decisions made is published in a series of volumes, the CCITT Yellow Book and the CCIR Red Book (as they were called in 1985; the colors change with each revision). Each of these "books" comprises several volumes totalling about 6000 pages.

Since 1973 the ITU has compelled the publishing division of the General Secretariat to be self-supporting.[6] At the 1973 Plenipotentiary, Canada proposed a resolution to achieve this goal. Several observers have pointed out that this step was not made to penalize the Third World or hinder telecommunications development, but to put an end to rumors that the General Secretariat was using the publishing division budget to conceal a variety of fairly irrelevant expenses. By making the division self-supporting, the ITU could be seen to be making itself both more fiscally accountable and more "efficient."[7] Consequently, the CCITT Yellow Book sold in 1985 for nearly SFr 1700.[8] LDCs in particular and even smaller organizations in the developed countries, such as university libraries, often cannot afford to spend that kind of money on books that must be replaced every four or five years. Since only a small number of developed country telecommunications administrations can afford to purchase these volumes, sales of the books remain limited, which in turn ensures the publishing costs and prices charged will remain high. Moreover, the sheer volume of recommendations issued in the volumes demands detailed and professional consideration. Often LDCs lack the highly trained personnel required to interpret the CCI books.

The seemingly minor point of CCI publication costs illustrates the much greater conflict within the CCIs between North and South, or the developed and developing members. This has been and will continue to be the central area of concern within the CCIs. CCI members consist of not only government telecommunications administrations, but also recognized private operating agencies (RPOAs), scientific and other international organizations, and other standard-setting organizations. CCI delegations are comprised of governmental—RPOA—other agency "teams." For example, at the 1979 CCIR Plenary Assembly only 36 countries from the Third World out of a possible 117 were represented. Conversely, the US sent 16 delegates, Canada sent 14, and Japan fielded 65 delegates.[9] The situation is slightly better in the CCITT but remains inadequate from the Third World perspective and a serious concern to all those involved in CCI affairs.

The paramount concern of developing countries within the CCIs is that the standardization process will bypass their interests entirely and widen the already vast technology gap between North and South by recommending standards that require major investment or advanced telecommunications infrastructures. This places the CCIs in a Catch-22: any "standard" must promote the most advanced, efficient, innovative state of the technology and reflect the needs of the major telecommunications users. Yet the CCIs also wish to actively promote developing country access to worldwide telecommunications services, which for many countries exist only at the most tenuous level. Only a handful of developing countries have any CCI representation. These tend to be the newly industrializing countries (NICs) such as Malaysia, South Korea, or Brazil. These countries are increasingly significant to the CCIs. But the majority of developing countries lack substantial technical presence and seem to now believe that the only way they will be able to enhance their role in the CCIs is through becoming actively involved in the political process of CCI activity and administration.

It is difficult to envisage how purely political reforms might aid and address developing country concerns without damaging the professionalism and high technical esteem enjoyed by the CCIs. An example of the precarious value of reform is the decision at the 1982 Plenipotentiary Conference to allow the Plenipotentiary, and not the CCI Plenary, to elect CCI directors. Delegates from the United States, along with those of many developed countries, expressed grave concerns that this reform would lead to the appointment of "politicized" CCI directors who would disregard engineering principles and technical efficiency in favor of placating Third World political interests.[10] At worst, it is feared that new, post-1989 CCI Directors, heretofore always persons of substantial technical expertise, will be "politicos" from the more radical developing countries who could damage CCI credibility and, hence, endanger the standardization process.

More could be done to make CCI publications and technical expertise available to LDCs, and to generally improve the interaction between the CCIs and the Third World, but this would invariably entail some sort of increased financial commitment on the part of the developed countries. This is clearly out of the question. In fact, most countries are fully committed to a strict zero-growth budget for all ITU activity. This makes it increasingly difficult for the CCIs or other branches of the ITU to promote activity on their own accord. It may, however, also serve to compel the ITU to get individual affluent member countries and recognized private operating agencies (RPOAs) within these countries to do more to consider Third World needs in their own standardization process. Recommended standards could, to a greater extent than now takes place, consider the financial limitations existing in most LDCs where the replacement of existing obsolete equipment with new, invariably imported CCI approved equipment can be (and usually is) prohibitively expensive.

A further difficulty, not related to the North-South conflict, which has arisen as a consequence of the convergence of telecommunications technology with data processing technology—e.g., through the interconnection of data networks—is the question of jurisdiction over a proposed standard. There are several international standards organizations, such as the International Standards Organization (ISO) and the International Electrotechnical Commission (IEC), as well as international organizations that set specific standards within their bailiwick, such as the International Civil Aviation Organization (ICOA—aviation radio use safety standards) or the Universal Postal Union (UPU—transfer of electronic mail standards). Problems arise as these different organizations come to address concepts of computer data transmission technology which lack clear jurisdiction. Several organizations have differing definitions for key terms such as telecommunications and software. In the attempt to propose standards for the Integrated Services Digital Network concept (ISDN) through CCITT Study Group XVIII, difficulties arose over the existence of overlapping ISO, IEC, and CCITT Study Groups. An eventual resolution of the overlapping jurisdiction problem occurred through largely informal discussion, but the anticipation of future disputes served as a catalyst for the formalizing of a CCITT-ISO/IEC collaboration framework through Resolution Seven of the 1984 Malaga-Torremolinos CCITT Plenary.

The relationship between the CCIs and these complementary standards organizations is not always unconditionally cordial. The ISO and IEC are voluntary-membership organizations consisting of the national standard-setting bodies and RPOAs. Third World involvement in these two organizations is minimal. Yet these organizations issue standards on everything from paper clips to hydroelectric turbines to computer terminals, including much telecommunications equipment which is also seen as being under CCI jurisdiction. Difficulties arise as the CCIs and ISO/IEC have maintained markedly different processes of standardization and in fact have not yet agreed upon a common definition of the word "telecommunications."[11] Particularly in newer technologies such as ISDN or videotex where it becomes difficult and indeed a matter of controversy to discern whether a new development is a "service," a "concept," or a "device," the issue of which organization's bailiwick the new technology falls into becomes nightmarish.

The CCIs have also sought to formalize working arrangements with "voting regional groups" such as Europe's CEPT (European Conference of Post and Telecommunication Administrations). The CEPT telecommunications committee consists of 26 European administrations which seek to coordinate and harmonize regional telecommunications policy. CEPT "standards" may come about through a combination or ratification of existing European national systems. Regional groups become significant in a one-nation, one-vote structure such as the ITU as they will often pre-coordinate their position and vote *en bloc* at a CCI Plenary Meeting.[12] In addition, international user groups such as INTUG (International Telecommunication User Group) are becoming increasingly important in the development of international technical standards. Because of their non-governmental nature and broad, multinational corporate membership, these groups pursue a global approach to standardization which seeks to foster compatibility in policies, services, and equipment in a way "best suited to user needs at prices attractive to the user."[13] Considerations of cost and quality of service may therefore take priority over technological innovation in the formation of an INTUG standard recommendation. INTUG enjoys close, chiefly informal cooperative ties with the ITU.

But the CCITT and INTUG met for formal discussions for the first time at an ITU-organized meeting in October 1984.[14] Some divergence in approach between the CCITT and the user organizations surfaced at a 1985 "Usercom" Conference in Munich. Major users complained that within standard-setting bodies such as the CCITT, telecommunications engineers and technicians tended to favor highly advanced technologies and systems at the expense of practical world communications. Users "want the Land Rover, not the Mercedes of technologies," as one observer stated.[15] The position of the major user is thus remarkably similar to that of most developing countries where, to stretch a metaphor, only a Land Rover will work.

To explain how these curiously structured consultative committees became a federal component of the ITU, and not a function of the ISO or IEC, requires a brief review of the history of telecommunications standard-setting. The CCIs can only be understood in light of the technical and administrative developments that comprise their part.

Telecommunications Standard-Setting Prior to 1925

Compatibility in telecommunications standards has been an integral part of international telecommunications activity since the first international telegraph signals were dispatched in the 1850s. Prior to the establishment of the ITU in 1865 the scope for differing telegraphy standards was limited by the primitive state of the technology: there could, in effect, only be one kind of wired telegraph. International standardization problems were less technical and more concerned with rate structures and languages to be employed.[16]

This continued to be the case for many years after the foundation of the ITU in 1865. In fact, wired telegraphy posed few technical standardization problems during the era of its supremacy. The physical linkage of national systems in Europe was easily achieved, and just as easily cut in wartime. In North America, private American companies formed telegraph networks cutting across the Canadian and Mexican frontiers, forming a de facto single network.

As telephony developed in the late years of the nineteenth century, technical standards began to differ from country to country as national networks and domestic sources of equipment developed. The most notable and predictable differences emerged between the private American Telephone and Telegraph (AT&T) Bell System of North America and the government–post office administered telephone systems of Europe, which in turn began to differ from one another as each country sought to ensure the well-being of its incipient domestic equipment manufacturers. Virtually every country possessing a telephone system felt the need to produce all of its own technical equipment in order to build up a domestic industry and minimize vulnerability to outside influence in an area as important as basic communications. Many countries continue to retain this view of telecommunications autarky, no matter how economically inefficient such "industries" may be.

While telephony remained chiefly a domestic telecommunications issue until the 1920s due to minimal interconnection between countries and a negligible exchange of telephone equipment, the emergence of radio in the 1890s posed a new set of international standardization questions. The new technology was first employed for maritime radiotelegraph communications, and quickly proved to be a great aid to safety at sea. The development of the medium had been dominated by one large firm, Marconi, which discouraged the inter-governmental ITU from involving itself in the new technology, despite the obvious complementarity and commonality between wired telegraphs and radiotelegraphs (see Chapter 1 above). International radiotelegraphs, at least in the early years, thus operated in a largely unregulated environment.

Early radio standards were set in a de facto manner by the radiotelegraph leader and virtual monopolist in the world radio equipment market, the Marconi Company. Marconi exerted strong control over both development of radio communications equipment and determining how that equipment would be employed. Potential competitors in Germany and the United States were not pleased with the rise of this Anglo-Italian monopoly. The German Administration, exasperated at the lack of international action, convened a nine nation Preliminary International Radio Conference in Berlin in 1903 to establish an International Radiocommunications Union on ITU lines. In attempting to draft a protocol the German delegation sought to combat what was seen as the latest abuse by the Marconi giant: discrimination of interconnection. This phrase described a policy dictated by the Marconi Company to maritime users of its equipment which forbade them to communicate with other ships or land stations not employing Marconi equipment. The Marconi argument, advocated by the British and Italian administrations, insisted that the Marconi technical standard was far more efficient and the Marconi Company was merely facilitating implementation of the best technology on a worldwide basis. In fact, this discrimination was endangering maritime safety.

The Final Protocol of the 1903 Conference obliged signatories' coast stations to "be bound to receive and transmit telegrams originating from or destined for ships at sea without distinction as to the systems of radio used by the latter."[17] This resolution was reiterated at the Berlin Radio Conference of 1906, which drafted a Convention and Radio Regulations establishing periodic Radio Conferences as a complement to the ITU (see Chapter 1 above). Until the founding of the CCIR, the Radio Regulations set and maintained all internationally recommended radio communication and frequency use standards. Such standards at this time related chiefly to radio service use, which languages would be employed, call signals, and station call letters, as well as various other universal rules of the road. To this extent the Radio Regulations continue to serve this standardization role. Such "standards" are outside the purview of today's CCIs.[18]

Throughout the early part of the twentieth century, standards concerning telecommunications equipment remained uncoordinated between countries, particularly in telephony. Any international standardization that did take place was achieved through common equipment suppliers or through common ownership. For example, telephones in Canada were first established as an extension of the American AT&T Bell System, thus achieving de facto North American telephone standards. But no deliberate attempts were made at creating united international technical standards or even at coordinating independent telephone networks.

Part of the problem, of course, rested with the primitive state of telephone technology. Telephones remained the telegraph's poor relation well into the early part of the twentieth century. As national telephone networks in Europe expanded, however, technology progressed rapidly and the need to cross international frontiers arose. The different choices made earlier by different countries resulted in a plethora of incompatible national standards which did little to facilitate interconnection.

The ITU had first established international telephone regulations at the 1885 Berlin Telephony Conference. These were expanded at subsequent conferences, leading to a fairly comprehensive set of regulations by the close of the 1903 London ITU Conference. At London the French delegation submitted proposals recognizing aspects of telephone regulation that were of a different nature than those governing international telegraphs. The acceptance of these proposals illustrated the importance of the new technology and the ITU's recognition of this importance. France, along with Hungary, also took the opportunity offered by the London Conference to suggest the implementation of regular meetings between the engineers and specialists of various member countries. The model for such discussion was a national US conference held periodically to bring together specialists from the many private American telephone companies. Such meetings at the international level were immediately opposed by most members, however, as it was believed such coordination could reduce the power and authority of their incipient national telephone administrations.[19] It was as yet too early for international telephony to be envisaged by the majority of either administrations or users.

A related danger involved the protected "infant" state of the telephone equipment industries of most ITU member countries. The nations of continental Europe feared British or American domination of equipment standards and they were dubious of any sort of cooperative international system that could hinder their ability to control the home markets. Different standards and minimal interconnection may have been costly and inefficient but were seen as the sole effective means of exercising domestic control over national telephone systems.

It was nevertheless from Europe that the first efforts at international telephony standardization came forward. At the behest of the Hungarian Administration, delegates from 14 European countries met in 1908 at the First Conference of Telegraph and Telephone Engineers. The Hungarian delegate expressed the lofty sentiment that "telegraphy and telephony know no political or national frontiers but serve the interests of all mankind, and we must concentrate our efforts to ensure that scientific progress is put to good use everywhere and, as far as possible, in the same way and at the same time."[20] Actual discussion of standardization at the Conference was in fact less than sensational, centering on the pros and cons of manual versus automatic telephone switching. No decisions were reached at the Conference, apart from an agreement to meet again in two years time.

The Second Conference of Telegraph and Telephone Engineers of 1910 was a larger affair, involving 22 European countries and the major telephone companies of the United States. Again, however, no decisions were made. These conferences, it must be recalled, were compelled to consider only the most general of principles due to the primitive state of international telephony at the time. Long distance telephony prior to World War I was accomplished through crude overhead circuits which could not even be weatherproofed. Underground cables were just beginning to be used over long distances and then only within domestic systems (the longest pre–World War I cable connection being the 378 km New York–Boston circuit).[21]

World War I led to the cessation of many European interconnections, but also led to dynamic growth in telephone technology. Standardization became a by-product of interconnection within the countries of the Allied and Axis powers. A standardized system was implemented allowing unhindered military telephone links between Allied General Headquarters at Chantilly, near Paris, and the Italian Army Headquarters at Turin. Likewise, a similar system connected Berlin and Vienna with Constantinople.[22] Progress achieved in America during the war, particularly in the establishment of a transcontinental overhead line between New York and San Francisco, was applied in late 1917 by the US Army Signal Corps for communications between American military installations in Europe. The improved technical systems employed by the Americans were soon adopted by the allied European Administrations. This was an era in which standardization was determined by high-profile technical developments pioneered by one dominant administration or company. The setting of standards was therefore easily accomplished without an international regulatory superstructure.

Two Recovery Conferences in 1920 and 1921 sought to re-establish telephone and telegraph connections severed during the war. It was recognized that certain technologies, such as radio and telephony, would enjoy unprecedented growth during the 1920s. The Recovery Conferences, however, satisfied themselves with the objective of restoring the pre-war status quo ante.

Less than one year later the President of the Institution of Electrical Engineers of Great Britain, Mr. Frank Gill, made a strong speech describing the velocity of growth and expansion taking place within the European international telephone service. He prescribed the establishment of a single cooperative European international telephone communications company which would be granted a monopoly and the full responsibility of operating a standardized, uniform European telephone network. Another option proposed by Mr. Gill was the establishment of a cooperative company which would be owned by government telecommunications administrations and operated on their behalf.[23] Remarkably similar to the Intelsat satellite consortium that was to emerge 42 years later, Mr. Gill's proposals were based on the promise that the international telephone system could and should be standardized as well as unified. In the United States the methods employed to install, maintain, and operate the national network were by this time standardized, despite the continued existence of many small telephone companies in often far-flung regions of the country. This standardization was in no small part due to the AT&T monopoly which, through sheer size, breadth, and economies of scale, became the world leader in telephone technology and development. To apply such standards in Europe appeared, technologically, to be the obvious solution. Yet it soon became evident that European states were reluctant—in fact intractably so—to realize what many administrations feared would be tantamount to a relinquishing of sovereignty over national communications.

But the goal of a single European telephone network was growing among technical experts who now saw such a development as both desirable and inevitable. In 1923 the French PTT called together delegates from Belgium, France, Italy, Spain, Great Britain, and Switzerland to form a Preparatory Technical Committee. This committee unanimously proposed what was to become the first ITU Consultative Committee. Delegates argued that "a single organ is required consisting of officials generally having a high rank in each of the administrations and familiar with technical and, so far as possible, administrative questions. . . ."[24]

Establishment and Evolution of the Consultative Committees

The International Consultative Committee on Long Distance Telephone (CCIF) achieved official status as a part of the ITU in September 1925, when the Paris ITU Conference decided to recognize and affiliate itself with the CCIF. Heretofore the CCIF had been a sort of private, provisional organization.[25] The Paris Conference also established the Telegraphy Consultative Committee (CCIT). The functions of these new components of the ITU were to promote uniform and efficient technical standards. From their inception the CCIs consisted of member administrations and telephone and telegraph operating agencies. The CCIs existed through periodic plenary assemblies and, between plenary meetings, ad hoc study groups. In 1926 CCI organization was rationalized and made more consonant with ITU structure, but its autonomy was recognized through the affirmation of a specialized CCI secretariat.[26]

The successful operation of the CCIF and CCIT for five years led the Washington Radio Conference to propose and establish a Consultative Committee on Radiocommunications (CCIR). Such a committee had originally been proposed by the unsuccessful Preliminary Conference on Electric Communications in 1920 (see Chapter 1) and had been agreed upon in principle. Curiously, seven years later those who had been the keenest proponents of such an organization, chiefly France, Britain, and the United States, now vociferously opposed establishment of the proposed CCIR.

The United States, by then the world technology leader but still averse toward what was seen as a highly Eurocentric club of imperious functionaries, feared a CCIR would create too rigid a regulatory order and hinder technical development. The justified concern that the CCIR would favor European interests could not have been absent from the minds of the American delegates. France feared that CCI approval could confer undue commercial advantage on certain private companies and national administrations. France was still annoyed at the moving of the committee from Paris to Geneva and believed that "internationalizing" the body would only diminish the power of France and impede the growth of a domestic telecommunications industry. Britain, arguing from a technical standpoint, stated that a radio CCI, if organized like its telephone and telegraph counterparts, would be useless as periodic meetings could not hope to keep up with the rapid developments in radio communications technology. Germany, still searching for any international forum in which to restore its legitimacy, and Italy, keen to defend the rights of the Marconi interests against rapidly growing competitors, emerged as the chief proponents of the CCIR, arguing that rapid developments in technology were in fact the chief reason why such a standardizing body was needed. In the end the CCIR was created at the Conference by a close vote.[27]

At the Madrid Conference of 1932 the CCIR, along with its parent radio conferences, were merged into the new International Telecommunication Union. The *modus operandi* of the three CCIs was standardized as much as possible to ensure the smooth operation of the committees. One of the most noteworthy technical achievements of this time was the overall standardization of the European telephone networks by the CCIF, which by 1939 allowed "any European subscriber . . . to speak to any other European subscriber with generally highly satisfactory conditions of audibility without having to wait on average more than 15 minutes for the connection."[28] While equipment and modes of operation still differed, often substantially, between European countries, this achievement in an era of declining political relations and increasing hostility spoke well of the ability of the CCIF to circumvent non-technical issues.

A skeleton staff kept the CCIs alive during World War II, but all constructive and substantive work ceased for the duration. Developments in technology did not cease during the war, of course, and the immediate postwar years saw the CCIs coping with the need to restore standardized services destroyed or hindered during the war as well as considering new telecommunications technologies such as radar, which were a product of the war effort. During World War II the American Forces employed their own military telephone system throughout Europe. This system was of the same specification as the US civil network.[29] This created a de facto upgrading of the ravaged European telephone network to the latest CCIF standard. The CCIF Plenary of 1945 was one of the first ITU activities to take place after the end of hostilities.

By the time of the 1947 Atlantic City Conference, the CCIs had enjoyed over two decades of nearly unbridled success. At the conference the record of the CCIs was lauded and the CCIF rated special mention by the Swiss delegate as being exemplary in its flexibility and usefulness. Perhaps the most important change to take place at Atlantic City regarding the ITU's role in standardizing international telecommunications was a change so subtle it passed virtually unnoticed at the time—and indeed for years afterward. This change consisted of amending the definition of the terms of reference of the CCIF from "relating to international telephony" to "relating to telephony."[30] This apparently trivial change was in fact indicative of the CCI plan for a single standard global network in which national and international systems would be technically indistinguishable. It also enabled the CCIF to aid and advise newly independent and developing countries in studies relating to establishing and maintaining domestic national networks.

The Buenos Aires Plenipotentiary Conference of 1952 and subsequent CCIF and CCIT Plenaries expressed the view that the separation of the telephone and telegraph committees was increasingly unnecessary. The CCIT was at first opposed to a merger of the two committees, perhaps sensing that telegraphy would be the weaker partner in a single committee. The CCIF, on the other hand, believed that "considering the increasing similarity between new techniques of telegraphy and telephony; that the international telegraph and telephone services are to an increasing extent using the same arteries: the merger of the CCIF and CCIT is in the interest of the ITU."[31]

In 1956 the CCIF and CCIT were merged to form the International Consultative Committee on Telephone and Telegraph (CCITT). The year was significant in that it was also the founding year of the first transatlantic telephone cable, TAT-1. This signified a new era in telephone by finally placing it on a worldwide footing. Prior to this point the CCIs had, despite an ever-widening membership, focused chiefly on the interconnection and standardization of European systems. This Eurocentrism began to wane rapidly after the structural changes made to the ITU system at the Atlantic City Conference in 1947. This was not as much due to any explicit changes made to the CCIs—the changes made to CCI structure at Atlantic City were minimal—but to the new worldwide scope of the ITU caused by its affiliation to the UN system and the "winds of change" which were increasing ITU membership at an unprecedented rate.

By 1959 the CCIR and CCITT viewed their role as that of studying technical, operating, and, in the CCITT's case, tariff questions relating to telegraphy, telephony, and radio communications. The objective of CCI study remained facilitation of international telecommunications through standardization of telecommunications equipment and delivery.

The Current ITU Standard-Setting Order

The CCIs do not issue formal standards but merely make considered recommendations regarding how to best facilitate international compatibility for new services and how to best improve compatibility for existing services. It is, for the most part, highly specialized, technical work. The

CCIR does this work for all wireless services including radio, television, microwave communication, and satellite communication. The CCITT issues recommendations for wired services such as telephony, telegraphy, computer data transmission, and optical fiber delivery systems. As the CCIs are the sole global bodies entrusted to study international telecommunication standardization problems, their recommendations are influential.

While occasional calls to merge the CCIR and CCIT have been put forward in the past, the division of "wired" and "wireless" technical study groups makes a certain amount of sense. This becomes apparent when viewing the unique problems faced by each Consultative Committee, how each facilitates resolution of these problems, how successful each has been at avoiding North-South or East-West political polarization, and, ultimately, how effective each has been at achieving global standardization.

Just as many of the difficulties confronting the CCIs are common to both committees, so too are many CCI objectives common to both. Chief among these is the commitment to *efficient telecommunication through global standardization* of the means of delivery. This is consonant with one of the central purposes of the ITU as expressed in Article 4(b) of the 1982 Nairobi ITU Convention: "To promote the development of technical facilities and their most efficient operation with a view to improving the efficiency of telecommunication services, increasing their usefulness, and making them, so far as possible, generally available to the public."[32]

The CCIs have been largely successful in their work. There are limits, however, beyond which the CCIs find themselves powerless against national, political, and economic interests which may act as disincentives to standardization. Despite the undeniable success of the CCIs, there has been increasingly harsh criticism of the time-consuming character and growing expense of CCI procedures. Worse, the CCIs continue to be distrusted and criticized by certain developing countries who view the committees as Northern/MNC-biased and neglectful of Third World concerns.

The latter criticism is warranted and remains a cause for concern within the CCIs. Unlike other components of the ITU which the LDCs either dominate (Plenipotentiary) or greatly influence (IFRB, Administrative Council) the CCIs are strongly oriented toward Northern interests. CCI work requires technical expertise. CCI structure allows participation by both telecommunications administrations and recognized private operating agencies (RPOAs) such as AT&T or Cable and Wireless. In sheer numerical terms—numbers of delegates at a CCI Plenary, number of submissions made, numbers of recommendations originating from a given country—this obviously skews the entire system in favor of not an amorphous "North" but the six or eight major telecommunications technology leaders.

Moreover, given the CCIs recommendatory role, it must be at the cutting edge of new technological developments. This unavoidable and necessary element of CCI work effectively excludes Third World participation. There are exceptions, of course, as some LDCs, notably South Korea, Malaysia, Brazil and India are becoming growing telecommunications powers, with an increasing facility for innovation and independent research and development.

This is not to say that much of the current tension and mistrust could not have been avoided or at least minimized in the past. Perhaps due to this Northern dominance and the lack of LDC representation at the Plenaries, there has been a tangible neglect of Third World interests in certain CCI policies. The price of CCI publications, as has been mentioned, is a seemingly trivial cause for complaint which has become a contentious issue and, ironically, is not even the fault of the CCIs. Another more serious problem is the accusation that most CCI Recommendations promote technical efficiency over universality of access to new technology or affordability. Particularly in this era of rapidly evolving technology— nowhere more notable than in telecommunications services—this contributes to the LDC perception of being caught at the wrong end of an increasing technology gap.

The LDCs are not the sole critics of the CCIs. The chief technological powers are often exasperated at the time-consuming character of CCI deliberations. The development of most CCI Recommendations on standards take anywhere from 18 months to over four years. Given the rapidly evolving state of telecommunications technology, this time-lag diminishes the value of CCI Recommendations. By the time a recommendation is issued, a de facto standard may be so firmly entrenched that the CCI will only be able to verify a fait accompli or, worse, issue a contrary standard that may end up irrelevant and widely ignored.

To understand why the CCI recommendatory process is so lengthy, it becomes necessary to observe how the CCIs currently operate. The general procedure commences with a plenary assembly at which a list of questions to be investigated is drawn up by the participants (administrations, RPOAs, SIOs) and then apportioned to relevant study groups. Any administration or RPOA can be on any study group subject to plenary approval. The study group members work from their home countries and deal with questions through correspondence to the CCIs in Geneva. When the study groups meet, they tend to be high-powered sessions dealing with questions each member has considered for some time. The study group commitment to consensus may, on matters of controversy, further delay the issuing of a recommendation.[33] The CCIs are aware of the time-lag problem. Efforts to rectify the situation however, have not been entirely successful. The final and interim meetings of CCIR Study Groups comprise a three to four year process, instead of taking up to five years as had once been the case. Some delegates argue, however, that holding plenaries as close together as every 18 months disregards the technical imperatives of detailed study and leads to a general decline in the quality of papers submitted and work completed. One unforeseen consequence of shortening the period between plenary meetings has been a dramatic increase in the number of study groups that cannot finish their mandated work in the allotted period and must continue into another period. This diminishes the value of the plenary meetings and *adds* to the amount of time required to achieve a recommendation.

Two compromise solutions to the time-lag problem, apart from shortening the time period between plenary meetings, have been instituted, although neither is particularly effective from a technological standpoint. Since 1972, the CCIs have been able to issue a "Provisional Recommendation" after one or two years when circumstances suggest a great deal more time will be required before a new full recommendation can be issued. When a Provisional Recommendation is proposed, the Secretary General will request that members approve it by correspondence, obviating the need for a special meeting. Of the hundreds of recommendations issued each year, Provisional Recommendations comprise an infinitesimal part. The CCITT issued only two Provisional Recommendations in 1984.

A second type of compromise is provided by the issuance of "multiple standards." Since the 1984 Malaga-Torremolinos CCITT Plenary, the CCITT has viewed multiple standards as a policy of last resort. A multiple standard exists when the CCIs approve two or more recommendations covering a single function. How this may come about is detailed below. Multiple standards create difficult choices for developing states and others seeking to adopt a single national or regional standard. A multiple standard becomes in fact somewhat of a contradiction in terms. A standard, by definition, implies a certain uniformity, particularly given the ITU's goal of increased harmonization through standardization. When, due to the length of the CCI decision-making process, several incompatible systems arise in different countries, the CCIs are left with no choice but to confirm existing national standards as acceptable on an international basis. Such an option may not be graced with "Recommendation" status by the ITU. If a multiple standard seems inevitable, the CCIs may simply present the incompatible systems together in a single *report*. The three different worldwide color television standards which emerged in the 1960s, for example, are contained in a CCI Report, not a Recommendation.[34]

Fortunately, multiple standards occur rarely. Nevertheless, those examples of multiple standards arising tend to be related to major technological developments. Multiple standards come about in those areas where nations, while sincere in their general commitment to global technical standardization, suddenly draw the line when standardization threatens the political strength or economic vitality of the nation. This introduces a fundamental conflict: a global commitment to standardization for improved telecommunications may conflict with recognition of a country's sovereign right to exercise domestic control over the establishment of technical standards.

Two categories of telecommunications standards can be identified. Most CCI Recommendations are of a straightforward nature: an improvement or innovation has been submitted by a telecommunications agency, an RPOA, or by the CCIs own laboratories to the plenary. The CCIs will then recommend that this new standard be adopted universally. The CCI Recommendations thus become rules of the road documenting technical specification and the means by which world communication can take place.

The second type of standard, usually involving entire systems, concepts, or expensive technologies, is not as easily promulgated. In some cases, illogically from a technical viewpoint, administrations fight new technologies and resist new CCI Recommendations. If these administrations possess their own version of a new technology, they may promote their version to the exclusion of other, perhaps more efficient, systems. Since the CCIs seek consensus, their job is made infinitely more difficult by the recalcitrance of certain states. If no compromise can be reached, a multiple standard may ultimately be issued in either a CCI Recommendation or, more likely, through the publication of a report.

Why are countries willing to struggle for years to defeat a recommendation that may facilitate world telecommunication? Two examples—one from the CCIR, one from the CCITT—will illustrate that it is neither malice nor a desire to weaken the ITU which motivates recalcitrant states. It is, however, a desire to have one's own national standard or system given the CCI worldwide "seal of approval." Ironically, countries are willing to allow a weakening of CCI credibility through multiple standards because, as yet, those recommendations from the CCIs carry a great deal of influence. A CCI Recommendation is a sign that the recommended standard is in the vanguard of technology.

The confidence inspired by CCI approval confers a strong marketing advantage to the manufacturers and suppliers of the recommended system and hence it may be of economic benefit to the recommendation's country of origin. For those systems heavily supported by their home governments, it may be necessary to have a system approved by the CCI simply in order to prevent domestic political disaster. Conversely, if the CCI approves a foreign competing system, the national standard-setting agency may simply adhere to the CCI-rejected domestic standard; either in violation of CCI standards or as part of a multiple standard. In either case the home standard becomes a de facto non-tariff barrier (NTB) to trade. There is no technical reason why Western Europe should have until 1987 possessed six incompatible cellular car telephone systems. The different standards existed in the car telephone case because cellular car telephones in each European country were distributed by PTT monopolies which employ "buy domestic" policies. Different systems evolve in different countries and the natural selection of a single standard in the marketplace is made more difficult even with a technology as obviously international (in Western Europe) as cellular mobile telephones by national administrations seeking to protect their domain.

The CCIR and CCITT have, particularly in recent years, evolved into quite different organizations, notwithstanding the differences dictated by their mandates. Arguably the most successful components of the ITU, the CCIs nevertheless find themselves now confronted with concerns and issues that question their basic premise and structure. Each committee is pursuing different approaches in reconciling new, inchoate technologies with the economic and political commitments of the major technological powers, often with the opposite aspirations of the developing countries.

The CCIR: Indispensable or Indistinct?

The International Radiocommunications Consultative Committee (CCIR) studies technical and operating questions relating specifically to radio communication issues. It is a large mandate, covering all aspects of wireless telecommunication. Unlike the CCITT, the CCIR Recommendations often relate not to specific devices or telecommunications equipment but to services and systems facilitating international communications. These are often issues of basic compatibility, such as maritime or aviation radio standards. In much of the CCIR's work the ratification and recommendation needed is so obvious that consensual agreement is usually a foregone conclusion.[35]

While the CCITT views itself as an active promoter of standardization, CCIR personnel are not always comfortable with being so described. The CCIR prefers to see itself as active in the technical policy planning process before WARCs and in the study of new radio communication systems. Its mandate is viewed as far more policy oriented and of a wider scope than the "nuts and bolts" sort of standard achieved by the

CCITT. Yet the CCIR is also involved in specific issues of basic radio communication compatibility that are not terribly exciting but are nevertheless fundamental to international telecommunication. This dichotomy in how the CCIR is seen—and sees itself—leads to the title of this section. Despite the "indispensable" nature of the bulk of the committee's work, a lot of what the CCIR does is increasingly viewed, whether justly or not, as too esoteric and not particularly relevant to real world concerns. The CCIR is seen by many developing countries as a clique of about 35 to 40 leading technological countries that cannot adequately address the concerns of the majority of ITU members.

This view suggests that the CCIR is fading in power and influence due to a failure to encompass developing country aspirations and a consequent inability to evolve with the times. The most visible example of this "fading" is the relative neglect of CCIR preparatory work at WARCs. The CCIR is rightfully proud of the high caliber of technical expertise that goes into the CCIR Conference Preparatory Meetings (CPMs) and Interim Working Parties (IWPs) that precede WARCs and RARCs. Depending largely on major administration research, these conferences produce extensive studies of each technical option available to a given WARC or RARC. For example, in preparation for the 1985 and 1988 Space WARC, the CCIR held exhaustive four week CPMs which produced detailed reports of considerable erudition and worth. Instead of comprising a valuable technical guide at the WARC, however, these reports were largely ignored by both conference delegates and the relevant technical committees at the WARC.[36]

Why is the substantial contribution of the CCIR neglected in this way? The central reason rests with the heavily Northern, major developed country bias of the CCIR. Of the nearly 160 ITU member countries present at a WARC, many—the majority—see the CCIR as a high technology "club" to which they cannot obtain entry and from which they cannot expect much consideration. This view, of course, is not entirely just. The CCIR does attempt as much as possible to take global interests into account. The committee has recently established a fund to enable larger numbers of developing countries to send delegations to CCIR meetings. CCIR publication costs have been substantially lowered. At the same time, the CCIR attempts to forge a purely technical path and avoid political or social concerns. By addressing purely technical issues, however, it contributes to claims that it is neglecting the Third World. These technical blinkers also leave the committee at a disadvantage when it is forced to consider the political or social implications of its technical decisions.

Ironically, some developing countries have accused the North of "politicizing" the CCIR. Even some Western developed countries have accused the United States of using the committee's CPMs as a "first line of offense"[37] in preparing for WARCs by skewing CCIR Recommendations in its favor. When the CCIR is seen as representing a small group of influential interests instead of the majority, no matter how unfair that view may be, the credibility of the committee's recommendations and the soundness of its advice immediately become suspect.

Two developments at the 1982 ITU Plenipotentiary Conference further aggravated this unenviable situation. First, a decision was made to elect CCI Directors at the Plenipotentiary Conferences, starting in 1989, instead of having them elected at CCI Plenary Assemblies, as had been done in the past. This decision may have a dramatic impact on the future development of the committees. In the case of the CCIR the effect may be more positive than in the CCITT, where it is feared an overtly political director from one of the more radical developing countries could endanger the innovative, high technology work of the CCITT. As the CCIR's work is less specific, a wisely chosen director from a developing country might help to bring in greater LDC input and enhance Third World trust in the committee, without sacrificing the quality of CCIR technical studies.

This was in fact the desired and anticipated objective of the developing countries in establishing a CCI directorate elected by the Plenipotentiary.[38] The potentially hazardous side-effects of this decision—politicization, diminished quality of work, dilution of CCI autonomy—are at least recognized and can be circumvented to the greatest extent possible. Such is not the case with the second noteworthy decision to come out of the 1982 Plenipotentiary. This decision originated in the immense mandate of the 1979 General WARC, when several specific spectrum management issues were deferred to later Special WARCs. At Nairobi it was decided to make the Special WARCs all two-session conferences, where the first session would pursue a more technical bent and, in its Report to the Second Session, set a technical framework for the policy decisions to be made at the second session. The unforeseen consequence of two-session conferences has been to remove much of the rationale behind CCIR preparatory work, as this is now the role of the first session of a WARC. The 1984 CCIR CPM for the First Session of the 1985 GSO-WARC has been described as the "opening session" of the WARC and a "mini-WARC" in itself.[39] While this role could be valuable, the neglect with which the Report of the 1984 CPM was treated by the First Session of the WARC suggests that two-session WARCs may be contributing to the increased disregard of the CCIR.

A further indication of this is the almost exclusive role given to the IFRB in completing WARC intersessional work. The IFRB has "benefited" from its amicable relationship with the Third World and the high degree of objectivity seen to exist in the Board. But the IFRB is overworked by its intersessional mandate, and the CCIR could be put to greater use in this area.

The role of the CCIR in providing much needed technical and policy preparation for WARCs may thus be merging into the mandate of the WARCs themselves. Two-session WARCs eliminate the need for a significant portion of the CCIR's preparatory work. While this was not actually foreseen in 1979 or 1982, it is not an unwelcome development to many Third World countries.[40] These countries would rather shift this work to the WARCs and the IFRB, both of which enjoy a high reputation for impartiality and responsiveness to Third World concerns.

The South, as is by now apparent, is not a major actor in the CCIR. This fact has already served to diminish the CCIR's important contribution to WARCs. But as the controversy over "fat cat domination of the CCIR"[41] continues, the actual work of the radio committee goes on unhindered. Many of the key standardization issues within the CCIR in the late 1980s centered on technologies that will be applied—at least in the short-run—almost exclusively in the developed, industrialized world. Such technologies include high definition television and cellular mobile radio services. From a technical standpoint this is natural and should not be a cause for concern. The CCIR, as a technical body, cannot realistically address why Japan, West Germany, or the USA should be technically innovative while Bolivia and Rwanda are not. The committee attempts to "denationalize" new technologies through dispassionate study and CCIR worldwide recommendations. The CCIR tries to ignore country of origin and focuses instead on the technologies themselves. But the actual dissemination of a new global technology, while facilitated by CCIR standardization, is not a direct goal—or responsibility—of the CCIR.

Of course, even as "professionals who fight for better telecommunications and enhanced trade,"[42] CCIR delegates seek to promote national and regional interests. The lack of Third World participation leaves developing countries suspecting that the "dispassionate, denationalized" forum of the CCIR will—even if unintentionally—only reflect First World concerns. Yet at least one group of developing countries are increasingly involving themselves in CCIR activities. These are the newly industrializing countries (NICs), such as South Korea and Brazil, that are undertaking a greater portion of their own research and development, with a consequent increase in their contribution to CCIR work.

In recent years even the advanced Western technological powers have come to question certain elements of CCIR activity. These concerns have been the cost of a marked increase in Eastern bloc participation on the committee. The Soviet Union has, not surprisingly, traditionally been a major actor in the CCIR. But in recent years Hungary, Romania, and the GDR have risen within the committee as major contributors. From a technical perspective this has been a beneficial development for all countries and the ITU in general. The technical nature of the CCIs facilitates East-West cooperation. Irrespective of ideology, demographics and geography dictate that the countries of Eastern Europe will share many common interests with their Western European counterparts, just as the USSR will have a surprising commonality of technological interests with the United States. In CCIR meetings and plenaries the two super-powers often side together.[43]

Concerns arise as the growth of Eastern bloc involvement in the CCIR is viewed as a double-edged sword. The Soviet Union and other Warsaw Pact countries have repeatedly attempted to introduce non-technical "peaceful use" and "peace and disarmament" resolutions into CCIR Recommendations. At one point during 1985, the United States delegation to the CCIR had to bring in several disarmament specialists from the State Department in order to intelligently discuss and debate a Soviet proposal for, *inter alia*, "a commitment to the peaceful use of telecommunications in the disarmament process. . . ."[44]

The CCIR is therefore not the close-knit regional club that is sometimes portrayed by observers. Even within the traditional "clique" of the CCIR—Western Europe, North America, Japan, and Oceania—the distribution of markets, the nationality of major manufacturers, and the origins of technical research can lead to conflict within the CCIR decision-making process. These are not problems that pervade all CCIR work. In much of what the CCIR does, particularly in establishing rules of basic compatibility for radio services, agreement between all parties is a foregoing conclusion. Likewise, CCIR preparatory work for WARCs is not *in itself* controversial. It is the position of the CCIR in relation to the WARC that has caused the controversy discussed above. The CPM reports are themselves technically valuable and are achieved in an atmosphere of professionalism and consensus.

What kinds of issues promote conflict or dissuade consensus within the CCIR? Not surprisingly, such issues tend to be those related to nascent technologies or systems that involve major political and economic interests within the developing world. One of the most famous of these disputes was the color television "war" of the 1960s.

The first operating color TV system was the American NTSC (National TV System Committee) system which began regular operation in the US in 1954. NTSC was developed to operate with American television technology and remains the color television system used by countries operating on that system.[45] Relatively little technical adjustment was believed to be needed to modify NTSC for European use.

In the late 1950s, French television pioneer Henri de France developed a technically superior color TV system, SECAM (Sequentiel a Memoire) to be used with differing European technology. In 1962 AEG-Telefunken of West Germany developed a system employing some of the best elements of NTSC and SECAM, calling it PAL (Phase Alternation by Line).[46]

By the mid-1960s three wholly incompatible color television broadcasting systems had come into widespread use, each closely tied to its nation of origin and each vying for the increasingly lucrative world export market. Fearing a costly and limited future for color television if standardization did not take place,[47] the European Broadcasting Union (EBU) launched an ad hoc group in late 1962 to compare the systems and choose a single standard. At this point the CCIR became involved with EBU Study Group XI:

> The result was that conflicting international political and economic interests interceded in debates about color TV systems. Representatives to the CCIR and EBU were generally national technical broadcasting experts. However, during the color TV system debate when each nation voted in favor of one system or another the representatives heading the delegations were politicians. Their primary loyalty was not to the International Organizations but to the domestic industrial and political interests in the countries from which they came. This conflict eventually made agreement upon a single color TV standard impossible.[48]

French domestic policy in the promotion of the SECAM color system followed the 1960s Gaullist strategy of using technical standards as nontariff barriers (NTBs) to foreign (especially American) penetration of the French market. This policy had been reinforced by the 1964 takeover of the French computer firm, Bull, by American General Electric and by related fears induced by Jacques Servan-Schreiber's book *Le Defi Americain*.[49] Servan-Schreiber perceived America to be quietly, unconsciously colonizing Europe. The reactive French policy consisted of reasserting France's technological leadership through costly "nouvelles cathedrales" such as the Concorde airplane, the first tidal power plant, the TGV express train, and SECAM color television.

Servan-Schreiber, along with many others, believed that European unity was a prerequisite to answering the American (and later the Japanese) challenge. But while the Gaullists were keen advocates of European unity, they were equally committed to French supremacy within a United Europe. That this was primarily a political viewpoint is illustrated by the two centers of opposition to SECAM within France. The French television equipment industry feared that SECAM would end up being adopted solely in France, and, while that could guarantee control of the domestic market, it would preclude access to export markets. The ORTF (predecessor to Telediffusion de France) asserted that, as the nation's broadcaster, it had jurisdiction over which color television standard would be adopted. Technical personnel within the ORTF strongly opposed politicians forcing the costly and unknown SECAM system upon them. While ORTF engineers decried the "politicization" of technical standardization, much of their opposition to SECAM could be traced back to purely non-technical factors, such as personality conflicts between scientists.[50] Moreover, the ORTF had no say in the original development of SECAM and remained resentful of that fact.

By the mid-1960s each of the three color TV systems was, at the very least, established in its country of origin. The question of which system would be adopted as the worldwide standard was to be decided by the 1965 CCIR Plenary Conference in Vienna. What CCIR officials failed to realize was the importance of what was at stake with this new technology. PAL, SECAM, and NTSC all have powerful corporate backing as well as government support. Potential export orders worth millions of dollars were riding on the CCIR decision. Moreover, the decision would—for France (SECAM), West Germany (PAL), or the United States (NTSC)—be a major political victory; a confirmation of technical leadership and superiority. At least the politicians could claim as much.

French officials realized that some "coup" would be necessary to irrevocably establish SECAM as a growing *international* technology and as the natural European standard. It was hoped this would convince the majority at the CCIR conference. President De Gaulle's exclusion of Britain from the European Economic Community (EEC) ruled out one potential SECAM market, and the Netherlands, Scandinavia, Switzerland, and Belgium seemed committed to the German PAL system. The Italian government found itself impossibly cross-pressured, ultimately deciding to defer any decision-making until an international standard was recommended by the CCIR.[51] Finally, France found a willing partner in the Soviet Union.

The 1960s had witnessed an increased degree of economic and political exchange between the USSR and France. The Soviets were, moreover, in the market for a color TV system, and, while Soviet scientists had mixed emotions about SECAM, it was not politically desirable for the USSR to adopt the American NTSC, as it would have symbolically ceded technological superiority to the USA. PAL was not seriously considered as the Soviets did not wish to assist West German recovery and prosperity. SECAM was politically the natural choice. A Franco-Soviet accord in which the two countries agreed to "cooperate" on the adoption of a color television system was concluded in March 1965,[52] several months before the CCIR was to meet in Vienna to decide on a single system.

The Soviet-French agreement established SECAM as a major contender for the title of "world color television system." The Americans and West Germans reacted by hastily combining PAL and NTSC support into a package called QUAM, which sought to eliminate technical differences between PAL and NTSC through creating one compatible system. This was accomplished in the weeks leading up to the conference in an atmosphere of frantic activity. One consequence of the reigning disorder was that many countries were unaware of QUAM's background and so believed it to be a fourth contender.

Despite the resulting confusion, the voting patterns of the 1965 CCIR Vienna conference reflected pre-existing groupings and linkages. France's SECAM received 21 votes against 18 for the German-American QUAM hybrid. SECAM's slight edge could be attributed to the votes of the USSR and Warsaw Pact countries as well as the votes of four Francophone African countries. None of the four African countries supporting France had any sort of domestic television service at the time. The other Western Europeans, as well as Britain and Australia, supported PAL. The Americas, predictably, rallied behind NTSC.[53]

CCIR disillusionment over the apparent deadlock led to a discussion of the color television standards problem at the Eleventh Plenary Assembly of the CCIR at Oslo, 1966. By this time a further complication had arisen. The Soviet Union, while now committed to acquisition of the French SECAM system, was unhappy about the political ramifications of such an obvious admission of its inability to develop a Soviet color TV system. The USSR added a few patented circuits to the system which, curiously, brought the system closer to the PAL and NTSC systems. The Soviet-modified SECAM, dubbed SECAM-IV, allowed the Soviets to now claim that they possessed a "Soviet" color television technology that had been developed "with French cooperation" instead of merely possessing a modified French system.

One side-effect of the new Soviet system was that it presented a fourth option to the Oslo conference. A few delegates—not just the Soviets and their allies—viewed SECAM-IV as a potential compromise system which could perhaps be modified to make it compatible with PAL-NTSC. The former loyalties held, however, as SECAM-IV only drew the votes of three delegations. The final tally gave 15 votes to the French SECAM and 12 to PAL. NTSC was not formally in the running at Oslo as it had been decided to limit the conference to adoption of a color system compatible to the European 625-lines standard.

Even the narrowed parameters of the Oslo conference could not preclude breakdown, dissent, and deadlock. The conference, like that in

Vienna one year earlier, ended without an agreement on the European color television system. The CCIR resigned itself to the irrevocable and entrenched existence of three incompatible "standards." Significantly, at both Vienna and Oslo CCIR Meetings, delegates were chosen not for their technical expertise but for their political ability to proselytize their cause. The ability to compromise and eliminate minor technical differences was not highly valued in such a setting where important international economic gains were at stake.

Standardization of the best technology and efficiency of transmission took a distant second place to the guaranteed survival and growth of home manufacturing industries, assuring potential export sales, and enjoying the political prestige of being chosen "world standard" in color television technology. Compromise and consensus could not be reached as national delegations held opposite policies, goals, and strategies. The CCIR sought to establish a recommendation on one world standard. They could not have confronted the color television standard issue any earlier than they did without freezing or at least hindering the technical developments which led to the PAL and SECAM color standards. By the mid-1960s no one of the existing systems could claim to be either technically superior or more internationally acceptable than its competitors. Yet any preferential decision made by the CCIR would confer the ITU's "stamp of approval" on one system, greatly aiding the future of that system. Most LDCs and several developed countries (e.g., Italy) had not chosen a color television system by the mid-1960s. Thus, the export advantage conferred by CCIR approval would have been considerable.

The CCIR eventually published a multiple standard report allowing the three incompatible systems to coexist. PAL and SECAM (and to a much lesser extent NTSC) have engaged in fierce competition as LDCs have, one by one, selected color TV systems. The choice of a system often has little to do with superiority of technology. A stronger motive may be a desire to forge closer links with one of the three countries identified with the three systems (France, West Germany, USA), the sort of financial arrangements which can be negotiated, and/or a desire to adopt a different system than unfriendly neighbors (e.g., Turkey has PAL, Greece has SECAM).[54] "It appears when governments have no similar technology to promote, export, or license, their support for compatible technical standards approximates current political interests and objectives at the national level."[55]

Two reasons suggest why the CCIR may be at times ineffective in establishing international telecommunications standards recommendations and why national administrations may support incompatible technologies.[56] First, the maintenance of domestic telecommunications industries can be jeopardized by adoption of an international or "foreign" standard. Country A may possess a superior system to country B or C, and may get CCI approval. But if B and C have competing telecommunications industries to maintain, they will be loath to scrap their non-standard system, damage their industry, and sacrifice jobs, all in the name of technical efficiency and compliance with CCI standards.

Second, a concern for national prestige can hinder acceptance of a single standard. The Gaullist promotion of SECAM color television involved more than the securing of economic advantage through CCI approval. The prestige of the country—the vision of France as a world leader in a vanguard technology—was at stake. Likewise, the Soviets could not adopt the American NTSC system as it would have added to the prestige of a rival power and could have been viewed as a diminution of their own technological abilities.

In the case of color television standards and the CCIR, the above description illustrates how countries attempted to circumvent CCIR channels with well-timed, outside agreements (e.g., the France-USSR SECAM sale) and through the replacement of technically minded CCI conference delegates with politicians less prone to compromise. Color television standards also illustrate CCIR's inability to prevent the major technological powers from developing de facto standards and successfully promoting international use of such standards, irrespective of whether or not the de facto standard is the most technically efficient or best choice.[57]

The color television disputes took place over two decades ago. As has been described, the CCIR has undergone some dramatic changes over those 20 years. Yet the nature of the dispute illustrates points which remain valid in discussing CCIR activity. Conflict that hinders CCIR standardization tends to be between major Northern telecommunications powers. An equally dramatic recent example of this can be found in the on-going CCIR discussions relating to high definition television services (HDTV).

HDTV consists of a highly improved television picture and the means by which such a picture may be broadcast. Two CCIR Study Groups have focused on the adoption of "advanced" television standards such as HDTV. In 1982 a CCIR Interim Working Party was established, which recommended adoption of a single world HDTV standard. By the mid-1980s a fully developed HDTV studio system existed.[58] This system was developed, over the course of fifteen years, by NHK of Japan. The Japanese system has been extensively tested by administrations in Japan and Italy, and by various independent firms in Canada, France, and the United States. Japan was keen to have the NHK system adopted as the global HDTV standard. A strong ally was found in the United States, which does not possess its own HDTV technology but leads in the production of complementary systems such as enhanced-videoscreen technology for scientific and medical use. American officials were amenable to supporting a single HDTV system, even one of Japanese origin, as it could lead to a single worldwide television reception standard. If such a system existed, it would then become far easier for American program producers to exploit lucrative export markets. US officials have suggested that television program production has now become the forte of the United States, and they are willing to cede to Japan the position of "leader" in television transmission and equipment technology.[59]

The Europeans, however, have not been as gracious in accepting the technical ascendency of Japan. Europe's television manufacturing industry, long buoyed by incompatible color standards (see above) and an imposing array of tariffs, feared being excluded from any future television technology. The vision of Japanese dominance of technology and American dominance of program production was profoundly disquieting to the Europeans.

When the CCIR met in Dubrovnik early in 1986, Japan, along with its Asian and Oceanian neighbors as well as North America, hoped, with some optimism, that at least a firm protocol leading to a CCIR Recommendation—and a global standard—could be achieved. European opposition was led by the television equipment manufacturers Philips (Holland) and Thomson (France). In addition, the CEPT—the regional association of 16 European administrations—had soundly insisted on development of a European HDTV system. European concerns were expressed through the EEC as well. Brussels was adamant in refusing to allow Japan to dominate Europe's television industry through the "stealth" of new technology.[60]

The European position at the CCIR Dubrovnik meeting has been described by one American observer as "a day late and a dollar short."[61] While national administrations, the CEPT, and the EEC all opposed the submitted Japanese HDTV standard, some European broadcasters startled their administrations by embracing the Japanese system. Italy's RAI-TV had even purchased and experimented extensively with the Japanese system prior to the 1986 conference.

Yet the Europeans were able to get their way at Dubrovnik. The Japanese HDTV system was not adopted as a recommendation but instead listed in a report. Recommendation status would be suspended for another two year "study period." The Japanese were keenly disappointed.[62] This was, nevertheless, a hollow victory for Europe. Two years could not provide Europe with time to improve upon Japanese technological gains. It could, however, give the Europeans time to develop a nascent, evolutionary standard called MAC. The advantage of MAC rests in its ability to be phased in slowly, through gradual stages, and—above all—the fact that MAC is compatible with existing TV sets. But the development of MAC is at least several years behind that of the NHK system, and the best the Europeans could get out of the CCIR in 1988 was yet another two year deferral. This was nevertheless a victory for Europe.

Why did Western Europe dominate these CCIR meetings? The residue of Eurocentrism in the CCIR is certainly a factor. The Western Europeans are far more comfortable within the CCIR than their overseas cousins. The structure and style of the committee is familiar to those coming from European PTTs. In addition, the regional strength of the CEPT serves as a formidable voting bloc, the power of which cannot be matched by informal associations between other countries. It must be recalled that the size of the Japanese and American delegations are swelled by RPOA (recognized private operating agency) representatives, but that *only* officials from national administrations can vote at CCI meetings. Europe's administrations can thus still comprise a numerical majority, particularly as few developing countries involve themselves in the CCIR. The relative inexperience of Japan in dealing with the CCIR, despite that country's overwhelming technological strength, may also have been a factor. As in the videotex dispute within the CCITT (see below), Europe was still able to defer the setting of a CCIR Recommendation despite the attempts of Japan to rally support among allies in Asia and the Americas. But these lobbying efforts were weakened in the US by similar European efforts and by the European acquisition of much of what was left of the US television receiver manufacturing industry—Thomson purchased RCA and Philips took over Magnavox. The NHK HDTV system, however, is rapidly gaining ground in worldwide markets. The virtual acceptance of the system by the North American market and by several European broadcasters indicates that the marketplace has to an extent already decided. Further European research in developing improvements to current systems remains valuable, but when this is combined with deliberate attempts to hinder the CCIR standardization process the effects could be damaging to both the promotion of the technology and to the credibility of the CCIR.[63]

In the HDTV example the role of potential global markets became a factor in both promoting the NHK standard and as a catalyst for European reaction against it. What about instances where an emergent technology is closely associated with one country or region and then, only after exploiting its home market, submitted to the CCIR for tacit international approval? In such a case a country may merely be seeking the export advantage conferred by a CCI Recommendation. This has occasionally placed the CCIR in a difficult and unfamiliar position. In the case of the color television dispute, each of the proposed systems was too firmly entrenched in its home market for any sort of worldwide standard to evolve. There was no one dominant system, yet countries were pursuing a CCIR Recommendation in the hope that their system could somehow be made dominant.

A similar situation currently exists in the efforts to establish a global CCIR recommended standard for a cellular mobile radio system. This technology was originally developed in the United States, where, as in Canada and Australia, expansive geography dictates the need for effective mobile point-to-point communication. Until the early 1980s the European market for this type of radio communication was, by comparison, minimal. Requirements and standards for the systems used in North America were largely developed by the early 1980s. In Europe, however, the situation remains inchoate. In essence, the North American and European markets are "out of sync" in that many Western European markets for cellular radio remain embryonic while in North America the same markets have fully evolved.

This dichotomy in the needs and the state of the European and North American marketplace provides a strong disincentive to standardization. As cellular radio technology is applied through mobile telephones, the discriminatory domestic purchasing policies of most West European administrations have led to the employment of incompatible technical standards as non-tariff barriers (NTBs). Consequently, there were by the mid-1980s seven incompatible cellular radio standards being used in Western Europe.[64] Several of these systems are just different enough from one another to provide a rationale for a "domestic" system and cellular radio industry. While incompatibility also exists between the US, Japanese, and Hong Kong standards, the situation is considered particularly grave in Western Europe given the geographical proximity of the incompatible systems and the nascent demand for mobile telephones that can be used when travelling to other countries. As most of the systems employed in Europe have at least been inspired by some of the early American systems, the US has been pushing hard to obtain a CCIR Recommendation for its "tried and proven" system. RPOAs within the CCIR such as Motorola are particularly keen to obtain approval for the systems they design and manufacture.

Western Europe is largely hostile toward any attempt to establish a CCIR cellular radio Recommendation in the near future. This opposition does not entirely stem from concerns of maintaining national markets for domestic telecommunication industries, for progress has been made during the late 1980s at forcing a regional European cellular radio standard. Advances in digital technology have led to many innovations in cellular radio technology in recent years. The current feeling within the CCIR Interim Working Party studying the matter is that the next few years will witness a great deal of revision to the cellular radio status quo, and that the American position put forth by Motorola and the other RPOAs in the CCIR is not tenable.[65] To decree a standard at this stage could hinder the development of the technology.

The rapid growth of demand for cellular radio—from one third of Western European mobile radio sales in 1985 to a predicted 60% by 1990—has led to calls on both sides of the Atlantic for standardization *now*. Some observers feel this position is untenable, given the incipient state of digital technology, a lack of data on how sizeable international cellular radio needs might be, and the possibility that a single global standard might come to be easily dominated by the powerful Japanese equipment manufacturers.[66] Others believe that cellular radio will never reach its marketing potential unless worldwide standardization takes place soon. Delays will lead to further fragmentation which could, in the long-run, preclude this technology from ever being employed beyond the affluent telecommunications manufacturing powers. Standardization would facilitate the dissemination of the technology, particularly in developing countries and newly industrializing countries (NICs). These two positions leave the CCIR in a quandry and subject to strong criticism no matter what position it takes. The cross-pressures from—and within—delegations to the CCIR meetings will make this a turbulent issue within the CCIR until well beyond the end of the decade.

To the developed countries the CCIR remains a vital standardization body, not just for the newer and economically influential technologies but also for basic international service standards necessitated by safety and security considerations. In this latter role the CCIR provides recommendations which serve as technical ground rules for all international radio communications. This is of vital importance to all countries. Yet the LDCs largely view the CCIR as a Northern club which does not adequately address their concerns nor welcome their contributions. CCIR attempts to redress this situation illustrate how unfair some of the accusations against the committee are. The fact remains, however, that Northern countries *have* exploited the purely technical CCIR in seeking commercial or political advantage. This is particularly evident to developing countries in CCIR preparatory work for WARCs, and the chief reason why developing countries have chosen to neglect much of this high quality work. The position of the CCIR relative to the WARCs is further jeopardized by the emergence of two-session WARCs, which remove much of the need for CCIT CPMs. CCIR work in studying new radio communications technologies like HDTV or cellular radio remains the most valuable component of the committee's efforts. Indispensable to this work are CCIR mediating efforts between the technology power centers in North America, Europe, and Japan. CCIR involvement may sometimes be necessary for international radio communication to take place at all. Yet, by nature of its structure and its highly technical work, the CCIR will never achieve the IFRB's global perspective nor its enviable reputation. A "Northern club" it was born, and a "Northern club"— albeit with a less Eurocentric focus and increased NIC involvement— it must remain, as any marked change could imperil its technical effectiveness.

The CCITT and the Videotex Dispute

The CCIR, as has been mentioned, often considers matters of a broader nature than the CCITT. The CCIR engages in service standards and WARC policy preparation while the CCITT, focusing on matters of "wired" communication, has traditionally existed as the one purely technical committee. Its work in telephony and telegraphy has been invaluable and largely successful. This success is in part attributable to the limitation of discussion in the plenaries to specific technical matters. More significant, however, is a genuine worldwide commitment to the creation of a single global telephone system.[67] Among OECD countries this unified network is largely in place. The CCITT, through its recommendations, has successfully established worldwide standards for telephone systems and instrument specifications, despite the "buy domestic" policies of virtually all developed countries and the temptation to ensure maintenance of current market strength through the employment of incompatible technical standards as non-tariff barriers.

From the inception of the CCITT's predecessors in the 1920s until the 1960s the work of the committee focused on the interconnection of European telephone networks. The advent of transoceanic telephone cables in the late 1950s heralded a new desire to achieve worldwide equipment standards through the ITU. As satellites pioneered new means of relaying a substantially enlarged volume of telephone traffic, the goal of standardization became an imperative. The chief technical question concerning telephony remains elimination of differences between ITU-CCITT standards, often of European origin or adaptation, and "Bell" North American standards, the product of seventy years of isolated evolution prior to the establishment of undersea connection between the continents.[68]

The most serious political issue confronting telephony concerns the widening technical disparity between North and South. Most LDCs have unreliable, incomplete, archaic telephone networks which, when they work at all, are available to only a very small segment of the population. The ITU has addressed this important political concern through the establishment in 1982 of the Independent Commission for World Wide Telecommunications Development (The Maitland Commission), discussed in Chapter 1. The CCITT is not mentioned in the report, despite the obvious and significant role it could play in facilitating worldwide access to telephone systems. This neglect of the CCITT is illustrative of the ITU's desire to keep CCI work limited to the strictly technical level. By not analyzing or including the work of the CCITT in the Report of the Maitland Commission, the ITU may have missed an opportunity to prove to the Third World that the CCIs *can* actively encourage development of telecommunications in the South.

The CCITT is viewed as being on the cutting edge of new telecommunications technologies like ISDN, fiber optics, and digital transmission. From the perspective of the developed world this makes the CCITT one of the most important elements of the ITU structure. To the Third World, however, it often appears that the CCITT is promoting these new standards at their expense. Some of the central concerns of the New World Information Order (NWIO) and New International Economic Order (NIEO) relate to the apparent widening of the technology gap. Nowhere is this gap more visible than in telecommunications technology, which is enjoying a period of rapid progress.

The velocity of technical change now far outpaces the CCITT's ability to make detailed consideration of proposals. As has been mentioned, this difficulty has been compounded, ironically, by efforts of the ITU to speed up standardization through shortening the time periods between study group meetings. Consequently, many groups meet without sufficient preparation and must defer decision-making to the next study group meeting, adding considerable costs in money and time to the process.[69] The CCITT must necessarily resort to dual standards, multiple standards, provisional recommendations, and reports, if only to reduce the backlog. The problem of securing uniform standards is exacerbated by the unwillingness of national administrations to compromise when the proposed standard poses significant implications for political prestige and economic well-being.

As with disputes in the CCIR, the process of recommending standards by the CCITT can also devolve into a battleground for a number of competing standards proposals, often each possessing great technical merit. Again, such confrontation is not characteristic of the majority of exchanges within the CCITT. Indeed, as with the CCIR the bulk of the CCITT's activity takes place within an admirably cordial, professional atmosphere where agreement on evident improvements or pioneering technologies becomes a foregone conclusion. But in recent years, as the CCITT has had to consider systems and technologies of increasing

economic importance—videotex, teletext, ISDN, open systems—the political influence of the major technological actors has been enhanced.

The growth of political, economic, and social concerns within the
standard-setting process does not preclude success in achieving technical
standardization. But it does require CCITT delegates to look beyond
purely technical criteria and recognize the differing concerns of the
aspirant South, the centralized "national strategy" approaches of Europe,
Japan, and many other countries, as well as the non-governmental,
informal telecommunications structure of the United States.

The history of CCITT Recommendation X25 provides an example of
a technical "battleground" that was turned around into a successful
standard. Recommendation X25 is entitled "Interface Between Data
Terminal Equipment (DTE) and Data Circuit Terminating Equipment
(DCE) for Terminals Operating in the Packet Mode on Public Data
Networks." This unwieldy title essentially describes a technically improved packet switching system that facilitates connection between
terminals and computers. The recommendation describes a physical
system or network, not a medium for transmitting data.

Beginning with American and British research in the 1960s, by 1975
packet switching concepts had emerged in the United States, Canada,
Britain, France, Japan, and Spain. The development of these systems
occurred separately from one another but at all times there existed a
high degree of similarity between the systems and a substantial international exchange of knowledge and ideas on the concept. As a consequence of the rapid growth of the technology, "tremendous pressure"[70]
was exerted on the CCITT to act to develop international protocols and
a global recommendation.

In 1972 the CCITT established a Study Group to survey the issue.
The meeting held by Study Group VII, as it was known in the early
1970s, attracted far more attention and far greater input than had any
past single CCITT issue.[71] This signified the maturing of the CCITT into
much more than the "telephone and telegraph" group and set a trend
that continues to this day. The CCITT is now viewed as the most
technically progressive arm of the ITU which is increasingly responsible,
through its recommendations, for the "internationalizing" of complex
telecommunications delivery systems, particularly as communication
problems within computer networks become more acute.

The CCITT Study Group VII of 1972–76 realized early in its existence
that it would be able to issue a recommendation. The North Americans
and Japanese were keen to achieve CCITT approval for a packet switching
system and were willing to compromise to achieve their goal. The nature
of the technology facilitated this progress as major equipment producers
largely believed that they could successfully sell compatible systems in

a global marketplace. Within Europe, the main buyers of these systems would be the national telecommunications administrations. France had developed a comprehensive national strategy to promote its "Transpac" X25 system.[72] Therefore, European equipment suppliers were more concerned with exploiting domestic potential than in securing export markets. They promoted the X25 standard because of its technical merits and because, through facilitated interconnection with other countries, it would create demand for the system at home.

A satisfactory CCITT Recommendation was achieved in 1976. Recommendation X25 has been considered an "extraordinary event"[73] by some observers, yet what it accomplished is merely illustrative of the CCITT at its best. Given a potentially controversial and technically inchoate technology, the CCITT was able to effect an admirable degree of international cooperation and compromise in order to achieve a sound yet flexible standard.[74]

National interests can, at times, prove to be insurmountable obstacles to international standardization. Such occasions are uncommon, but the battle over videotex in the early 1980s is illustrative of some of the problems the CCITT may confront when various standards proposals are influenced by the political and economic interests of the countries supporting them. In many ways the CCITT is discovering in the 1980s some of the limitations to its effectiveness that were revealed to the CCIR in the color television disputes of the 1960s. The CCITT had believed its narrow focus spared it from such political concerns or international conflict. By addressing solely engineering and technological problems in a "professional" atmosphere the CCITT staff hoped that regional coalition formation and voting blocs based on non-technical considerations and trade-offs could be minimized, as they had been with Recommendation X25. But the emergence of new wired technologies such as videotex and their implications for domestic political prestige and economic well-being rapidly created an environment in the CCITT which closely paralleled that in the CCIR twenty years earlier.

Videotex is a standardized computer layout and graphics system which may be defined as "the process of sending and retrieving text and graphics primarily over telephone lines between a central computer and a terminal or personal computer."[75] This definition is necessarily vague. The CCITT itself has yet to determine a comprehensive definition of all that videotex entails.[76] As an increasing number of enterprises employed an ever-widening variety of computer equipment, such a standardized communication system between computer systems became imperative. As with color television, three competing, incompatible systems emerged, each in its own way technically meritorious, and each enjoying the strong financial and political support of the country promoting it. The systems which had evolved in the late 1970s came from Canada, Great Britain, and France.

The Canadian system, Telidon, had commenced as a joint project between the Canadian Department of Communications and the private telecommunications industry in Canada. It was newer and in some ways technically superior to its existing competitors, the British Prestel and French Antiope systems. The idea for Telidon stemmed from a laboratory project carried out by the Canadian Communications Research Centre. A belief by the Government of Canada that this system warranted development led to the establishment of a strategy for the Telidon program entailing, among other items, (1) subsidization of a series of field trials, (2) encouragement of related research and development, (3) "promotion of the acceptance of Telidon technology in national and international standards forums on at least an equal basis with competing systems,"[77] and (4) use of Telidon by the Government of Canada ("buy domestic" policy).

Telidon's competitors in Britain and France had adopted similar strategies to promote their systems.[78] The European systems had already been presented to the CCITT for consideration when Canada introduced Telidon to the committee in late 1978. Canada let it be known that it was willing to allow Telidon to coexist as one of several CCITT recommended standards, along with the British and French options.[79] Britain and France, however, were not amenable to a "live-and-let-live" solution and wished to have one of their systems adopted by the CCITT as the sole recommended industry standard.

Irrespective of the financial resources Britain and France had already invested in their systems, why were the Europeans so adamant about forcing the CCITT into adopting one system? Unlike the color television wrangle, at the back of the minds of each proponent of a videotex alternative there rested one consideration: CCITT approval could ensure delivery of the potentially immense American market for videotex. Through the 1970s the standards situation in the United States remained unresolved. While AT&T had toyed with the idea of developing an alternative of its own,[80] by 1980 it was apparent that the United States would not be developing its own videotex system, thus opening their market for the Canadian, British, and French systems.

From the beginning the Telidon system was developed with the US market in mind. The Canadian Department of Communications conducted a simultaneous strategy of marketing and standardization—basing much of the latter on the needs of the former. Representations were made to US government agencies and lobby groups as well as to major American telecommunications firms such as AT&T, GTE and others.[81] While some experimentation with the European systems had taken place in the

United States, Telidon was rapidly accepted as the sole North American standard.

When AT&T decided in 1981 to adopt a Telidon coding system, the American National Standards Institute (ANSI) joined forces with the Canadian Standards Association (CSA) to draft a single Canadian-based videotex standard, known as NAPLS (North American Presentation Level Syntax).[82] By the end of 1981 Telidon/NAPLS enjoyed the support of all major American and Canadian computer manufacturers and telecommunications companies as well as many large scale investors in electronics equipment such as Exxon Office Systems and the Canadian Bankers Association.[83]

Canada was thus pursuing the strategy of creating a de facto North American standard while simultaneously seeking CCITT approval. Ensuring acceptance of Telidon in the American market was as high a priority as gaining CCITT approval, but the two were viewed as inexorably linked—neither was possible without the other. Movement to "catch-up" with the European systems first gained momentum in 1978–79. At this time the British and French governments had already committed themselves to full-scale development and worldwide promotion of their systems. A cornerstone of this commitment was of course the submission of detailed proposals to the CCITT.

While Canada was willing to allow Telidon to coexist as an alternative standard to Britain (Prestel) and France (Antiope), the Canadians were not willing to accept anything less than equal recognition for Telidon from the CCITT. At the final meeting of CCITT Study Group VIII on competing videotex systems, held in June 1980, Britain submitted a Delayed Paper calling for the "deletion of the . . . Telidon coding section from the draft recommendations" and for "making the alpha-mosaic coding (Prestel) *the* international basic system. . . ."[84]

Britain submitted this strong statement without any prior warning and without co-opting any supporters. It is difficult to understand what the delegation hoped to achieve through such a confrontational missive. The statement forced countries that had been equivocating to take a stand, and Canada gained the support of the United States, Japan, and France. French support of Telidon may seem surprising, given France's own Antiope system, but French support for the Canadian position was in fact fuelled by a desire to prevent the victory of the British system, which was still viewed by France as the *real* competitor. France also persuaded West Germany and Sweden to support their stand against Prestel by threatening to delay and fight certain CCITT teletex (terminal-to-terminal) proposals the Germans and Swedes were eager to see realized. The British Delayed Paper was therefore a self-defeating gesture.

It prompted a period of frantic but, for France and ultimately for Canada, highly profitable dealing and negotiation.[85]

Since the British proposal had been put forward through a Delayed Paper, the rules of procedure allowed any delegation a right of veto over the entire standard Recommendation. Canada was ready to exercise this option if the need arose,[86] but such a veto was not necessary as Canada handily won majority support. Backing for Telidon by the United States, which by now viewed Telidon as the natural North American standard, and by Japan, which was shocked at Britain's lapse of protocol and attracted to the Canadian technology, greatly assisted Telidon's quest for legitimacy in the CCITT.

Britain "did not concede defeat gracefully."[87] Still reeling from its sound defeat in Study Group VIII, the British delegation in Study Group I placed on record its "strong reservation against the alpha-geometric (Telidon) system as part of the CCITT Standard because it is a system used only by one administration."[88] This statement was in fact erroneous as by mid-June 1980 the United States had accepted Telidon for standardization field trials. Moreover, the British statement was procedurally out of order, earning censure and a firm rejection from the Study Group Chairman (from Switzerland) as well as the CCITT Senior Counsellor.[89] The CCITT Draft Recommendation passed despite British protestations.

A further complication confronted the CCITT in the summer of 1980 when British Telecom began advertising Prestel as the videotex system "preferred by international standards organizations."[90] Many countries raised vigorous objection to these erroneous claims including a strongly worded letter from the Canadian Minister of Communications to the Managing Director of British Telecom. Neither British Telecom nor the British Government ever completely retracted their statements. They did nevertheless agree to support the CCITT Draft Recommendations on videotex, thus removing the last barrier to worldwide recognition of multiple systems.

By 1981 the Europeans perceived a need to present a unified CCITT negotiating position to thwart what was evolving into a united USA-Canada-Japan bloc supporting Telidon. The logical European forum for reconciling technical differences between Prestel and Antiope was the Council of European Post and Telecommunications ministries (CEPT). A CEPT "standard" was achieved by mid-1981, but was not technically viable as it combined incompatible elements of the British and French systems. In essence, it was not a standard but merely a listing of the two separate systems in a single document.

The CCITT 1981–84 Study Period sought to accomplish the reconciliation of the two European negotiating positions with both each other and with the North American position. The goal, not actually articulated until 1983, was a "World Wide Unified Videotex Standard" (WWUVS). From the earliest meetings, Canada and the United States were willing to merge many of the CEPT and NAPLS/Telidon features in order to placate the Europeans. With the exception of the Netherlands, the European administrations did not accept this compromise and continued to amend the CEPT standard, making it even more incompatible with Telidon.

Inability to compromise was at least in part a result of disunity and maneuvering within the European CCITT delegations, and not due to any particular aversion to standardization *per se*. France, vying for the adoption of Antiope as the sole CCITT standard, co-opted the support of the Netherlands and, in a surprisingly visible display of European disunity, attempted to block the CEPT Recommendation from being introduced into the CCITT. Britain and West Germany continued to promote a single European CEPT standard and attempted to resolve intra-European rivalries. With France maneuvering against the CEPT, however, hopes for European unity on the videotex issue were doomed.

One consequence of such visible disunity was a loss of European credibility within the CCITT. By the end of 1981 Japan had introduced a videotex system called CAPTAIN which enabled Japanese and Chinese lettering to be incorporated and programmed into the display. CAPTAIN employed chiefly NAPLS/Telidon technology.[91] When Japan, a recognized world technology leader, chose NAPLS, any hope harbored by the CEPT countries or France to establish either of the European systems as sole CCITT recommended standard was dealt a fatal blow. The Europeans remained adamant, however, creating a looming dilemma for the CCITT: "(The) European countries were willing to have NAPLS change but would not themselves give an inch. . . ."[92]

The CCITT, seriously divided, decided to sponsor a series of three conferences in 1983 to hammer out a world system (WWUVS). The weakness of adherence to the principle of equal status of the separate systems and the assurance of no economic harm to countries with vested interests was compounded by further French attempts to block the CEPT Recommendations from CCITT consideration and a general European reluctance to compromise. The Europeans argued that the North American standard resulted in expensive terminal equipment and was not as well suited as the CEPT Standard for mass-marketing. Proponents of the North American system retorted that as of 1983 even mass market consumers expected high quality, high resolution, and high capability performance in their computer systems. Technical arguments against NAPLS/Telidon were hence weak.

Throughout the debates the Europeans showed no willingness to back down. For Britain and France to capitulate on this issue would have indicated weakness in the high-technology field at a time when the governments and politicians of both countries were claiming that the new information technologies were going to revolutionize their economies and supplant their declining traditional heavy industries.

In seeking to explain why Britain and France remained unable to resolve their differences on this issue, it should be remembered that while "high-tech" enjoyed a remarkable political salience in the early 1980s the perennial issue of European unity was somewhat discredited, although it was to enjoy a strong revival in the late 1980s as a consequence of the "single European market" strategy of the European Commission under the leadership of Jacques Delors. As of 1983, however, over twenty years of conscious efforts to present a European front in all matters, reflected in telecommunications through the EBU and CEPT, had merely resulted in a widely publicized perception of top-heavy bureaucracies and ill-advised subsidy programs.

In fact, when the Europeans had collaborated, particularly in organizations like EBU or CEPT, the results had been largely successful and beneficial to all Europeans. Nevertheless in the early 1980s perceptions in Europe were not amenable to this view, and "European solutions" were not actively sought. As the 1980–84 Study Period concluded with the 1984 CCITT VIIIth Plenary Assembly at Malaga-Torremolinos, the divisions that had existed prior to the WWUVS Conferences not only remained but had been exacerbated by the generally intransigent tone of the conferences.

The 1984 Plenary was to have been a watershed conference. After combing through the 700 pages of CEPT, NAPLS, and CAPTAIN standards data, the participants were to make a final recommendation.[93] France entered the Conference still hoping to remove NAPLS from the list of CCITT alternatives. France's political commitment to Antiope continued to preclude any hope of compromise, even with the other European countries. France insisted that the Preamble to the CCITT Recommendation include a reservation retaining a commitment to study the French Antiope system. Antiope was retained for the study period 1985–88, prolonging the struggle for another four years.

Given the high level of disagreement surrounding the three systems, the CCITT could not recommend one system over another. Had it done so, the disappointed parties would simply have contravened the recommendation and continued to support their systems. Backed into a corner, the CCITT exercised what could well have been its sole feasible option and issued a multiple standard recommendation. In Recommendation T-101 of 1984, the three competing videotex standard proposals, as well as the Japanese NAPLS variant, were "recommended" as global standards. France argued that Recommendation T101 was not "mature" enough to be a full CCITT Recommendation. Their point might have been more sympathetically received had French obstinancy over Antiope not been one of the chief obstacles to a compromise.

Many members of the CCITT were not particularly pleased about the outcome of the videotex dispute.[94] No standardization had been forthcoming after seven years of study and negotiation. The most intensive work by the CCITT, that of WWUVS in 1983, actually reversed what very little compromise had occurred. By early 1984 it was possible to say that "the result of the exercise has been that world videotex standards are now far more incompatible than they were in November, 1982, due primarily to the Europeans."[95]

As with color television, videotex is a technology which is, in the short-run, to be employed domestically. Only in Western Europe can it be technically possible for a single videotex system to be integrated on a multinational basis. Yet as videotex technology continues to develop, global systems will become increasingly feasible. But the existence of separate and incompatible systems can only hinder the progress of videotex. North America and a few other regions share NAPLS/Telidon. The Japanese–East Asian CAPTAIN is easily rendered compatible with its NAPLS cousin. Ironically, the one region where videotex integration would be most likely—Western Europe—continues to be the primary source of incompatibility. Throughout the first half of the 1980s changes were constantly being made to the CEPT standard rendering it *more* incompatible with NAPLS or CAPTAIN. Moreover, changes within the CEPT Recommendation allowed many sets of incompatible dual standards to be incorporated into the CEPT system. This was done to present a re-emergence of the bitter Prestel-Antiope dispute. The compromise placated British Telecom and the French PTT but provided a strong disincentive to recognition of the CEPT Recommendation as a viable worldwide videotex standard.

The Canadians never attempted to create a single world standard with Telidon/NAPLS. France and Britain had entrenched commitments to their own systems before Telidon appeared on the scene. For Canada to adopt a combative strategy would have been unwise and self-defeating. Yet, undaunted by the potential of the Telidon late-comer, France and Britain themselves adopted "domination" strategies against Telidon and against each other. The Canadian administration realized that the technical strength of the Telidon system would discourage any pro-Prestel or pro-Antiope alignments within the CCITT. In that respect Canada showed faith in the ability of the CCITT to make sound decisions based on technical principles. Yet Canadian negotiators were not unaware of the political significance France and Britain attributed to Antiope and Prestel. Without forfeiting its vital interests, Canada was willing to accept a

CCITT multiple standard. Neither France nor Britain were amenable to such a solution, though intransigence on their part made a multiple standard inevitable. Canadian confidence was aided from an early date, however, by the knowledge that it had secured the American market and had hence created a de facto North American standard.

No fundamental change to this situation emerged at the end of the current CCITT Study Period in 1988. Any hope of compatibility between existing systems remains in the fairly distant future, although the current pace of technological change means that any prediction would be highly tentative at best.

The videotex saga illustrates how the standardization mandate of the "narrowly technical" CCITT can be undermined by the maneuverings of key actors within the system. When political prestige, domestic economic welfare, potential export markets, and existing technologies are threatened by proposed standardization, states will dig in their heels to prevent standardization. All major technological powers promote their domestic objectives within the CCIs. There are thresholds beyond which, for even the most amiable members, compromise becomes impossible. Thus, in the videotex debate Canada adopted what it called a "live-and-let-live" approach: a willingness to allow a multiple standard to incorporate Telidon and the two European stytems. To allow either or both of the Europeans systems to dominate or supplant Telidon, however, would have been unacceptable to the Canadian administration and the Canadian CCITT delegation. When the United States and Japan adopted the Canadian strategy in support of Telidon, the British and French lost any realistic chance of gaining acceptance of their systems as exclusive worldwide systems.

From a domestic, political viewpoint the employment of incompatible technical standards to ensure domestic industrial stability, maintenance of markets, and "prestige" may be viewed as worth the cost. Had France forfeited SECAM color television to some trans-European compromise system, it would have greatly benefited French television equipment buyers, aided the spread of color television in Europe, and made international television broadcasting far easier. It would, however, also have doomed the French television manufacturing industry to an early demise through German, and later Japanese, competition. Obduracy over SECAM has yielded the French telecommunications industry billions of dollars in export sales. Companies such as Thomson have survived through exports to Eastern Bloc and Middle East countries employing SECAM,[96] and the French SECAM authority benefits from sizeable royalties paid by foreign users of the system.

Whether different national color television standards can continue to protect home industries is doubtful. The lower trade barriers negotiated by the GATT and the sheer lack of competitiveness of much of the European consumer electronics industry relative to that of Asian competition are rapidly making the color television industries of France, Britain, and Germany obsolete. The video equipment market in Europe is now dominated, despite unique European standards and high tariffs, by either Japanese marques or European marques of Asian manufacture. This, when combined with global advancements in television technology, makes the continued existence of the incompatible television systems less viable. Maintenance of the separate systems will come to yield far greater costs than benefits.

The future of the videotex situation remains as yet inchoate. A single North American standard exists, with its CAPTAIN variant for Asia. Divisions exist in Western Europe between French and British systems, and the systems employed remain incompatible. Nevertheless videotex was by the late 1980s only beginning to be employed to any extent on an international scale. In fact, on most domestic markets the spread of videotex has been at best sluggish and has been disappointing to the technology's proponents.[97]

Ironically, the sole exception to the depressed state of videotex is found in France. Most English-language literature on videotex dismisses the French Antiope system as technically inferior to the high resolution, high performance Telidon. When the issue was under debate in the CCITT Study Group, France and to a lesser extent Britain argued that Telidon would be too costly for many users. Telidon proponents believed that medium- to large-sized corporations would be the bulk users of the technology and would find benefits in the system to compensate for its rather high cost. The French strategy was to promote the less advanced but less costly Antiope as a personal, home-based information retrieval system. Administered by the monopoly PTT, the domestic "Minitel" videotex network in France had by early 1986 1.4 million terminals installed in households and businesses nationwide, processing 22 million calls a month. In 1985 alone monthly usage of the system had increased by 400 percent over 1984.[98]

The degree of success enjoyed by the French Minitel videotex system surprised even the system's promoters. The most popular service offered over the system—and the chief catalyst of its success among individual users—has been a service package called "le Kiosque" which includes over 200 separate services enabling consumers to read news synopses, classified advertising, sports results, and entertainment listings as well as conduct banking and information exchange services.[99] The success of Minitel illustrates how videotex can be successfully employed at the national level. If other Western European countries established similar systems, it would only be a matter of time before the inevitable linking of services took place. Should other European countries adopt systems incompatible with the French Antiope (e.g., Britain's Prestel), this interconnection could be postponed.

The success of Minitel might be viewed as vindication of French recalcitrance during the CCITT discussions. Telidon has the technical advantage but is still judged by consumers to be too costly. The French have seized their cost advantage and have been actively promoting export sales of the Minitel system. By early 1986 about 35,000 French videotex Minitel terminals had been exported to markets as diverse as South America, Australia, New Zealand, and, significantly, the United States.[100]

The examples of X25 and videotex illustrate the diverse factors which may assist or hinder CCITT work. Despite the disappointing result of the videotex dispute, the undeniable authority and expertise of the CCITT, along with the quantity and quality of its achievements, assures the future significance of the committee. Unlike the CCIR, which faces an increased sense of anomy as elements of its mandate merge into the IFRB or other groups, the CCITT seems to be growing in prestige and confidence.

Exemplifying this is CCITT Study Group XVIII, which is seeking to develop a recommendation on an integrated services digital network, or ISDN. ISDN, as the name implies, is a concept which, in its ultimate fruition, would create a revolution in wired telecommunications by introducing a new generation of capabilities and capacity through fiber optic networks and digital transmission. The study group, despite the voluminous work that has gone into it, has yet to fully explore the myriad of possibilities suggested by the technology. The potential importance of Study Group XVIII has been alluded to by former ITU Secretary-General Mili:

> We are on the threshold of a new era in which electronics will reign supreme. . . . The traditional concept of the telecommunications network will have to give way to that of an integrated network. . . . This gives us an inkling of the dimensions of the challenge.[101]

That the CCITT believes it can master the indistinct concept of ISDN gives an indication of the optimism and determination with which the CCITT regards its mandate. One entire volume of the CCITT Red Book is devoted to ISDN studies and recommendations. Study Group XVIII made several recommendations in 1980 which sought to define and chart the evolution of ISDN conceptual principles. Definitive ISDN standards remain years away. But the CCITT wishes to act as the global coordinative body channeling and supervising the dissemination of information and research on ISDN. A strong concern on the part of CCITT personnel is to make certain that the evolution of ISDN does not irrevocably exacerbate the technology gap between North and South.[102]

One consequence of this has been the creation of a dichotomy of CCITT objectives. The desire to be an integral part of exciting new developments such as ISDN which could revolutionize wired telecommunications exists uncomfortably beside the basic objective of adequate global access to telephone service and the need to provide practical, feasible telecommunications. This has led to accusations from developing countries and even user groups such as INTUG that Study Group XVIII and the pursuit of ISDN is, as one observer cited, an idea that is both ahead of its time and slightly beyond the CCITT's ability to control it.[103] Restructuring of Study Group XVIII and a narrowing of its mandate may become necessary.

The dispute over CCITT Study Group XVIII and questions concerning the scope of CCITT activity have been further aggravated by the lack of clear lines of demarcation between its jurisdiction and the computer technology committees of the ISO and IEC.[104] At the Seventh Plenary Assembly of the CCITT, the Director of the committee, Mr. Burtz, commented on the need for better clarification of roles in order to avoid duplication of effort:

> Will the CCITT be able to go on ensuring that its authority and expertise are duly recognized in all sectors within its competence, in face of the many initiatives taken by numerous bodies with growing involvement in telecommunications, even though they do not have the major responsibilities which are vested in the ITU as the internationally acknowledged official organization in this field?[105]

As has been mentioned, these concerns have led to the formalizing of relations between the CCITT and the ISO, IEC, and other relevant international organizations.

The CCITT has grown rapidly in significance, largely due to the need for computer data communication standards. This has suggested a need to reevaluate and restructure the committee. The difficulties over videotex and ISDN led in 1984 to the establishment of CCITT Study Group V, which will by 1989 seek to develop a new structure for the CCITT more commensurate with the committee's evolution beyond mere telephony and telegraphy. Many of these changes will be discussed at the 1989 ITU Plenipotentiary.

The urgency with which this issue is handled in 1989 will be determined by the revision of the Telephone and Telegraph Regulations at the 1988 World Administrative Telephone and Telegraph Conference (WATTC).

The last WATTC had been held in 1973. Unlike the WARCs, WATTCs have traditionally not tended to be conferences of much drama or import. In 1973 the Telephone and Telegraph Regulations were, by consensus, pared down to the most vague and inoffensive principles of international telephony and telegraphy. The 1988 Conference will be a marked departure from this placid history, however, as this WATTC will be the first major ITU conference on international issues raised by the integration of telecommunications and information systems.[106] The goal of the WATTC is to remold the 1973 Telephone and Telegraph Regulations in *Telecommunications* Regulations. This step is considered to be necessary as recognition of the significance of new technical developments and the expanded role of the CCITT.

To the dispassionate observer this would appear as a fairly straightforward task, particularly given the minimal, general nature of regulations emergent from a WATTC. The two preparatory meetings held by the CCITT up to mid-1986, however, proved to be contentious and littered with divergent opinions. Some CCITT and ITU officials fear that too revolutionary a scope for the WATTC could create political and legal complications beyond the conference's competence. As one recent analysis surmised, "the WATTC process raises the vital question of how to draw the regulatory boundary line between the telecommunications sector and other business sectors. As telecommunication and information processing activities become increasingly important to the transactional capabilities of many industry sectors . . . careful attention must be devoted to whether and how telecommunications regulations could affect the functioning of these industries."[107]

A group of countries led by Japan and Scandinavia rejected such caution by calling for a "broad international legal framework for all existing, emerging, and future new telecommunication services."[108] But others warn that "the greatest risk is that the WATTC-88 will adopt a legal regime that is too rigid to accommodate ongoing national efforts to restructure the telecommunications market and to redefine the relationship between telecommunications and other business sectors. In this event . . . the WATTC-88 might sow the seeds of the eventual demise of this important institution—or at least, its descent into irrelevance."[109]

As early as the 1982 ITU Plenipotentiary Conference, when the resolution calling for the 1988 WATTC was proposed and passed, the alignments which promised to dominate the conference were visible. The Nordic countries and Canada, along with Algeria and a handful of other developing countries, were the first to call for the conference. The motives behind this early call were cited by proponents as the need to reconcile the obsolescent Telephone and Telegraph regulations with emergent technologies as well as the promotion and safeguarding of efficient telecommunication systems.[110] The problems of CCITT Study

Group XVIII on ISDN regarding nuclear or overlapping jurisdiction with other international organizations confirmed the need to iterate, in a convention, the ITU's jurisdiction as the *sole* worldwide organization responsible for all aspects of telecommunications. Other Western European countries rapidly followed the lead of their northern confreres in the 1986–88 time period.[111] The 1982 Plenipotentiary, in Resolution 10, resolved that a WATTC would be held following the CCITT Plenary Assembly Meeting in 1988.[112]

Support for this comprehensive WATTC was not universal. The United States has, since 1982, insisted that the scope of the conference is excessive. American opposition stems from the American desire to minimize the number and breadth of regulations. Several American officials have expressed the sentiment that the spartan regulatory framework established after 1973 was the ideal sort of WATTC product; basic user guidelines and principles that do not constrain domestic regulations or users.[113]

In the CCITT Preparatory Committee meetings held in the years leading up to the conference, the divergence in viewpoints between that of United States and that held by other countries became more explicit, and highlighted the ambiguous wording of Resolution 20 of the 1982 International Telecommunication Convention which sets the 1988 WATTC to "establish, to the extent necessary, a broad international regulatory framework for all existing and foreseen new telecommunications services."[114] Regulatory activists prove this wording obligates the WATTC to develop a new comprehensive and revolutionary set of regulations. Opponents maintain that the phrase "to the extent necessary" leaves the conference free to decide to what extent new regulation is needed, if at all.[115]

Britain has drifted toward the American position and has stated that the expansion of the WATTC regulatory order, as proposed by France, Canada, Japan, and Sweden, may be motivated by a desire to restrict new service suppliers to the same conventions and regulations administrations must follow or, in other words, they are seeking to use the WATTC to restrict competitive access to the marketplace.

The British delegation at the Second WATTC Preparatory Conference in March 1986 also showed an appreciation for the effect an irreconcilable dispute on the desirability of regulation could have, not only for the 1988 WATTC, but also for the credibility of the CCITT and the ITU. As Anthony Rutkowski has stated, the comments of the British delegate "soberly captured the very essence of the WATTC-88 dialogue":

> There are currently different national philosophies about how telecommunications should be provided. The approach currently being adopted by those arguing for a more all-embracing Regulation inevitably means

that one group of countries would be obliged to give up a significant area
of national sovereignty. It is difficult to see a consensus being achieved
on this basis. If this is accepted, the Committee might find it more fruitful
to return to the approach which it implicitly adopted at its first meeting—
a simple set of general principles which preserves the world order whilst
permitting national diversity.[116]

The ability of the 1988 WATTC to address the desire for a more
explicit regulatory framework for wired telecommunications will determine the treatment of the CCITT at the 1989 Plenipotentiary. The
developing countries in particular are carefully watching for possible
Northern biases within the CCIT or for the passage of WATTC resolutions
that do not adequately consider their requirements. If the developing
countries emerge dissatisfied from the WATTC, there is a greater chance
that the new CCITT Director elected at the 1989 Plenipotentiary will
be an overtly political Third World spokesman. There is a risk of this
occurring no matter how the WATTC concludes, as 1989 will be the
first occasion where the Plenipotentiary and not the CCI Plenary has
elected the CCI directors.
  Within the Northern countries, the fate of Study Group XVIII on
ISDN and the ability of the CCITT to determine its jurisdiction vis-à-
vis the ISO, IEC, and other international organizations will continue to
dominate concerns regarding the CCITT well into the 1990s. The fundamental value of the CCITT has never been questioned. The committee
provides an indispensable and remarkably efficient standardization process which has enabled international telecommunications to take place.
A US government report published several years ago provided what is
perhaps the best synopsis of the CCITT's value:

> . . . the CCITT emerges as an international forum to which the telecom-
> munications experts of the world can bring together a plethora of ideas,
> attitudes, national backgrounds and biases, techniques and technologies;
> from the widely diverse arena that results, they can forge the standards
> which the world—by and large—adopts for its telecommunications net-
> works. One outstanding example of their success is direct dial signalling
> for international calls; it stands as both a symbol of the CCITT itself, and
> a tribute to the skill of the CCITT members to come to agreement.[117]

Conclusion

International standardization of telecommunications services and
equipment has been at the heart of the ITU's ability to facilitate international communications. For much of the history of the Union this has

been largely a "reactive" process whereby CCI Recommendations emerge as the evolutionary application of established domestic technologies to the international level, or the application of new, obvious developments in technology for which acceptance as an international standard is a foregone conclusion.

The examples of HDTV and cellular radio in the CCIR or that of ISDN in the CCITT illustrate that the CCIs are now being compelled to undertake an increasing "proactive" role in standards development. Toward this end the CCIs are becoming involved in nascent technologies at an early stage so that they may supervise and coordinate international research and development. The CCIs have discovered that they can provide an ideal forum for exchanging technical ideas and information, and thus facilitate standardization from the earliest stages of a technology's development.

Where the CCIs have neglected early technical development of specific technologies, the cost has usually been seen in a greater difficulty in achieving collaboration—and hence a near impossibility in obtaining standards—at the international level. Color television and videotex are illustrative of technologies which developed in isolation at the national level and were only with great difficulty reconciled at the international level. It might seem both illogical and unethical for a country developing a potentially international technology to refuse to coordinate or compromise with fellow ITU member countries in order to achieve standardization. In the cellular radio dispute of the mid-1980s, one saw the same unwillingness and inexplicable incompatibilities that accompanied the furor over the Marconi discriminating radio communications policy back in 1900. Yet, as the CCIs have discovered, countries do not oppose standardization without cause. Their positions are in fact rarely illogical or unthinking. Simply put, international standardization can be to a country's disadvantage or, more likely, can be seen by national administrations as disadvantageous.

Certain factors will serve as disincentives to international standardization. The CCI's ability to achieve a recommendation on a standard will be hindered when: (1) two or more members from different countries have developed—and heavily invested in—incompatible means of achieving the same goal. This was the case with color television and videotex; (2) where a technology is not perceived as international in nature and hence can be "protected" against foreign competition through using incompatible standards as non-tariff barriers (NTBs); (3) where a telecommunications equipment manufacturing industry may be threatened by foreign competition, incompatibility may also serve as an effective NTB. This was the case with high definition television (HDTV) and cellular radio, where Western European manufacturers and administrations feared Japanese domination of markets; (4) where basic philosophical differences concerning the need for standardization cannot be reconciled. Increasingly, the United States has questioned the need for certain regulations and standards that, it argues, could emerge more efficiently within the natural competition of the marketplace. Often cited as an example is the greatly decreased standardization role of the FCC and the deliberate refusal to select an AM stereo broadcast technology in order to allow a marketplace solution. Other countries do not share this view, believing it is an invitation to chaos and monopoly. In the AM stereo example, many American observers and most foreign observers believe the "marketplace" selected a standard technically inferior to other alternatives then available, due to the overwhelming strength of the large corporation promoting the "chosen" standard. Other countries may select different standards and global compatibility may well be rendered impossible; (5) how the CCIs are viewed by the ITU membership. Much of the valuable preparatory work of the CCIR for WARCs is not given the attention it deserves from LDCs because they believe the CCIR is hopelessly biased toward Northern needs and concerns. The nature of the structure and work of the CCIR and CCITT has so far precluded strong Third World involvement. Many developing countries cannot afford to purchase the CCI publications, much less send delegations to conferences and take an active role in the standardization process. This leads to distrust on the part of developing countries toward the recommendations produced by the CCIs and a feeling that Third World needs are not being adequately addressed. Distrust, when combined with a technical inability to interpret new standards, does not facilitate the standardization process.

This litany of negative factors might suggest that the CCIs are confronted by almost insurmountable obstacles. Such a view would be entirely inaccurate. Despite a plethora of challenges, the CCIs remain the most successful, least aggravated component of ITU activity. In the early 1980s, when certain American officials were clamoring for a US withdrawal from the ITU, these same officials were always quick to add a proviso saying the United States would "of course" remain active in the CCIs. The committees are simply seen as indispensable to international telecommunications. At the core of their success is the stark fact that factors predisposing international standardization strongly outweigh the disincentives. Standardization is promoted by factors that are more central and more vital than the factors dissuading standardization, such as:

(1) International telecommunications. Simply put, international telecommunications are impossible without a basic framework of common technical standards. The bulk of the recommendations in the CCIR and

CCITT books are achieved without dissent. They are merely the international confirmation of new developments that will facilitate telecommunications between countries. Agreement to accept a new recommendation and hence an improved standard is usually a foregoing conclusion. In the nature of telecommunications technology there exists a strong imperative for technical homogeneity. Only in a very few instances can that imperative be overcome by domestic economic, social, and political concerns.

(2) Markets. Particularly in recent years, there has been an increasing tendency to presume a global market for new technologies. New products and services are designed from their inception with export markets or worldwide integration in mind. The "proactive" role of the CCITT in the channeling of Recommendation X25 and the development of ISDN from an early stage is an attempt to make certain that the evolution of the technology does not fragment and that, ultimately, a single network emerges. Major export markets such as the United States create an international mind-set on the part of developers of new technologies, as in the videotex case, where designing systems for export and worldwide use was viewed as equally if not more important than merely satisfying domestic needs.

(3) Dominant firms. Especially in the CCITT, recognized private operating agencies (RPOAs) play a vital role in research and development. Private firms are responsible for most technical innovations that find their way into CCI Recommendations. By nature of their global size and breadth, major multinational corporations can create global de facto standards which the CCIs then recognize through their recommendations. This type of standard is often less innovative and not necessarily at the forefront of new technology. Conversely, standards "set" by multinational corporations are often more pragmatic and cost-effective than the more pioneering, technically exciting systems the CCIs prefer to study, and may thus be more acceptable to users in the Third World. In an ironic twist, multinational corporations, through pursuit of economies of scale, have forced the CCIs to become more "worldly" and less technically zealous in their recommendations. Both developed and developing country users prefer their standards to be practical and achievable. "Users want the Land Rover, not the Mercedes-Benz of telecommunication technologies."[118]

(4) A belief in the value of international telecommunications standards. This point cannot be overestimated. All ITU members believe in the merits and necessity of international standardization. When countries fight standardization, they do not do it with pride or bravado. More often than not they will not cite the real reasons why they oppose standardization. In the examples of color television, HDTV, and videotex,

opponents to a CCI recommended standard concealed their arguments behind a facade of technical respectability, claiming that a standard would be "premature," or that "more study is needed," or that "we've a better proposal for a standard."

Standardization is integral to international telecommunications. Despite controversy and the occasional inability to achieve standardization, the overwhelming benefits of standardization are universally recognized by national telecommunication administrations, manufacturers, system providers, and users. As the CCIs survey their future, witnessing the constraints of zero-growth 1980s austerity budgets, an escalation in the velocity with which technical change occurs, and the notably complex nature of much new telecommunications technology,[119] the CCIs mandate of "producing standards at the right time in the right way" in an atmosphere of technical consensus and professionalism will be tested as never before. Theo Irmer, the director of the CCITT, maintains that the CCIs can and will successfully adjust to the changed telecommunications environment and that the CCITT, like its CCIR sibling, ". . . is the *only*—and this is important—*worldwide* organization capable of providing telecommunications standards."[120]

Notes

1. L. Burtz and E. Hummel, "Comment: Standard Setting in International Telecommunications," *Telecommunications Policy* (March 1984), p. 3.

2. CCITT, Document *AP VII*, No. 110 (1980).

3. Interview.

4. ITU, *International Telecommunication Convention* (Geneva: ITU, 1982), p. 11.

5. Ibid.

6. Ibid.

7. Interview.

8. The CCIs have done all in their power to reduce the cost of the books, and the 1985 Series sold for one-third the price of the 1980 Series.

9. George A. Codding, Jr. and Anthony M. Rutkowski, *The ITU in a Changing World* (Dedham, MA: Artech House, 1982), p. 103.

10. Leslie Milk and Allen Weinstein, *United States Participation in the ITU: A Study of Policy Alternatives* (Paper prepared for US Department of State, Washington, D.C., 1984), p. 34.

11. Interview, Geneva.

12. Nine regional voting groups exist in addition to the CEPT: (1) Arab Telecommunication Union (ATU); (2) Association of South East Asian Nations (ASEAN); (3) Committee for Inter-American Telecommunications (CITEL); (4) Technical Commission for Communications in Central America (COMTELCA); (5) European Broadcasting Union (EBU); (6) Economic Community of West

African States Telecommunications Subcommittee (ECOWAS); (7) Pan-African Telecommunications Union (PATU); (8) Pacific Basin Development Council (PBDC); (9) Pacific Telecommunications Council (PTC). Examples of the kinds of standards emerging from these organizations are the development of telex standards for the transmission of Arabic language characters and certain African regional standards relating to the use of telecommunications equipment in humid, tropical climates. See D.M. Cerni and E.M. Gray, *International Telecommunication Standards: Issues and Implications for the 80s* (Washington, D.C.: National Telecommunication and Information Administration, US Department of Commerce, 1983), pp. 45–46.

13. Ibid.

14. Interview.

15. Interview, Washington, D.C.

16. One of the earliest accomplishments in this regard was the standardization of Morse code at the 1865 founding Conference of the ITU.

17. George A. Codding, Jr., *The International Telecommunication Union: An Experiment in International Cooperation* (New York: Arno Press, 1972), p. 86.

18. An example of a radio service standard found today is the CCIR-ICAO joint standard recommending the exclusive use of the English language for all international civil aviation services.

19. Robert Chapuis, *The CCIF and the Development of International Telephony (1923–1956)* (Geneva: CCITT Reprint Series, 1976), p. 19.

20. Kolossvary in Chapuis, Ibid.

21. Ibid.

22. Ibid.

23. Ibid., p. 20.

24. Ibid., p. 21.

25. Ibid., p. 23.

26. Known until 1947 as a CCI General Secretariat.

27. Codding, op. cit., 1972, p. 122.

28. Chapuis, op. cit., 1976, p. 31.

29. Codding, op. cit., 1972, p. 297.

30. ITU, *Final Acts of the International Telecommunication and Radio Conferences, Atlantic City, 1947* (Geneva: ITU, 1947), p. 9.

31. Chapuis, op. cit., 1976, p. 38.

32. ITU, *International Telecommunication Convention (Nairobi, 1982)* (Geneva: ITU, 1982), p. 3.

33. Interview.

34. Interview.

35. Interview.

36. The relevant committee was Committee Five.

37. Interview.

38. Established in Article 11, *International Telecommunication Convention (Nairobi, 1982)* (Geneva: ITU, 1982), p. 11.

39. Interview, Ottawa.

40. Interview.

41. Interview.
42. Interview, Washington, D.C.
43. Interviews, Geneva and Washington, D.C.
44. Interview, Washington, D.C.
45. NTSC is the color standard employed by most countries in North and Central America, along with Japan, South Korea, Taiwan ROC, the Philippines, most Caribbean countries, and several South American countries.
46. R.J. Crane, *The Politics of International Standards: France and the Color TV War* (Norwood, NJ: Ablex Publishing, 1979), p. 12.
47. By 1962, color television was still not an unqualified success, even in the United States. Receiving sets were costly and picture quality was mediocre at best. Color television was dismissed by many as a fad and color sets remained slow-selling novelities. This situation did not change until the end of the 1960s, by which time the majority of programs were broadcast in color and transistor technology allowed a sharp drop in the price of color sets.
48. Crane, op. cit., 1979, p. 20.
49. Ibid, p. 38.
50. The foremost of these disputes concerned the developer of SECAM, M. de France, who was not a graduate of the Haute Ecole Polytechnique.
51. In fact RAI-TV, the Italian state television network, was unable (or unwilling) to select a color television system until 1975.
52. Crane, op. cit., 1979, p. 74.
53. Ibid., p. 75.
54. Ibid., p. 83.
55. Ibid., p. 84.
56. To state that administrations may prefer incompatibility is a significant qualification. Certainly, the pursuit of *incompatible* standards will not yield any benefits to consumers nor contribute to technical or economic efficiency.
57. For example, many computer equipment standards—the domain of the CCITT or ISO—are set *de facto* by IBM. The reason for this is not because IBM is more technologically progressive: in fact it is not, generally employing proven technologies. IBM is a standard-setter because it is the largest computer manufacturing entity in virtually every major market, particularly in the United States. Perhaps the most famous example of an inefficient standard which is inexorably entrenched is that of the QWERTY typewriter keyboard. Many far better keyboard configurations allowing much faster typing speeds have been designed and patented but never employed. No manufacturer would be willing to market a non-QWERTY typewriter or computer system in a world so accustomed to the QWERTY system. Likewise, the ISO would be highly reluctant to approve new systems, no matter how superior, for fear of opening a heretofore stable, standardized system to disorder.
58. Interview, Washington, D.C.
59. Interview.
60. Interview, Washington, D.C.
61. Interview.
62. As of late 1988, NHK remained eager to establish a national HDTV broadcast network as soon as possible. The 1986 Dubrovnik decision was a

hindrance to the NHK planners, but the end of the 1980s saw Japanese broadcasters and manufacturers moving ahead with plans to begin full HDTV services by the early 1990s.

63. Nick Snow, "Leaving It to the Engineers," *Television Business International* 1:1 (February 1988), p. 64.

64. The seven incompatible cellular radio systems were found in the British Isles (TACS), the Nordic countries and Switzerland (NMT 450/900), the Benelux countries (NMT Variant), France (Radiocom 2000), Germany FR (C-Netz), Italy (Italtel), and Austria (C-Network). See Patrick Whitten, "Cellular: What Need for European Integration?," *Intermedia* 14:3 (May 1986), p 36.

65. Interview.

66. Whitten, loc. cit., 1986, p. 38.

67. The degree of commitment varies, and some countries such as the Soviet Union fear the political implications of a direct-dial international telephone system. Other countries such as Albania, Burma, and North Korea will have nothing to do with an international direct-dial system and have no desire to be plugged into the world network. See Rex Malik, "Can the Soviet Union Survive Information Technology?," *Intermedia* 12:3 (May 1984).

68. Bell Northern Research, *A Study of Telecommunications Equipment Standards* (Ottawa: Bell Northern Research, 1975), p. 96.

69. Interview, Ottawa.

70. Cerni and Gray, op. cit., 1983, p. 59.

71. Interview.

72. Cerni and Gray, op. cit., 1983, p. 59.

73. Ibid., p. 57.

74. Recommendation X25 was substantially revised in 1980. These revisions did not affect the basic principles of the Recommendation but did permit alternative systems to exist as well. These were not in fact competing standards or additional standards but merely technically different methods by which the same goal could be attained.

75. M. Epstein, "Et Voila! Le Minitel," *New York Times Magazine* (March 9, 1986), p. 46.

76. This work is done by CCITT Study Group I (Definitions).

77. Hussein Rostum, *Telidon and the Videotex Standard-Setting Process: Background Study No. 2 for an Evaluation of Telidon* (Ottawa: Teega Research Consultants, 1985), p. 4.

78. Ibid.

79. Ibid., p. 34.

80. Ibid., p. 48.

81. Ibid.

82. Ibid., p. 31.

83. Ibid., p. 50.

84. Ibid., p. 56.

85. Ibid., p. 17.

86. Interview.

87. Rostum, op. cit., 1985, p. 58.

88. Ibid.

89. Ibid.

90. Ibid.

91. NAPLPS/Telidon geometric coding was formally approved into CAPTAIN by the Japanese delegation and by Nippon Telegraph and Telephone (NTT) in November 1982.

92. E. O'Brien, *Final Report under DSS Contract OST83-00010 to Provide Technical Assistance to Study and Analyze Presentation Level Protocols* (Ottawa: Depatrment of Communications, 1984)., p. 4.

93. Ibid.

94. Interview.

95. O'Brien, op. cit., 1984, p. 6.

96. For example, in 1979 Soviet Television commissioned Thomson-CSF to exclusively provide an entirely new SECAM television system and all related equipment for television coverage of the 1980 Moscow Summer Olympics.

97. Epstein, loc. cit., 1986, p. 49.

98. Ibid.

99. Ibid., p. 48.

100. Ibid., p. 69.

101. A. Anderson, "Secretary Mili of the ITU Surveys the World Telecommunication Scene," *Telephony* 201:17 (1981), pp. 50–94.

102. Interview, Geneva.

103. One American observer used the analogy of the compact but unsuccessful Henry-J and Crosley automobiles of the late 1940s and early 1950s.

104. International Standards Organization (ISO) and International Electrotechnical Commission (IEC).

105. CCITT, T.D. Number 33 (1980).

106. Anthony Rutkowski, "Regulation for Integrated Services Networks: WATTC 88," *Intermedia* 14:3 (May 1986), p. 10.

107. Robert Bruce, Jeffrey Cunard and Mark Director, *WATTC 88 and the Future of the ITU: Realism About the Limits of Regulation* (London: International Institute of Communications Telecom Forum, 1987), p. 2.

108. Rutkowski, loc. cit., 1986, p. 11.

109. Bruce, Cunard and Director, op. cit., p. 4.

110. Rutkowski, loc. cit., 1986, p. 11.

111. ITU, *International Telecommunication Convention (Nairobi, 1982)* (Geneva: ITU, 1982), p. 239.

112. Interview.

113. ITU, *International Telecommunication Convention (Nairobi, 1982)* (Geneva: ITU, 1982), p. 238.

114. Bruce, Cunard and Director, op. cit., p. 17.

115. Rutkowski, loc. cit., 1986, p. 16.

116. D.M. Cerni, *The CCITT: Organization, US Participation, Studies Toward the ISDN* (Washington, D.C.: National Telecommunication and Information Administration, US Department of Commerce, 1982), p. 45.

117. Interview, Washington, D.C.

118. The most detailed recent example of CCIs successfully reaching agreement on a telecommunications technology of almost unprecedented complexity is found in the work of Study Group XVIII on Integrated Services Digital Networks (ISDN). The future of this technology, as envisaged by the ITU, is detailed in *CCITT Plan Committee for Europe and the Mediterranean Basin, Report R2: Report of the Meeting of the Plan Committee for the Development of the Telecommunication Network in the European and Mediterranean Basin Region, Nicosia, 28 September– 4 October 1983* (Geneva: ITU, 1984).

119. T. Irmer in Williamson, "CCITT Reviews Its Mission and Traditional Methods," *Telephony* (November 26, 1984).

120. Ibid.

Conclusion

After 120 years of survival as an international organization, the ITU remains unique in a myriad of respects, from its anomalous structure to its subtle politics to the sheer magnitude of what it actually achieves. The ITU is undeniably successful. It is not merely a talking shop, nor has it been co-opted or politicized by any of its member states. Our ability to telephone friends in Brisbane, send faxes to Berlin, watch satellite broadcasts from Baltimore, and find out what is happening in Brasilia—all within the course of a normal business day—is a tribute to the achievements of the ITU. Technologies which could have easily devolved into a parochial morass of incompatibilities have instead been coordinated to work in relative harmony.

But is it right to give such accolades to the ITU? Would this cooperation have existed without the ITU, simply because it would have been in states' economic and political interests to cooperate? In other words, if the ITU did not exist, would we have to invent it?

Even the most recalcitrant members of the ITU would argue "yes." The ITU is not without faults, but it provides an invaluable *global* forum for the advancement of international telecommunications. It is practically the sole meaningful avenue through which developing countries may address their telecommunications needs and concerns. It also sets the rules of the road by which all telecom administrations and radio spectrum users must abide.

But the degree to which the ITU achieves successful outcomes is utterly dependent upon a small number of pivotal factors. The following variables promote the strength of the ITU's regulatory accords:

(1) High salience to the viability of international commercial or business activities. If a particular sphere of activity requires regulation in order to facilitate international commercial ventures, then there will be a strong proclivity to accept regulation and international arrangements. Only in this way can commercial exploitation of the technology and the business goals of the actors involved be achieved.

This point is fairly self-evident when applied to international telecommunications standards. Without the acknowledgement of the CCIs, telecom technologies cannot be viably promoted abroad. The CCIs, for their part, must consider the commercial goals of broadcasters and telecommunications operators. Likewise, judicious frequency management will be increasingly important in an era of potentially rewarding international direct-to-home satellite television and competitive carriage of telecoms traffic. Satellite common user organizations such as Intelsat cannot fulfill their goals unless they work with the ITU through national administrations to ensure access to frequencies and orbital spaces.

(2) Large size of the financial investment in the activity. States will be reluctant to devote large sums to any particular enterprise unless they are certain of their ability to exploit opportunities in the designated international sphere. Most communications activities require at least the tacit consent—and more often the specific collaboration—of all the parties involved.

In this area state discretion wields great influence over ITU power. Adherence to the doctrine of prior consent and insistence on the right of the state to accede to incoming information flows has done more to delay the evolution of satellite television than any technological barriers encountered regarding frequency allocation. Having said that, it must also be noted that no party was willing to invest in direct television broadcasting by satellite (DBS) until the ITU had hammered out equitable frequency plans for all regions at Conferences in 1977 and 1983. In fact, because of the magnitude of investment required for DBS-TV, the ITU was under considerable pressure throughout the 1970s to rapidly—some would argue hastily—settle the issue of a frequency plan, particularly in Europe.

Nowhere is this question of investment more evident than with international telecommunications standards. Chapter 4 has shown the power and prestige of CCI approval in achieving international status for telecom systems. A cursory glance through the advertisements in telecommunications and broadcasting trade journals attests to the commercial power of being able to state "CCITT (or CCIR) approved standard."

CCI approval does not, of course, guarantee a healthy return on investment. In the videotex case, CCI backing did not prevent the Canadian Telidon system from remaining in the commercial doldrums while the less sophisticated French Antiope standard established itself as the preeminent industry norm. But without CCI approval *any* potential international commercial reward is impossible. This competition between technologies leads to a third point:

(3) Low salience to international competition for markets. When international arrangements are seen as favoring a rival's technology over one's own or if they are not considered to be in the state interest, it may be to a state's advantage to go it alone. This often leads, in the

area of standard setting, to multiple standards. Such was the case for color television and videotex standards, and will probably also be the case for high definition television (HDTV) and DBS-TV color standards. This disinclination to accept international agreement may also occur in the area of frequency management, usually—but not exclusively—on those bands used primarily for domestic broadcasting. In international radio broadcasting the drive to get the message through to the target audience will override the ITU's quest for technological order and efficiency. States that insist on "going it alone" in this area do so because of the perceived political rewards and the fear that any unilateral concessions would be unrequited.

(4) High concentration of technological expertise and capabilities. The more concentrated the skill and power, the fewer the number of parties that will have to compromise or negotiate to reach agreement. Problems of reaching accord increase with the number parties involved as important actors. When many states have conflicting interests and compromise is not seen as essential to the functioning of the medium, as in international high frequency radio broadcasting, then agreement is exceedingly difficult to reach. In the area of standards, most new technologies are evolutionary developments that can be clearly credited to one source. Consequently, consensus is a straightforward part of the bulk of CCI decision-making.

While this concentration leads to rapid, consensual decision-making on technological criteria, it also reinforces the Third World view of the CCIs as a First World club in which leading telecommunication administrations and multinational corporations work together with little regard to developing country interests. One consequence of the 1989 ITU Plenipotentiary Conference will be the diffusion of CCI power through the establishment of elected directors. This change is being made with the intent of enhancing developing country power in the CCIs, but it will inevitably render decision-making in the CCIs a less straightforward process. Whether this is "damaging" or "democratizing" remains a matter of opinion.

(5) Low salience of states' control of their own societies. ITU regulations which are seen to constrain a state's ability to maintain control over society are not likely to be met with widespread compliance, regardless of the potential economic rewards that compliance might offer. National autonomy remains a preeminent goal for states. When the regulation of a given sphere of activity is apt to curtail or constrain their own ability to govern their societies, states will oppose such regulation.

The jamming of international radio broadcasts, for example, is universally regarded as an expensive and unsuccessful activity. Even those who engage in it admit this point. Yet, after fifty years of failure, jamming continues. Jamming remains a last resort measure in attempting to control the media consumed by national audiences. More successful in this regard has been the acceptance of the doctrine of prior consent for satellite television services. Country A cannot beam TV broadcasts to country B without the latter's permission. If this permission is not granted and country A broadcasts anyway, country B may take measures to prevent the signal from getting through. "Prior consent" has not yet led to great difficulties for the ITU or its member states. But the rise of international television, particularly within Europe, and the definitional problems of what constitutes international television versus the international spillover of domestic signals will become a greater problem to the ITU as the 1990s progress. This issue is at the heart of state control over domestic communications as a component of national social and cultural policy.

The salience of the above five factors determines the effectiveness of ITU regulation and, indeed, the likelihood of the ITU reaching an accord in a given area. The ITU has, over 120 years, tacitly accepted these norms and has sought to accommodate such "facts of life" in its behavior, negotiating contexts, structure, and regulatory functions. But even if there is a general acceptance of the limits of ITU ability, the Union must nevertheless accept the challenge of at least attempting to reach agreements in spheres of activity where the likelihood of success is remote. After all, the ITU exists to oversee all telecommunications. ITU activity must therefore include valiant efforts to, for example, create order in the chaotic world of international broadcasting or to effect improvements to the lamentable and worsening gap between First World and Third World telecommunications capabilities.

Through this vast scope of activity, certain jurisdictional properties have evolved and are now embodied in the activity of the ITU. The principles must accommodate the three reigning dependent variables that have been iterated throughout this book: the free flow of communications across borders, the concept of national sovereignty, and the doctrine of the common heritage of humankind as manifested through the "commons" of the radio frequency spectrum and the geostationary orbit. These principles are summarized as follows:

(1) The low salience of an issue to states' domestic control over their own societies is supportive of common heritage norms, freedom of the airwaves, and accord on international standardization. The management of the international aviation and maritime bands is an example of universal recognition of the value and need for compromise. But in any sphere of activity where national autonomy is seen as being forfeited or impinged upon, states will reserve their right to final discretionary power. As has been shown, the ITU permits states to do this in the literal sense through national reservations, international treaties, and

final acts. More often, however, states express their autonomy in this area through action, not words. They may sign ITU Final Acts or international protocols, but will continue to broadcast on unauthorized frequencies or employ non-standard technologies. This is not done out of malice or even out of a lack of commitment to the ITU, but simply because national imperatives—getting the message through, maintaining national telecommunications industries—outweigh any need to placate international organizations.

(2) Freedom of the commons depends upon the supply of the resources. The 1985/88 Space WARC was able to forge a more or less satisfactory allotment plan for the geostationary orbit because of the relative underemployment of the physical orbit and the portions of the frequency spectrum used for satellite communications. In fact, as we enter the 1990s it seems increasingly apparent that satellites may never become a problem area for the ITU. The growth of international private satellite telecoms traffic may well be matched by the transfer of other satellite traffic to terrestrial fiber optic cable networks. There should therefore be a generous supply of satellite spectrum space and orbital allocations for satellites well into the next century.

Such is not the case for most of the broadcasting bands, which must battle for frequencies for both international and domestic use. The swift rise in demand for radio and television frequencies in the 1970s and especially during the 1980s has, in radio, led to "air wars" where domestic and international radio services employ high-powered transmitters to cover their target audiences. The growth of new terrestrial television networks and stations (e.g., new national TV networks in several European countries and the growth of new urban stations in North America) has led to demands for the expansion of the UHF bands allocated to television. This is a perfect example of the zero-sum quality of most ITU frequency management, for this step would require reallocating frequencies currently used for the point-to-point utility services. Look at virtually any part of the terrestrial radio frequency spectrum and one will discover a struggle between competing uses for a given band. It is to the ITU's credit that a "breakdown of audibility," to use Donald Browne's phrase for international radio services, has *not* taken place across the bands.

(3) An absence of strong political hostilities is seen as promoting freedom of the radio frequency/orbital commons and the likelihood of standardization. This somewhat obvious point is reflected time and time again in the behavior seen at ITU conferences and in shaping agreements. Even where accord is virtually impossible, as in the international jamming of broadcasts, the fluctuations in great power relations are constantly reflected in the audible level and persistence of the jamming itself.

Similarly, it is no mere coincidence that Iran and Iraq or Greece and Turkey have differing color television standards.

(4) If states do not possess the physical ability to disrupt the activities of other states in a certain sphere, they are likely to go along with freedom of the radio frequency and orbital commons and international standardization. They have little choice, for they do not have the power to back any actions they may contemplate against activities they find disagreeable. A more level playing field could actually harm international communications. An example in this area is the tumultuous radio and television "wars" between the United States and Cuba. For all the grandiloquence and posturing put forward by Cuba regarding jamming and high-powered radio services, Cuba is not in fact willing to enter a technological battle they cannot afford.

The ITU provides, in instances such as these, a safety valve. Countries can express their displeasure with one another through the international forums only provided by the ITU. This advantage, perhaps the strongest characteristic of United Nations organizations, cannot be overestimated. What some states view as politicization of ITU meetings is in fact an important source of stability which obviates the likelihood of such political action being manifested in physical terms against states. Moreover, it gives all states a voice and a chance to be heard.

(5) A similar point shows that a concentration of technological capabilities is likely to promote freedom of the radio frequency spectrum and technical standardization because those countries with the capability are apt to want freedom of action. States not enjoying such capabilities, regardless of their preferences, will not have the ability to enter into the activity and shape its behavior. Moreover, even when states' collaborate to collectively create sufficient capabilities, their ability to act is often hindered by in-fighting and internal dissent within the cooperative body. So far, European cooperation has yet to create truly common European positions vis-à-vis the ITU. This is not to say such positions will not later be the case, particularly given the new enthusiasm with which the European Community is pursuing the goal of a single internal market and harmonization of social and broadcast policy.

(6) When jurisdiction over a particular area is salient to the viability of commercial activities, then a state is likely to favor unilateral national action in order to guarantee the survival of this activity or to thwart international measures seen as interfering with it. Countries will be reluctant to place in the hands of others any power that might at some point deprive them of the ability to participate in profitable international commercial activities. This was the approach of France in the standardization battles over color television and videotex, and most states have behaved this way over certain technologies of national priority.

For over 120 years, the ITU has been a fundamental ingredient in the rapidly changing, unstable communications order. The ITU of the 1990s will little resemble its forebears of fifty or a hundred years ago, but there has been one constant: the ITU has always been the ultimate *international* authority in the regulation of international telecommunications. Promulgating order in technologies so innately international and so vital to international life has been, as we have seen, a far from easy task.

Moreover, the supremacy of electronic communications in daily life should not be seen as the apogee of ITU achievement. In many ways the toughest years for the ITU remain ahead. The technology gap between developed and developing countries continues to widen dramatically, despite the now half-forgotten efforts of the Maitland Commission. Serious questions regarding the outcomes of the High Frequency and Space WARCs of the 1980s have been deferred until well into the 1990s. The specter of politicization will inevitably follow the Plenipotentiary. Given the growing strength of new private international communications actors and the emergence of newly powerful regional blocs, as in Europe, new problems may emerge regarding the status of private entities in the ITU and the possibility of regional and coalitional voting blocs hindering ITU action.

To lionize the ITU would be as mistaken as labelling it irrelevant. The ITU has been neither dramatically good nor dramatically bad. It has, in fact, attempted and succeeded in not being dramatic at all. Like the frequencies, telecom lines, and standards it oversees, the ITU seeks, above all else, to be transparent. Like the telephone on your desk, the radio in your car, and the television in your home, it is taken for granted. All evidence seems to suggest that it prefers to be so.

The ITU does not attract the sort of attention—and analysis—received by other international organizations such as the GATT or the UN General Assembly. The apparent lack of drama at the ITU is one reason. Another involves the self-proclaimed technological nature of the Union, which intimidates many journalists and academics. But the importance of telecommunications to modern society makes the ITU too important to ignore.

The issues detailed in the above chapters, while of political interest themselves, all have vast implications well beyond the field of telecommunications. The ITU makes decisions every day determining the fate of the global commons, the free flow of information and ideas, the survival of industries employing thousands, and the balance of technological power. The ITU, as one of the preeminent actors in the international telecommunications regime, will be hurled grudgingly into a higher profile as the millennium approaches. It will enter the 21st century with a fundamentally different character: leaner, more open to non-governmental organizations, cognizant of emerging regional organizations, and more open to the international role played by private telecommunications entities.

The remaining years of the century find the ITU at a crossroads. Mistakes have been made, conferences have not always enjoyed successful outcomes, and perceptions of the ITU among some member states are still often at odds with reality. Conversely, even the most recalcitrant participant in the international telecommunications order would admit that the ITU is necessary. It is not flawless, but it is surprisingly effective. Applying the ultimate test to it, it is fair to say that if the ITU did not exist, we would have to invent something very much like it.

Index

AM radio. *See* Medium-frequency broadcasting
AT&T Bell System, 56(n28), 172, 174, 176, 198, 202, 203
Austro-German Telegraph Union, 28

BBC World Service, 92, 93, 94, 161(nn 3, 10)
discrediting, 133–134
jamming, 134, 135, 139, 141, 150, 159–160, 163(n33)
and the Third World, 146, 164(n64)
Bern Bureau, 29
Frequency List, 67, 69–70, 72, 77, 123(n15). *See also* Soviet Union, Bern Bureau Frequency List and role of, 30, 37, 57–58(n59), 70–71

Canada, 71, 99
videotex and, 202–208
See also North America
CCIF. *See* International Consultative Committee on Long Distance Telephone
CCIR. *See* Consultative Committee on Radiocommunications
CCIs. *See* International Consultative Committees
CCITT. *See* International Consultative Committee on Telephone and Telegraph
Cellular radio, 196–197
Center for Telecommunications Development (CTD), 17, 49, 50–51

CEPT. *See* European Conference of Post and Telecommunication Administrations
Common user organizations (CUOs), 107, 114, 115, 116–117, 118, 119, 127(n113)
Computer technologies
development of, 1–2, 3
ISDN, 210–211, 223(n118)
packet switching systems, 200–201, 221(n74)
regulation and, 16, 17, 170–171, 211, 220(n57)
videotex, 201–208, 209–210, 222(n91)
See also International Consultative Committee on Telephone and Telegraph
Consultative Committee on Radiocommunications (CCIR)
and cellular radio, 196–197
and color television, 189–193
Conference Preparatory Meetings (CPMs), 18, 185, 186, 188
establishment of, 177–178
and HDTV, 193–196
and the HF band, 99
publications by, 168–169, 185
role of, 6, 18, 19, 25, 40, 45–46, 61–62, 121, 167, 168, 179, 180, 184–188, 197–198
and space services, 80, 106, 114
and the Third World, 26, 121, 169, 216
See also International Consultative Committees; International Frequency Registration Board